Inspiring | Educating | Creating | Entertaining

Brimming with creative inspiration, how-to projects, and useful information to enrich your everyday life, Quarto.com is a favorite destination for those pursuing their interests and passions.

First Published in 2022 by Cool Springs Press, an imprint of The Quarto Group, 100 Cummings Center, Suite 265-D, Beverly, MA 01915, USA.
T (978) 282-9590 F (978) 283-2742 Quarto.com

Cool Springs Press titles are also available at discount for retail, wholesale, promotional, and bulk purchase. For details, contact the Special Sales Manager by email at specialsales@quarto.com or by mail at The Quarto Group, Attn: Special Sales Manager, 100 Cummings Center, Suite 265-D, Beverly, MA 01915, USA.

26 25 24 23 22   3 4 5

ISBN: 978-0-7603-7571-6

Digital edition published in 2022
eISBN: 978-0-7603-7572-3

Library of Congress Cataloging-in-Publication Data Available.

Design: Cindy Samargia Laun
Cover Image: Jordan Brannock
Illustration: Christopher Mills on page 28

Printed in China

THE VEGETABLE GARDENING BOOK

Your complete guide to growing an edible organic garden from seed to harvest

JOE LAMP'L

COOL
SPRINGS
PRESS

PRAISE FOR *THE VEGETABLE GARDENING BOOK*

"Joe Lamp'l has done it again! Not only does he tell you how to make a superb vegetable garden, he also explains why his recommendations work as well as they do. Joe claims that this beautifully illustrated book does not answer every question about vegetable gardening, but I am skeptical; it certainly answered all of mine."
—DOUG TALLAMY, author of *Bringing Nature Home, Nature's Best Hope*, and *The Nature of Oaks*

"In this long-awaited garden guide from the man with the greenest of thumbs, 'Joe Gardener' walks the reader through his garden from artichokes to winter squash, sharing tips he's amassed over decades of tending his own plots. Be prepared to have your muck boots knocked off!"
—LISA STEELE, founder of Fresh Eggs Daily and author of *Gardening with Chickens*

"Joe breaks down everything you need to know to create a productive food garden using modern techniques. As a naturalist concerned about pollinator and songbird decline, I can say Joe's advice on managing pests and using natural gardening practices is spot on. This is now my go-to vegetable gardening book."
—DAVID MIZEJEWSKI, Naturalist, National Wildlife Federation

"If you're a beginner to vegetable gardening, I definitely recommend this book. If you have already experience growing vegetables, again, I recommend this book. Clearly, and with oodles of informative and luscious photos, Joe Lamp'l covers everything from where to site your garden to soil care to tips on growing individual vegetables to harvest, and everything in between."
—LEE REICH, author of *Growing Figs in Cold Climates, The Pruning Book*, and *Weedless Gardening*

"Precise, concise, and full of actionable advice, Joe's book is my go-to guide for growing a greener world and a more beautiful and bountiful garden no matter where you live! His sage wisdom continues to inspire and educate gardeners in the Bronx and all around the world! Read the book and you too will MAKE EPIC HAPPEN!"
—STEPHEN RITZ, Founder of Green Bronx Machine

"A well-researched, carefully organized, and beautifully written book, Joe is a true gardening scholar who has done an amazing job of taking the knowledge he has gained over a lifetime and putting it into an easy to read and understand form that even beginning gardeners can use. This is destined to be *the* go-to source for vegetable gardeners."
—JEFF GILLMAN, PHD, author of five gardening books and Director of the UNC Charlotte Botanical Gardens

"Joe Lamp'l demystifies the essential components of successful organic gardening in this well-organized resource. His vast knowledge will help new and experienced gardeners alike in their quest to grow healthy, productive edible crops!"
—SUSAN MULVIHILL, author *The Vegetable Garden Pest Handbook* and creator of SusansintheGarden.com

"Joe Lamp'l knows how to grow things; I've seen that up close and personal. I've spent time in his wonderful garden, had hours of garden conversations on the phone or on podcasts, and worked alongside him as we share our knowledge with our Growing Epic Tomato students. Even better, Joe knows how to impart his knowledge in a clear, direct and engaging way. Gardening is in his blood—it is his passion. This beautiful, comprehensive, well written book is a must read for all who wish to grow their own vegetables, no matter what the experience level."
—CRAIG LEHOULLIER, author of *Epic Tomatoes*

"*The Vegetable Gardening Book* pairs Joe Lamp'l's lifelong quest for knowledge and lush photos to create an easy-to-follow seed-to-harvest guide for the modern gardener. It exemplifies the joy and beauty gardening provides to communities and family tables alike."
—DIANE OTT WHEALY, Co-Founder of Seed Savers Exchange

"Joe Lamp'l's popular and pragmatic garden voice sings across the pages of this gardening tome. Illustratively photographed, beautifully organized, and concisely written, this is the resource I wish I had from the beginning. Joe's candor and expertise permeate every detail—he's thought of everything to help you grow your very best garden. A must-have gardening resource for every level of gardener."
—MEG COWDEN, author of *Plant Grow Harvest Repeat*

"A must have for all gardeners, this comprehensive vegetable guide is full of essential information and beautiful images. Joe has done a magnificent job sharing his lifelong passion for growing and is sure to inspire others to sow a few seeds and enjoy the harvest!"
—BRIE ARTHUR, horticulturist and author of *The Foodscape Revolution* and *Gardening with Grains*

"Joe is a lifelong vegetable gardener. He has the unique perspective of learning from his personal experiences in his own gardens and hosting a gardening podcast and TV show where he has gleaned tips from other expert gardeners. The result is this comprehensive, organic gardening book filled with Joe's inspiration and practical advice."
—CHARLIE NARDOZZI, author of *The Complete Guide to No-Dig Gardening*

CONTENTS

PREFACE

The Joy and Importance of Growing Your Own Food

One of the first deliberate plantings I tried was a single row of bush beans along the wall outside my parents' bedroom. I had no idea then about choosing the ideal location, soil preparation, sun exposure, or proper watering. I just cleared some weeds, dug a shallow trench, and sowed some seeds. A few hours later, I started checking for germination. Seriously. (I was eight.)

Three long days later, those seeds began to sprout. I was over the moon. After a few weeks, flowers began to bloom, the bees started to visit, and those treasured bean pods started to form. You can imagine my joy and pride when I got to finally savor every bite of the most delectable beans I had ever tasted. Beans I had grown myself. Decades later, I still get just as excited planting my vegetable garden as I did for that first crop of beans. The joy of growing what you eat from seed never gets old.

Beyond the personal satisfaction I get from such a healthy and fulfilling hobby, I now know

so much more. We know that most of the food grown for our consumption comes with many costs, starting with food miles—the distance food travels from farm to fork. Typically, it's 1,500 miles (2,414 km) or more! And throughout the growing process (and even before), nonorganic growers are dousing their crops and fields with pesticides (insecticides, fungicides, herbicides, etc.) and synthetic fertilizers. Suffice it to say that, given a choice, none of these chemicals are things we really want to go into our bodies or those of our family.

But here's the thing. We *do* have a choice. Growing our own food isn't hard, it doesn't require a lot of space, and there are edibles for nearly every growing environment. From sunny suburban backyards to urban patios and even apartment balconies, everyone can grow some amount of food. Food we grow ourselves has zero food miles, and it can be 100 percent free of potentially harmful chemicals.

Another important benefit is that organically homegrown vegetables are more nutritious and delicious. If you have any doubt about the better taste, try it on your children. Give them a homegrown anything (fill in the blank) and compare that to a store-bought version. You'll see that there is no comparison. I've witnessed this time and time again with my own daughters. Thankfully, they were spoiled at a very young age by the sweet, delicious taste of vegetables picked fresh from the garden. Growing them free of synthetic chemicals was icing on the cake.

And avoiding those chemicals is also vital for the health of our planet. While this may sound far-reaching, it's true. When plants are sprayed with pesticides, those chemicals, most of the time, do not differentiate between good bugs and bad ones. They're designed to kill everything they contact. Moreover, not only do all the bugs die, but sadly, much of the wildlife that relies on insects for their diet dies, too, thanks to a poisoned food source. Gardeners may think they're just eliminating nuisance hornworms or cucumber beetles, but they're also killing millions of backyard songbirds each year.

So, let's change that. If we knew that at least 97 percent of all insects on the planet are either beneficial or neutral (doing no harm to your plants), why then would we shower our plants with something that kills *everything*? Biodiversity depends on balanced ecosystems. We have a lot to do with that, starting with what we use (and don't use) to grow our gardens and maintain our lawns and landscapes. Consider the microorganisms living in the soil, lady beetles, honeybees, backyard songbirds, and beyond—they all play key roles in this, and much of their fate is in our hands.

But here's the good news. You can grow your food, free of harmful chemicals, while Mother Nature is doing much of the heavy lifting for you. While growing your own food is indeed personally fulfilling, it goes way beyond that. It's not all that difficult to grow enough to feed your family, share with neighbors in need, and lighten your environmental footprint, too. A backyard vegetable garden may be a simple thing, but it can have a genuinely profound impact on you, your family, your community, and the planet. Plant the seeds now. What you grow could last a lifetime. It has for me.

INTRODUCTION

My life as a forever-curious gardener began when I was eight years old. While I grew up in Miami, Florida, a place where everything grows easily, I was not raised in a family that did much gardening except for the lawn—my dad's pride and joy.

One Saturday after "helping" with yardwork, I was playing and accidentally broke off a branch from a shrub my dad had just finished manicuring. I panicked. I jammed that broken branch into the ground next to the plant it had come from, scooped some dirt around it, and retreated to a far corner of the yard to avoid suspicion.

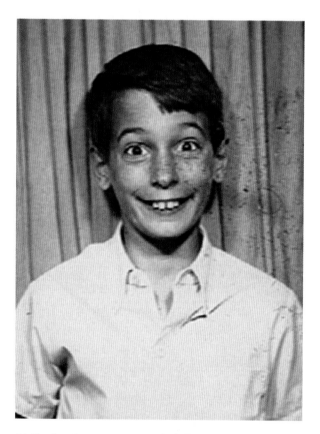

At the tender young age of eight, I had no idea what I wanted to do with my life. But I was about to find out.

A few months later in the yard again, having forgotten all about the incident, I rounded that same corner and realized that the branch I had snapped off was now sporting brand-new leaves. I gave it a gentle tug and it resisted. It had produced new roots and foliage. *It was growing again.*

I can say with absolute certainty, that was the defining moment that forever hooked me on horticulture. I simply had to know how that broken branch that I had left for dead and simply tried to hide had restored itself and, in fact, thrived when left to its own devices.

I started burying seeds. I broke (and then learned to cut) more branches, sticking them in the ground to see what would happen. I graduated to sowing beans (the ones mentioned just a few pages ago) and then flowers and fruit trees. Soon I had tables full of potted plants, my own little nursery that I cared for every day.
A few years later, I was volunteered to help my Uncle Ray with his yardwork. To this day, I'm not sure if it's because I did such a good job for my dad pulling weeds in our own yard—or just the opposite. But Uncle Ray had a passion for growing big, majestic hanging baskets of staghorn ferns. He made new ones by simply dividing and replanting them. I was fascinated. He and I made a dozen more of those hanging baskets, and I was sent home with everything I needed to make one of my own.

I ended up making hundreds more from that first fern. I even proposed a 100-year lease of some of my more prized specimens that my mom signed for the low price of ten bucks. (I was 10. I have no idea how I knew what a long-term lease even was.)

By the time college studies rolled around, my mother encouraged my initial idea of pursuing a horticulture degree, but she also pushed me to add a business degree, too. Moms are so smart.

A job hosting *Fresh From the Garden* suddenly cast me as the vegetable gardening instructor for a nation-wide audience, where failure was not an option.

Upon graduation, there were many more recruiters looking for business majors than there were opportunities for plant nerds.

I entered the business world but kept my feet in the garden, even starting a side business doing horticulture design and consulting work. And that's when I got an email, back when those were still relatively new, that changed everything.

A new cable channel called DIY Network (the sister station of HGTV!) was starting a series on vegetable gardening and was searching for a host. "They're looking for you, but they just don't know it yet," my friend had written. Although a fan of the many gardening shows on TV, I had never done anything like that before. I threw my hat in the ring anyway.

I was named the host of *Fresh From the Garden* before the show even had that name. I said goodbye to my career in the business world.

Overnight, I was teaching an audience of 40 million viewers that included all skill levels, from first-time novices to advanced master gardeners, how to be a successful vegetable gardener.

As my executive producer said on my very first day, "Failure is not an option." Not on TV, anyway. Failures, or "learning opportunities," as I like to call them, are part and parcel of growing anything in a real-world garden, but no one wants to watch a show about crops that don't make it. The point of the show was to demonstrate how to do it successfully.

Undaunted, that's what I did. Over three years, we shot fifty-two episodes, each one taking a single crop from seed to harvest, and we stopped only because there were no other edibles to cover on the show. And for the entire run, we never did have a failure. We had challenges, to be sure, but working through them made me a better gardener—and a better teacher of gardening, too.

Thirteen seasons of *Growing a Greener World*® have brought viewers from coast-to-coast into my own five-acre hobby farm, where I share my own organic gardening practices, tips, and advice.

And that's why I decided to write this book. I have two other gardening books already under my belt, but there was one more that I knew I needed to write. It's the one you're holding now.

After all, my work and love for growing food organically and producing thriving, bountiful vegetable gardens has continued to expand by leaps and bounds. I'm thirteen seasons into my own Emmy-award-winning, national, organic-gardening television series, *Growing a Greener World*®. I've raised my own five-acre hobby farm to be even bigger and more productive than the one we used for those three seasons on *Fresh From the Garden* so long ago. And by adopting all-organic practices, my plants are healthier, my soil is better, and the food I harvest is abundant in nutrients, free of pesticides and chemicals, and off-the-charts when it comes to flavor.

Learning to grow your own food, understanding the *why* behind the *how-to*, and feeling confi-

dent in your ability to grow your own food, all in an environmentally responsible and healthful way—that's powerful and important—now more so than ever.

I've been in the public spotlight for over twenty years now, gardening and growing food organically. And I'm happy to say, my track record is impeccable. Each year, I teach courses for thousands of students in my Online Gardening Academy. They rave about the results they get from what they've learned in my lessons. And while I would love for you to take a deep dive into mastering those skills at an immersive level, this is a great place to start! I am so glad you are holding this book in your hands. I know that once you've read this book, you, too, will become a better, smarter, more confident gardener.

There's magic in gardening. And it can be learned. Take it from a formerly freckle-faced eight-year-old with a broken branch in his hand.

ABOUT THIS BOOK

You may choose to read this book cover-to-cover, and that's fine. I assumed that most gardeners would use it, though, as a reference guide, by picking it up and flipping ahead to a chapter on a particular topic one day, thumbing through to find the answer to a specific question the next. That's why I've divided the book into chapters, each covering one aspect of gardening. If you need some help getting your seeds started, jump right to Chapter 6. The nuts and bolts of blending the perfect garden soil will be waiting for you back in Chapter 2 whenever you're ready.

The following is a brief look at what each chapter and section of the book covers.

Chapter 1: Start Here
This book starts where every gardener should—with a master plan. That includes everything from thinking through what edible crops you're going to grow, which flowering plants you should add to attract pollinators, considerations when choosing where to physically site your garden, and how to estimate how much of everything you'll need to get your vegetable garden up and running successfully.

Chapter 2: It's All About the Soil
Here's a "dirty" (wink, wink) little secret about vegetable gardening. It's not the plants or the vegetables themselves you should concern yourself with most, it's the soil they grow in. If you pour the majority of your time and energy and resources into building rich and fertile soil, the plants will take it from there and reward you mightily. This chapter will help you understand what actually makes soil rich and fertile in the first place. Then I'll guide you through testing your soil for essential nutrients, amending it accordingly, and creating your own compost (the closest thing to magic I've ever seen).

Chapter 3: Plant Basics
In this chapter, I'll run down the nonnegotiable things that your crops will need to survive, so you can roll with the punches that will inevitably come over the course of a growing season. I'll dive into the "golden rule" of gardening, define some terms that will help you select the best seeds or plants, and reacquaint you with the "cheat sheet" that too many gardeners take for granted.

Chapter 4: Where to Grow Your Food
A garden can take many shapes. Whether you plan to grow your edibles directly in the earth, build new raised garden beds, use a variety of containers, or are looking for something a bit outside the box, what you grow your vegetables in matters. I'll help you pick the perfect solution for your edibles—even if your ideal vegetable garden doesn't look like a vegetable garden at all.

Chapter 5: Feeding Your Plants
Fertilizer can be a tricky business. Too many gardeners use it like a fix-all, thinking if they spray enough of it over their plants, they'll overcome any deficiency or problem under the sun. Yes, it can give your crops a much-needed boost. But the truth is, sometimes the best fertilizer is no fertilizer. In this chapter, I'll help you understand what your garden needs from supplemental feedings. And I'll show how to decipher the labels you see at the store.

Chapter 6: Seeds and Seedlings
Some gardeners love to grow all of their edibles from seed, starting the process indoors in the dead of winter and then moving the whole operation outside when spring arrives. Others prefer to make one big trip to the nursery and bring home plants that already have a healthy head start. Whichever way you garden, this chapter will have everything you need to consider to get your crops started on the best foot possible.

Chapter 7: Getting the Timing Right

Timing plays a big part in successful gardening. You don't want to start your garden too early, but you'll be in trouble at season's end if you start it too late. This chapter helps you navigate the calendar to get your crops in the ground during that perfect window. I'll also share advice on staying ahead of things for maximum production all year long.

Chapter 8: Mulch Matters

If there was just one thing you could add to the garden that retains moisture, improves soil quality, controls erosion, regulates soil temperature, suppresses disease, minimizes weeds, and makes the entire garden look better, you would do it, right? Well, that one thing is mulch. There are no downsides to using it, as long as you pick the right kind. And there is no other single step you can take in the garden that pays so many dividends.

Chapter 9: Getting the Watering Right

Water is the lifeblood of the vegetable garden, but you must be careful with it. Overwatering kills more crops than underwatering. In this chapter, I unlock the mystery of finding that sweet spot in between. All you have to do is, literally, lift a finger. I'll help you water smart, in ways that are more effective for your plants and less hands-on for you.

Chapter 10: Extending the Season

The most successful gardeners have learned how to push the limits on the growing season, using clever techniques to get their plants started earlier than, or keep them growing strong well past, what the weather would seem to allow. This chapter demonstrates the best tricks for manipulating the growing environment to grow more.

Chapter 11: Insects and Bugs: Friend or Foe?

Gardening and bugs go hand-in-hand. But not all insects are a problem. In fact, the vast majority of insects you'll encounter in the garden are good. I'll use this chapter to (I hope) change the way you think about bugs when it comes to gardening. I'll help you identify which insects could put your crops in jeopardy and give you ways to manage those pests responsibly.

Chapter 12: Diseases: Managing the Inevitable

If you grow vegetables, you *will* encounter plant diseases. It's a fact of life. In this chapter, I'll walk you through ways to stay on top of issues that arise. You'll learn how to take both preventative and corrective measures, and also, when to let nature run its course. Combating disease doesn't have to be an uphill battle.

Grow Guides: The Fab 40 for Filling Your Vegetable Garden

Armed with knowledge of the first twelve chapters, you should be more than ready to start planting. Here I've included my forty favorite edible crops—from artichokes to zucchini, pumpkins to parsnips, tasty blueberries to all those wonderful kitchen herbs, and of course, the king of the backyard vegetable garden, the tomato. For each plant, you'll get a look at what it needs to thrive in the garden, special planting tips, a maintenance checklist, which pests and diseases to watch out for, and detailed instructions on how to harvest your crop.

Does this book comprehensively address every element of vegetable gardening and answer every conceivable question you'll have? Of course not. I'd need a lot more pages to do that. And truth be told, I couldn't do that with all the pages in the world. I've been seriously gardening for over four decades, and what I don't know still dramatically outweighs what I've learned up until now. That is the beauty (and sometimes the curse) of gardening—there's always more to learn.

But I definitely know enough to get you started on your vegetable-growing journey. And I hope that what I've included here will inspire you to roll up your sleeves and give you the confidence to jump in with both feet. I believe this book provides a sound base for anyone who wants to grow their own food.

And if what you read here encourages you to go seek out more answers for further success in the garden, I'd say I did what I set out to do.

START HERE

SO, YOU WANT TO GROW a vegetable garden. That's fantastic, but first things first. Before you grab the nearest shovel and just start tearing up a corner of your yard, there are some things you probably want to think through a bit that will (hopefully) make the whole adventure go much more smoothly.

This chapter is all about the plan. The more organized and focused you are up front, before your garden even takes physical shape, the better results you'll almost certainly have. If you're truly starting from scratch on your very first edible plantings, this is the place to begin. If you're looking to overhaul your existing garden and implement some big changes to the way you garden, this chapter may help you make some significant improvements.

GROW WHAT YOU LOVE TO EAT

Throughout this book, you'll discover that I'm big on explaining *why*. I could just list the step-by-step instructions on how to plant a garden, but I find it's far more helpful in the long run when new gardeners understand *why* they're going through the steps, *why* a certain technique works, and *why* some considerations are more important than others.

So, I want to start by asking you to consider the most important *why* of all. *Why do you want to grow your own food*?

Is it to adopt a healthier lifestyle, take more control over what your family eats, or reduce (or maybe even eliminate) your weekly grocery expense?

Maybe you just want to supplement what you buy with a few fresh-from-the-garden veggies, are looking to start a side hustle selling cucumbers or homemade salsa at the farmer's market, want to teach your young children more about where their food comes from, are looking for an activity for the whole family, or would like to bring your neighborhood or local community closer together with a shared garden plot.

Whatever the reason (and maybe there are several), I suggest starting with one basic premise—grow what you love to eat. It sounds silly, perhaps, but you'd be shocked at the number of gardeners I talk to who spend an inordinate amount of resources, time, and energy growing, let's say, eggplant. When they won't even eat it! Why? Sure, maybe they're growing it for someone else in the household, or they've planted a row of something they intend to donate to a food bank (a practice I highly recommend). Some edible plants can be just fun to grow from an ornamental standpoint or serve some other purpose in the garden (like luring certain pests away from the crops you care more about), but you still may need to stay motivated to maintain and nurse a crop along through some tough challenges. This is much easier when you care about the end result.

Start with what you enjoy eating, and you're more than halfway to caring deeply about what you choose to grow. "Because I love it" can often be the single most important answer to the *whys* that will inevitably pop up over and over through your gardening adventure.

SITING YOUR GARDEN

After asking yourself why you want to garden, you'll need to think about *where* you want to garden. Or, more accurately, where you *can* garden. This one is often out of your hands. Many would-be gardeners are prohibitively space-challenged, or at least they think they are. Even if you don't have access to a sprawling back forty of rolling farmland, you probably have ample space for a vegetable garden in some shape or form. You may just need to look at your property in a new light.

Think about the kinds of fresh food you and your family will want to eat and what you hope to get out of your garden. This will help you decide what to plant.

Many of the crops I grow are chosen as much for the beauty they provide to the garden as the food they'll produce.

A thriving vegetable garden doesn't have to occupy a massive chunk of your property. Even the smallest suburban lot can produce more food than you might think!

Start by finding the spot in your yard that receives the most sunlight. Eight hours per day is ideal.

Sunlight

Nearly without exception, your vegetable garden needs to be located in the sunniest spot you have to work with. Ideally, you're looking for an area that receives direct sunlight for eight hours a day. Maybe the most sun you can accumulate is five or six hours per day. Does that mean you can't have a vegetable garden? Not at all. It's just that your plants will get a less than ideal amount of fuel for things like flowering and fruiting. You can find a workaround for many variables when it comes to growing your own food, but if you don't have a spot that gets a lot of sun, it could be a long and uphill battle.

Grade

A level spot for gardening is a true blessing. Most of us have some degree of slope to our property, and depending on the steepness of your topography, a slope can make gardening a real challenge since it dictates how the water drains.

If your garden spot has a severe slope, building raised beds may be a way to create level planting areas.

If your garden might require some kind of fencing to keep critters out, think it through now, before the garden is planted.

You can chip away at the natural grade, digging and carving out a level spot or terracing the area into a series of flattened planes. Raised beds, though, are often an easier way to deal with a slope. We'll talk about raised beds in greater detail in Chapter 4. Constructing your own garden bed gives you a practical way to create a level planting area that sits on even the steepest of slopes.

Convenience
It may sound trivial at first, but convenience and proximity to the house really does matter greatly. A good deal of gardening success comes simply from spending time in the garden. If yours is tucked away in a back corner of your property, you may find yourself not getting out there often enough.

Water
Garden hoses are wonderful...until you have to untangle them, fix a leaky connector, walk back to undo the kink, or string together several because one just doesn't reach. The point is,

a garden with easy access to water, right where you need it, minimizes a lot of hassle. Paying a plumber to run water supply lines to my own garden and then install a permanent spigot in every single raised bed was an expense, to be sure. But it was a more than worthwhile investment. Give early consideration about where your garden's irrigation will come from, and it's possible you'll never have to think about it again.

Predators
It's also worth remembering that your vegetable garden will be growing where other living creatures also make their home. Much of that wildlife would love a salad buffet created just for them. If your area has a high population of rabbits, groundhogs, gophers, raccoons, squirrels, mice, voles, or deer, you'll appreciate knowing that *before* you plant your garden. Siting it closer to the house may make it less attractive to some critters, but in many cases, you may also need to include fencing or other physical barriers in your planning.

Plan Ahead for Pollination

To bear fruit, many plants in the vegetable garden require a little outside intervention for pollination. Whether it's birds, bees, or butterflies, there are plenty of living things you actually *want* to attract to your garden. There's a long list of beneficial insects who will help you by patrolling your plants and keeping the "bad bug" population down.

These invaluable garden helpers may not show up on their own. You have to attract them. So, as you plan your garden, be sure to include flowering plants that will bring all the Bs (butterflies, birds, and beneficials) to the yard. Below is a list of ten flowering powerhouse plants I have in and around my vegetable garden to attract pollinators and beneficial insects.

Milkweed: Also butterfly weed, is a honeybee and pollinator magnet, and the host for monarch butterfly larvae.

Coneflower: This garden classic is attractive to a host of insects all summer, but the seedheads that remain at season's end feed the birds all fall and winter.

Black-eyed Susan: The yellow petals of this versatile plant light up the garden. The flowers bring in a ton of beneficial insects.

Joe Pye Weed: Its small, delicate flowers draw butterflies and other insects. A beautiful border plant in the early fall garden.

Goldenrod: Planted en masse, they create a sea of yellow flowers. Fall bloomers, they're also an important source of nectar for pollinators.

Asters: Another fall bloomer, you'll love the white, purple, or lavender flowers. Pollinators love the nectar they produce.

Foxglove: This tall, spiky biennial is typically pink to purple in color, but this tubular flower can be found in many other colors that draw in pollinators.

Mexican sunflower: A vigorous, drought-tolerant annual with bright orange to reddish flowers, it produces an abundance of nectar and pollen.

Anise hyssop: An attractive but short-lived perennial, the tall blue-purple flowers are a great source of nectar and pollen for many insects and hummingbirds.

Tickseed: So named because its seeds look like ticks, the daisy-like flowers give a long-blooming period and are a gift to pollinators. And they're deer-resistant to boot!

While you're at it, plant plenty of **herbs** and allow some to go to flower. Basil, dill, rosemary, fennel, and lavender are all attractive to nectar-loving insects.

This is a list meant to get you thinking early on about incorporating flowering plants into the vegetable garden. Seek out the plants that are native to where you live—they'll be what attract the local pollinators and beneficial insects.

By planning for pollinators right up front, you'll put your vegetable garden on the path to becoming a thriving mini-ecosystem that's teeming with (the right kind of) wildlife.

Milkweed is one of my favorite plants for attracting pollinators to my garden.

I enjoy the tiny flowers of the unfortunately named Joe Pye Weed, but butterflies and insects love it even more.

SIZING YOUR GARDEN

How big should your garden be? That's a loaded question, because most gardeners always want at least a little more growing space than whatever they currently have. But when you're planning a garden, my recommendation is always to *start small*, especially if this is your first foray into growing edibles. Allow for future expansion, sure, but remember that plants *want* to grow bigger and bigger. It's literally in their DNA.

Consider, too, how much you are trying to get out of your garden. Is it meant to feed just yourself or provide a few extra veggies for your family? Or are you trying to fully sustain a family of four for the entire season (or longer)? These are two very different-sized gardens.

I'm always reluctant to give new gardeners an actual number, because there is no one-size-fits-all answer to how much garden you need. But if you're looking for a basic rule of thumb, 200 square feet (19 m²) per person is a good starting point. If the garden is meant to feed one person, the plot could be 10 feet by 20 feet (3 m x 6 m). For a family of four, 800 square feet (74 m²) of growing space could be broken up as needed to fit your property.

Yeah, But…

It bears repeating that every gardener's situation and needs are unique. If you plan on doing a lot of canning and preserving, you may want a lot more than 200 square feet (19 m²) of space per person since you're not trying to eat all your harvest fresh out of the ground.

Additionally, there are plenty of gardening techniques designed specifically to coax more produce out of every square inch of growing space. If you practice interplanting (discussed later in Chapter 7), for instance, you're packing more plants into every bed than someone who's using by-the-book spacing. As a result, you'll get more out of your 200 square feet (19 m²), so you may find you don't need quite that much garden space.

Two hundred square feet (19 m²) of growing space per person is just a guideline. This is by no means a magic number. Gardening is, by and large, one giant experiment. Play with the size to come up with what works for you. As they say, your results may vary.

There's a big difference between a garden meant to grow a few extra tomatoes and one that's intended to feed a family of four all year long.

Space-strapped gardeners will find a myriad of creative ways to tuck additional plants in every corner and fill every blank space in their beds, making the most of every square inch.

If you're starting from scratch, there is no substitute for sketching out your ideas for a garden layout on a piece of graph paper.

Use your bed size to figure out exactly how much soil you'll need. Online calculators make this quick and much easier than guessing and being wrong later.

PUTTING IT ALL TOGETHER WITH A PLAN

If you've followed the previous steps, you should have an idea of where your garden should go, a fair approximation of how big it should be, and what you want to grow in it. At this point, I find it's always helpful (and for me, a ton of fun) to draw out some ideas on how you want that garden space to look.

When I moved into my current house, I had a 50 x 100 foot (15 m x 30 m) patch of flat ground right outside the door to my home office. My garden needed to feed my family of four as well as serve as a demonstration area for a national television show, so I determined that I wanted about 3,000 total square feet (279 m²) of growing space. Breaking that into raised beds (for reasons I'll help you think through in Chapter 4) of a good workable size, I aimed to ultimately fit sixteen beds in my garden.

At night after dinner, I would sit down with a piece of graph paper and just play around with different layouts until I came up with something I liked. Having it sketched out on paper certainly helped when it came time to do the work and install the garden beds, but it also made it easy to visualize where each crop would go, where my walkways should be situated, where things like water and electricity would need to be located for maximum convenience, and how it would all fit together in the finished garden.

How much do you need?

Armed with a plan, you can start creating your garden space. To fill that space, you'll likely need to do just a little bit of math to determine the necessary quantities of things.

If you plan to have a garden of raised beds, you'll be filling those beds with soil. And even if you intend to do your gardening in-ground, you'll want to get enough mulch to cover all of your bedspace. Thankfully, there are plenty of online calculators that compute how much of these materials you'll need. Use one you like from a source you trust. Plug in the width and length of the area plus the desired depth, and it spits out the proper quantity in cubic yards (or sometimes cubic feet). There are also sources online that will give you results in cubic metres.

Now I know how much to buy. Why does that matter? Each of my raised beds is 4 feet by 12 feet (1.2 m x 3.7 m), or 48 square feet (4.5 m²). The soil depth is 18 inches (0.5 m). That adds up to 72 cubic feet (2 m³) of soil. An average bag of soil from my local garden center is 2 cubic feet. I would need to buy 36 bags of soil to fill just one of my 16 beds. I'd much rather know that information up front than make multiple trips to the store because I'm guessing (but this also helps illustrate why buying in bulk and having it delivered makes so much sense).

You'll likely also want to preplan for how many seedlings or packets of seed you'll need. This keeps you from buying too much or worse, not getting enough to produce what you intended to have. A seed packet will often list its total yield, for example, the packet will produce enough for a 50-foot (15 m) row of plants spaced 4 inches (10 cm) apart. You can use that information to plot out how many packets to buy. The plastic tag in a seedling pot at the garden center will always list the spacing too. Again, use these recommended measurements to fill your garden space with the appropriate number of plants.

Keep in mind, too, the yield of each crop you're considering. Just one indeterminate tomato plant, for instance, which keeps producing new fruit throughout the season, will give you between 10 and 20 pounds (4.5 to 9 kg) of tomatoes. One carrot seed, on the other hand, produces one carrot.

What Will the Neighbors Say?

It's worth noting right up front that not everyone loves the idea of a vegetable garden. As crazy as it seems, many subdivisions and homeowners' associations have restrictions and covenants that expressly prohibit vegetable gardens. I've deepened many a friendship with a neighbor over my garden, and nothing breaks the ice quite like sharing some of my bounty with the folks who live on my street. But if it's against the rules, no homegrown tomato you can offer will make up for the hassle and heartache of ripping out a garden after you've installed it. If you live in a place that has rules on such things, check that out before proceeding with your garden planning.

That said, I also know die-hard gardeners who have figured out how to sneak edible crops into their well-manicured landscapes. It's a technique called *foodscaping*. One of my closest friends got started with it precisely because her homeowners' association wouldn't allow traditional vegetable garden beds in her yard. So, she planted a few tomatoes and herbs and leafy greens in and around her foundation shrubs and colorful annuals—and even won Yard of the Month!

FOODSCAPING: EDIBLE LANDSCAPING, THE BEST OF BOTH WORLDS

Here's an idea on where to grow your food that may seem quite radical at first blush. What if your vegetable garden wasn't confined to a garden at all? Foodscaping is the marriage of vegetable gardening and landscaping by incorporating food crops with aesthetic plants to create an edible landscape.

Many homeowners' associations have rules that prohibit residents from turning their manicured suburbia into (gasp!) something that might be confused for working farmland. Not to be deterred, many enterprising gardeners have started sprinkling things like tomatoes, lettuce, peppers, broccoli, garlic, and herbs in and among the boxwoods, hydrangeas, azaleas, and roses.

The foodscaping trend has taken off, and why not? Many of our favorite vegetable crops are grown as much for the beauty they add to the garden as the nutrition they provide. In my mind, a garden full of gorgeous eggplant or show-stopping okra blossoms (a relative of hibiscus) is just as pleasing to look at in a sidewalk bed as gardenias and daylilies. Mixing edibles and ornamentals gives you the best of both worlds.

Edible crops can even be a beautiful and productive part of a traditional-looking landscape. If a dedicated vegetable garden isn't an option for you, try foodscaping.

Is it a beautiful landscape or a productive vegetable garden? When you practice foodscaping, it can be both at the same time.

It's still important to put the right plant in the right place, so pay attention to what landscaping plants are doing well in their current location, and identify which of your favorite vegetable crops will also thrive in those same beds, based on the sun, soil, spacing, and moisture conditions.

Use taller crops in the back or strategically placed at focal points, and taper down to the ground level with shorter growers, just like you would with any basic landscape design. Crops that need a lot of attention should go in high-traffic areas. You can even plant crops like garlic and onions on the outer borders of beds to protect other landscape plants from critters like deer! As you harvest each crop, you're left with an opportunity to switch up the overall look with new plants.

Foodscaping is a great way to constantly rein-vent the overall look of your yard and opens up a whole new palette of choices for gardeners. It offers incredible flexibility to vegetable growers who may be strapped for space or bound by local restrictions.

THE IMPORTANCE OF PLANNING

You may be eager to get out there and start planting. I get it. The excitement over a new gardening season (and especially an entirely new garden) can make it difficult to wait even one more minute. But I hope you see the value in taking the time to develop a smart plan for your garden. Giving just a little forethought to things like sunlight, drainage, overall size, proximity to resources, and the purpose of the garden will help make all the thousands of subsequent decisions fall into place.

A comprehensive and well-thought-out plan for your vegetable garden is a wonderful start. But as long as we're starting from scratch, we should also spend some quality time talking about the single most important thing in your garden, the element that will make or break everything about your growing success—the soil.

2

IT'S ALL ABOUT THE SOIL

WITHOUT QUESTION, the single most important deciding factor to your garden's success is soil. Notice, though, I didn't say "dirt." For gardeners, there's a distinct difference between the two. Dirt is a blend of minerals comprised of clay, silt, sand, and a small amount of organic matter. But there's little to no oxygen in it. With no oxygen there's no beneficial organisms and no life.

Soil, on the other hand, is rich with oxygen and is light, fluffy, and porous. Healthy soil supports an astonishing amount of life, much of it on a microscopic level. If you could zoom in close enough to the soil in a healthy, thriving garden bed, you'd find an almost alien world of fungi, bacteria, protozoa, nematodes, and microarthropods mixed in with the earthworms, beetles, grubs, and other creatures you can see with the naked eye.

Fungi and bacteria mine the nutrients in the soil. Other microorganisms in soil prey on the fungi and bacteria, producing nutrient-rich excrement that, in turn, feeds the roots of plants. Plant roots put out new food for bacteria and fungi to eat, and the circle of life goes on. It's called the soil food web. It's what makes gardening possible. And amazingly enough, it's the plants themselves that control the whole cycle.

As gardeners, it's in our best interest to feed and nurture that soil food web. Introducing organic matter into our garden soils provides even more food for the microbes there and delivers a fresh population of new fungi and bacteria to join the workforce. The end result is bigger, healthier, more productive vegetables.

This chapter is all about what makes great garden soil and how to get it in your garden. Even if you do nothing else, improving your soil will make your vegetable growing adventures far more successful.

ASSESSING YOUR CURRENT SOIL

Before you can begin improving your soil, you need to have a good understanding of the current status of your soil.

No matter where you are, soil is almost always a mixture of sand, silt, and clay. What changes from place to place is the percentage of each component. One way to think about those three components is to assign each one a unique size. As simplistic as it may seem, imagine sand particles as basketballs, silt particles as tennis balls, and clay particles as golf balls.

If you filled a container with basketballs, there would be a lot of air space between the balls and water would run through the container easily. That's sandy soil. Fill that same container with golf balls, though, and there's very little air space left. That's clay soil. In a perfect world, you'd want equal parts of each type of ball to create optimal conditions for air and water drainage and retention.

Organic matter helps introduce various particle sizes to the mix, opening up the soil's structure. But it also helps bind soil particles together—in a good way—by, over time creating humus.

Giving a handful of your soil a good squeeze will give you a good head start in assessing your current soil's texture.

To assess your soil, try the squeeze test. Pick up a handful of soil and make a fist. You want the soil to bind together but then break apart easily as you run your fingers through it. There's more to great soil than this simple experiment, but ultimately, it is a good way to start assessing what soil texture you have.

Step Away from the Tiller

Compacted soil is bad for plants because it squeezes out the oxygen necessary for the soil food web to live on. Loose, fluffy, oxygenated soil is better. So why not quit reading and go fire up the garden tiller to just fix things right now?

Yes, tilling will break up compacted soil and incorporate oxygen. But it only aerates the top several inches of the surface. Everything under the tiller blades remains compacted and is, in fact, even a little worse off.

But the real damage comes to the living organisms in your soil. According to research, tilling destroys up to 50 percent of the organisms of the soil food web. And the organisms who survive will have a harder time doing their important job, since the tiller's slicing tines likely broke up much of the network of microscopic pathways they had been using to deliver water, nutrients, and oxygen.

Tilling used to be the universally accepted answer to soil compaction. But gardeners now know it does more harm than good.

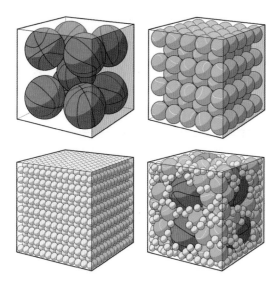

Think of the three components of soil as different-sized balls. Air and water drain through each type very differently.

The mighty soil test

In order for your vegetables (or any plants) to thrive, they'll need certain levels of nutrients in the soil. And to get a handle on what nutrients are present (or lacking) in your soil, you'll need a soil test.

A soil test uses samples of your actual soil, which are analyzed to give the nutrient levels present. Soil tests can also show the percentage of organic matter and your soil's pH. As you may recall from science class, pH refers to the acidity or alkalinity of a solution. Soil pH is measured in a range between 0 and 14. Anything below 7.0 is considered acidic, while anything above 7.0 is alkaline. The further away from 7.0 you get in either direction, the more acidic or alkaline the soil is. 7.0 is neutral, and most vegetable plants prefer soil that's fairly close to neutral.

Why does pH matter? Soil pH regulates the ability of plants to take up nutrients. If your soil pH is outside the preferred range for the crop you're growing, the nutrients in the soil, even if they're abundant, won't be available to the plants. While you can find basic do-it-yourself soil test kits at many garden centers, they generally won't give you the kind of detailed readings you'll need to truly improve your soil quality over the long run.

Many private soil labs sell kits that require you to dig small soil samples from your garden beds and send them away for analysis. Your local government agricultural facility or university extension agency also likely offers soil testing services that work the same way. (Note: Some of these locations even perform soil tests for gardeners for free!) Be aware that the shipping process takes time and depending on the volume of soil tests your private lab or extension agency is handling, you may be waiting several weeks or more to get your results back. Plan ahead so you have time to implement any recommended changes. Personally, I try to collect my soil samples and send them off about four months before my growing season begins.

When you get your test results back, you'll see the levels of the primary nutrients phosphorus and

A soil test is essential for helping you understand the nutrient levels available for plants, and what you may need to do to the soil to get them in the optimal range.

potassium. (Nitrogen is a primary nutrient, too, but it's notoriously difficult to accurately pinpoint in a soil test. Most tests measure the level of organic matter instead as a gauge of nitrogen levels.) You'll also typically receive suggestions on how to bring those levels within the preferred range of what you've told the lab you're trying to grow in that bed.

In addition, you'll get a reading on your soil's pH. Depending on where your soil falls on that scale of 0 to 14, you can adjust it by adding common garden products. Limestone or wood ash can be used to raise the pH in acidic soil, while sulfur, sphagnum peat, aluminum sulfate, or iron sulfate will lower the pH of alkaline soil. Even regularly adding compost and mulch will help bring your soil pH closer to neutral!

Finally, some soil tests will reveal the percentage of organic matter in your soil. (Be sure you know if yours does, or if you can add it on, before you order your report.) For all of my cheerleading

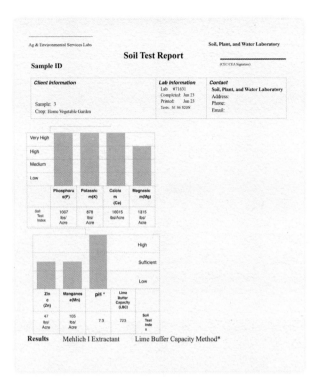

Soil Test Report

Ag & Environmental Services Labs

Soil, Plant, and Water Laboratory

_____
(CEC/CEA Signature)

Sample ID

Client Information	Lab Information	Contact
Sample: 3 Crop: Home Vegetable Garden	Lab #71631 Completed: Jun 23 Printed: Jun 23 Tests: S1 S6 S20N	Soil, Plant, and Water Laboratory Address: Phone: Email:

	Phosphorus(P)	Potassium(K)	Calcium (Ca)	Magnesium(Mg)
Soil Test Index	1007 lbs/ Acre	878 lbs/ Acre	16015 lbs/Acre	1315 lbs/ Acre

	Zinc (Zn)	Manganese(Mn)	pH *	Lime Buffer Capacity (LBC)
	47 lbs/ Acre	105 lbs/ Acre	7.3	723	Soil Test Index

Results   Mehlich I Extractant   Lime Buffer Capacity Method*

Soil Report
Soil, Plant, and Water Laboratory

Client Information	Lab Information	Contact
	Completed: Jun 23 Printed: Jun 23 Tests: S1 S6 S20N	Soil, Plant, and Water Laboratory Address: Phone: E-mail:

Results

Lab		71631
Sample		3
LBC [1]	(ppm CaCO₃/pH)	723.0
pH$_{CaCl_2}$		6.66
Equivalent water pH		7.26
N	(%)	0.8070
OM *	(%)	22.93
Ca	(lbs/acre)	16015
K	(lbs/acre)	877.7
Mg	(lbs/acre)	1315
Mn	(lbs/acre)	104.9
P	(lbs/acre)	1007
Zn	(lbs/acre)	46.91

1. Soil Testing: Measurement of Lime Buffer Capacity
2. Soil Testing: Soil pH and Salt Concentration
*Organic Matter is determined by the "loss on ignition" method for 3 hours at 360° C. Results are reported in percent by weight.

Your soil test results will contain a detailed analysis of exactly what's present in your soil.

about adding more organic matter, this number may not be nearly as high as you're expecting. Most of the time, a soil test will show organic matter as being around 2 or 3 percent! Even in nature, that number is usually about 5 percent. Make that your goal, too, and let the soil test guide you to get there. (There's more on adding organic matter toward the end of this chapter.)

Compost: How to make any soil better

Healthy soil is the key to healthy plants. And there is no single thing you can do that improves your soil more dramatically than adding compost. Seriously, if you learn nothing else from this entire book, remember this—there is no store-bought product that's better for the garden than compost. And I believe compost is the most important ingredient you can add for vegetable garden success.

Compost, put simply, is decayed organic matter, consisting of material you'd find around your yard, plus kitchen scraps from inside your house.

And compost is a major multitasker in the garden. In addition to creating that ideal fluffy soil texture mentioned earlier, compost also acts like a multivitamin for garden beds. It's loaded with vital organic nutrients that are released into the soil slowly over time. Plus, every tablespoon of compost contains billions of beneficial living microorganisms.

Finished compost adds organic matter to your soil and will dramatically improve your plants' health and your garden's production.

Continue to feed your garden beds with more compost occasionally throughout the growing season.

In addition, it's a known growth stimulant for plants, it protects plants from certain diseases, buffers toxins in the soil, helps moderate soil pH, feeds earthworms, and supports the beneficial microorganisms already (hopefully) living in your existing soil!

A little compost goes a long way in the garden. It's an amendment to your existing soil, not to be used as the growing medium itself. In fact, as little as ½ inch (1 cm) of compost mixed in the top layer of your current soil will do wonders. If you have more, even better. But in general, 1 inch (2.5 cm) or so of compost, top-dressed or worked in lightly on the surface of your beds a couple times a year is all it takes.

Compost can be found at some nurseries and garden centers by the bag. Alternatively, many municipalities have composting facilities that offer it to gardeners at a nominal fee, or even at no cost. This is a great way if you need a large quantity, especially if you're starting a vegetable garden from scratch.

That said, you can never be 100 percent sure of exactly what went into compost that you obtain from someone else. As an organic gardener, I don't want to bring home compost that might include pesticides, chemical residue, or even weed seeds! Commercial compost can be a time-saver but proceed with caution. Depending on the source, there may be a report you can access that provides details and a chemical analysis of the composted ingredients.

Killer Compost Alert!

Compost is always a huge benefit to the garden. Well, almost always.

When I first built out my sprawling vegetable garden, I had 16 raised beds to fill. And I was very excited to use the manure I'd been collecting and saving from my own horses, goats, and chickens. It was well-rotted and I had a lot of it. So, I plunged ahead, blending about 20 percent by volume into each bed.

It didn't take long to realize something was very wrong. The leaves on my new tomato plants were twisted and distorted. Other plants were severely stunted. It was only then, far too late, that I asked the farmer who grows the hay I feed my horses what type of herbicide he used on his fields. His answer confirmed my suspicion.

Active herbicide ingredients like picloram, clopyralid, and aminopyralid can remain active in hay, grass clippings, manure piles, and compost for an unusually long time—even after they've passed through the digestive tract of an animal feeding on it! Sometimes a complete deactivation and breakdown can take *years*.

The lesson? Never use compost, manure, or even hay as long-term mulch in your garden beds unless you know where it came from and what chemicals might be lurking in it.

I learned the hard way that my composted manure had been tainted by herbicides used on the hay I fed my horses. Lesson learned—the compost source matters.

The best compost, I'm convinced, is the compost that you make yourself. It's easier than you might think, and it's the ultimate way to control exactly what you feed the soil that feeds your vegetable plants.

Making great compost

Nutrient-filled compost takes just four ingredients, listed below. Combine generous portions of all four in a pile or bin and let it "cook" for several months. When the ingredients are no longer recognizable, the internal temperature is ambient, and the contents smell rich and earthy, it's ready.

Air Microorganisms can't live without oxygen that's already in the air. All you have to do is mix up your compost ingredients often (at least once a week) to keep it properly aerated.

Water Again, this is necessary to sustain life, but in the right proportion. Keep your pile at the moisture level of a damp sponge, and your compost will cook faster.

Green waste Recently living plant material brings nitrogen to the party. Examples include fresh grass clippings, plant trimmings, and food scraps like vegetables and salad greens. Even coffee grounds will work!

Brown waste Think of things that used to be living material: dried leaves, small twigs, shredded paper, newspaper, paper towel rolls, and brown paper bags. These supply carbon.

That's really it, though it's just the tip of the iceberg. There are plenty of resources on the finer points of composting, plenty of tools and gadgets and products you can buy that can help you perfect the process, and lots of ways to go about it on any scale you can imagine. Those four are all that's required for Mother Nature to produce the best amendment your garden could ask for.

There are a few things, though, that should stay out of your compost pile. Weeds going to seed, diseased plants, animal waste (from carnivores), chemically treated plants and grass clippings, and animal products (like meat, bones, grease, and dairy) are best left out of your compost pile.

What Can Be Composted

Brown Materials	Notes
Leaves	Shred or chop first for faster breakdown
Leaves – Oak	Acidic, slow to breakdown
Leaves – Black walnut	Initially toxic to some plants. Neutralized during composting
Sticks and twigs	The smaller the better. Slow to break down
Yard debris from dead plants	Cut or chop into small pieces
Hay or straw	May contain persistent herbicide residues. Use with caution
Pine needles	Acidic, slow to break down
Sawdust	Small particle size is best
Wood mulch (natural)	Slow to break down
Citrus and fruit waste	Includes rinds, seeds, peelings
Corncobs	Shred or chop first, slow to break down
Cardboard; egg cartons	Tear or cut into small pieces
Paper; paper towels	Shred first, avoid glossy paper
Natural fiber materials	Cotton, burlap, bamboo, or wool

Green Materials	Notes
Yard debris from living plants	Cut or chop into small pieces
Manures	High in nitrogen. Use caution when using horse manure due to risk of persistent herbicide residues.
Pet bedding	Small animals including hamsters, rabbits, guinea pigs. Herbivorous animal bedding only.
Vegetable kitchen scraps	Peelings and trimmings
Coffee grounds and filters	Balance with more dry ingredients to keep bin from getting too wet
Lawn clippings	Only collect grass clippings from untreated lawns
Hair	Human or animal
Seaweed/kelp	Rinse with fresh water before adding to bin

Vermicompost: The Gift of Worms

The lowly worm just may be the king of your compost pile. Worms devour food scraps, paper, cardboard, coffee grounds, and the like, breaking those materials down faster than they would biodegrade on their own. As that material passes through a worm's digestive system, what comes out the other end is called "worm castings." *Vermicompost* is the technical term, and it's like gardener's gold (even though it's deep black in color).

This worm manure is such a powerful nutrient source that many gardeners (myself included) maintain a separate bin away from the compost pile just for housing my millions of worms and the scraps I feed them. The bottom of my worm bin is lined with wire mesh, allowing the vermicompost to collect and the liquid runoff (called *leachate*) to drain into aluminum pans. Once I have enough, I use water to dilute the coffee-colored liquid at a 10-to-1 or even 20-to-1 ratio and apply it every two weeks or so in my vegetable garden.

It's as close to magic as anything I've ever seen. All the key nutrients are present in this rich elixir, along with a healthy dose of minerals and billions of good microorganisms. Now that I've seen first-hand what vermicompost can do for my soil and the vegetables I grow there, I'll never relegate worms to a strictly underground role in the garden again.

Worms are the behind-the-scenes (or under the ground) magicians that produce the most incredible nutrient-rich compost your plants have ever tasted.

Biochar is much more than just burned wood. It's a supercharger for garden soil when mixed in with compost and added to beds early.

ADDITIONAL AMENDMENTS

While compost is the best thing you can add to your garden soil, it's not the only additive that can be beneficial to your beds. As you experiment with ways to improve your soil, here are some other amendments to check out.

Biochar Made of pure carbon, biochar is wood chips, lumber waste, or animal manure. It has been burned in the absence of oxygen and at super-high temperatures to eliminate everything flammable, leaving only beneficial carbon behind. Biochar keeps nutrients bound in the soil and ready for plant roots to absorb. It also helps retain soil moisture. It's a supercharger for soil productivity, and it literally lasts a lifetime. But beware though, it's not cheap and it must be mixed with compost or organic fertilizer a month before it can go in the garden. Biochar with a high ash content can also raise your soil pH.

Minerals Typical soil is made up of about 45 percent minerals—sand, silt, and clay. While they don't provide primary nutrients, minerals are nonetheless essential to plant growth. And without minerals like calcium, magnesium, zinc, and manganese in the soil, the vegetables you grow in that soil will be missing them, too. A good soil test will break down your soil's mineral content and help you understand how to carefully add to it with amendments like granite dust, greensand, lime, and gypsum.

Organic matter Shredded leaves, straw and hay, arborist wood chips, and grass clippings can all be safely added directly to soil (once biodegraded) to increase your organic matter content. If you add it before it's broken down, it will temporarily draw nitrogen from the soil (to finish the decomposition process) instead of *feeding* it to your plants. Those things can also be used on top of the soil as mulch (See Chapter 8) or as ingredients in your compost pile, too. It's all about where in their natural breakdown process they are that dictates where you use them. Mushroom compost is what's left over after the mushrooms have been harvested. It's a wonderful feeder for healthy soil. And properly composted cow or poultry manure supplies nitrogen and other nutrients.

My Perfect Raised Bed Soil Recipe

Over many years, I've experimented with everything mentioned in this chapter—and many more things that didn't make the cut—in an attempt to come up with one perfect soil recipe for raised beds. I think I've come awfully close. If you want to skip some of the science and get right to bigger, better, healthier vegetables, try this in your raised beds as a rich and nutrient-packed starting point for your own gardening adventure. Here's my raised bed soil recipe:

- 50% high-quality topsoil
- 30% high-quality compost
- 20% organic matter (I mix and match from the following: well-aged, shredded leaves, mineralized soil blend, vermicompost, mushroom compost, aged ground bark, and composted manure. Don't worry about the percentages just use what you have to reach about 20% by volume—although you get bonus points for diversity.)

Blend all ingredients together. Use the same mix to top-dress the soil in your beds each subsequent season.

They may look like weeds growing in your garden beds after the growing season, but intentionally grown cover crops will add nutrients back to the soil after they're cut down and left in place.

GREEN MANURE: GROWING COVER CROPS FOR BETTER SOIL

One of the best things you can grow in your vegetable beds may be something you don't even eat! A cover crop is grown specifically to be cut down and worked into the soil later. Sow a cover crop across your garden bed after the harvest or even work it into the empty spaces between plants during the growing season! While the crop itself can be grains (rye, oats, or wheat), legumes (clover or vetch), or broadleaves (buckwheat, mustard, or alyssum), the ultimate goal for all of them is the aeration, organic matter, and nutrient content they return to the soil once they're turned in. Cover crops provide so much benefit to the soil that they're often referred to as "green manure."

THE DIRT ON GOOD GROWING SOIL

As you can see, there's a lot more to the soil in your garden than just "dirt." And there's nothing better you can do than be constantly mindful of your garden's soil. From regularly assessing what you have, to always enriching it with the right ingredients, taking care of your soil should be a never-ending endeavor. Your vegetable garden may have a growing season with a start and an end date each year, but improving the soil is a 24/7/365 process. Now that you know more about the soil that gives your garden life, you're ready to dive into the crops themselves.

3

PLANT BASICS

YOU CAN SUCCESSFULLY grow a garden without understanding how it works. And honestly, I could argue that no one fully understands the sheer magic of how or why plants grow at all. But I also firmly believe that the more you know, the better you'll grow.

I don't pretend to understand all the intricacies that go into making my car work. I insert my key, I follow a set of predetermined steps, and things typically just work the way they're supposed to. The point is, I don't have to understand *how* a car works in order to get where I want to go.

But the best drivers learn to know what's happening under their hood. And the more they know, the better they can respond with proper care and maintenance and get the most out of the engine. They're in tune with how things are supposed to run and when there is a problem, they're able to troubleshoot the issue quickly.

It's the difference between knowing *what* to do and innately understanding *why* to do it.

Having a similar grasp (or at least a little) of the science behind plants will make you a better, smarter, more confident vegetable gardener. This chapter is designed to give you a crash course in what makes plants tick (so to speak) so that you can more effectively and efficiently keep your garden running like a finely tuned machine.

THE BASICS PLANTS NEED TO THRIVE

Every crop in your vegetable garden (and every plant anywhere, for that matter) has a very specific set of requirements that, when given just the right conditions, yields the best and most productive possible version of that plant. Cracking that unique code for each edible plant in your garden is probably why you've picked up this book.

Boiled down to simplest terms (and with only a handful of exceptions), there are three non-negotiable basics all plants need to thrive—whether we grow them to put food on our tables or to complement our landscapes.

Light

For our purposes, there are no plants that we'll grow in our vegetable gardens that don't require direct sunlight. In fact, when it comes to edibles, more is better.

"But wait, Joe," I can hear you saying. "What about shade-loving plants?" That's a little bit of a misnomer. The plants that we call *shade-loving* don't actually *love* the shade. They're just more tolerant of low-light conditions than others. All plants must have enough foliage to photosynthesize (convert sunlight into food). And for most edibles, they're also producing flowers and fruit, which increases their demand for energy. The more sunlight, therefore, the more growing power. The plants we think of as shade-loving still need light—they've just adapted to process the light they need more efficiently.

Water

All plants need water. But just as there are plants that tolerate shade, there are also plants that can handle a relatively dry growing environment. We'll cover watering in more depth in Chapter 9, but the general rule of thumb for most vegetable garden plants is 1 inch (2.5 cm) of water per week, whether that comes from rain, supplemental watering, or a combination of both. Some crops like a little more, some prefer a little less.

It's important to note, though, that plants that receive deep, but less frequent, waterings tend to perform better than plants who get very frequent but light waterings. It's not how often you water; it's how deeply you water that matters most. Plant roots will grow deep underground in order to seek out moisture. This makes for stronger roots that can handle dry spells. Frequent shallow watering at the soil's surface makes the roots lazy. They have no need to grow deep to find water because it's already right there at the surface. It may be enough water for the plant to survive, but you're not doing them any favors when drought or hot weather comes. In those times, evaporation can pull water from the soil almost as fast as it's being

While there are a few crops we'll discuss that like a little dappled shade, more is almost always better when it comes to sunlight for the plants that you'll grow in your vegetable garden.

Water is essential for plant growth. Aim for 1 inch (2.5 cm) per week for most plants and remember that watering deeply is better than watering often.

applied, so it doesn't take long after the irrigation stops for the soil to become dry again. Deep watering encourages stronger, deeper roots.

Nutrients

You thought I was going to say soil, didn't you? The truth is, even though I just spent all of Chapter 2 telling you "It's all about the soil," soil isn't even required for plants to grow.

In traditional gardening, soil serves two purposes. One, it's there for the roots to anchor the plant in place. Two, soil serves as the primary medium for delivering water and nutrients to the plant roots. It's the nutrients that ultimately matter most, not the delivery method. Soil just happens to be the delivery method that most home gardeners utilize, and good-quality soil actually *creates* nutrients for plants. And that's why we make building healthy soil such a lifelong endeavor.

There are sixteen essential nutrients for plant life. Carbon, hydrogen, and oxygen are primary nutrients that are delivered to plants via air and water. Nitrogen, phosphorus, and potassium are the other primary *macronutrients* that you'll see listed on fertilizer labels. We'll get into those in detail in Chapter 5. Calcium, magnesium, and sulfur make up the secondary nutrients. They're necessary but used by plants in smaller amounts.

The micronutrients are also important but needed in even smaller quantities: boron, chlorine, copper, iron, manganese, molybdenum, and zinc.

Essential Plant Nutrients

16 essential nutrients	Amount required by plants (most to least)
Carbon, hydrogen, oxygen	Primary nutrients (supplied by air and water)
Nitrogen, phosphorus, potassium	Primary macronutrients
Calcium, magnesium, sulfur	Secondary nutrients
Boron, chlorine, copper, iron, manganese, molybdenum, zinc	Micronutrients

Each of the sixteen nutrients play a specific role in a plant's overall health, vigor, and productivity. A deficiency in any one of them will result in a plant that cannot reach its full growing potential. But excessive nutrients can also be harmful to plant life—the key is balance.

To figure out the balance of the nutrients in your soil, a soil test is the only way to be sure. Refer back to Chapter 2 to get into the nuts and bolts of this critical bit of garden preparation.

Tag, you're it: My cheat sheet for gardening success

There is a lot that goes into "the basics" of what plants need to thrive. It can be a lot to try to remember for every crop in your garden. If only there was a handy cheat sheet that spelled out just what you needed. There is. I'm talking about the tag that's stuck right in the pot of seedlings you bring home or the label that's printed right on every packet of seeds.

Check the Date

Seeds have a certain "best before" lifespan. The older they are, the less viable they become. Just like you wouldn't want to drink long-expired milk, you're setting yourself up for heartache and extra work down the road if you plant old seeds that are no longer viable.

A seed packet or pot tag will tell you many details: the proper season for planting based on your growing zone; whether to start your seeds indoors or direct-sow them outside; how deep to sow seeds or plant seedlings; and how much space to leave, not only from one plant to the next, but also between rows of plants. Most important of all, the tag or packet lists the sun, water, and light requirements for that specific variety. Think of plant tags and seed packets like user's manuals for your vegetable crops.

There's a lot of timing information there, too. How many days will it take, on average, for those seeds to germinate? How many days after planting outside can you expect to have mature fruit? These are critical details that keep gardening from being just a total guessing game.

Plus, there may be some information that's unique to certain seeds or seedlings such as special techniques that will aid in germination or tips for more successful mid-season growth. Additional questions are often answered such as does that crop need to be thinned after it sprouts? Should it be staked as it grows taller? Would it benefit from being placed under a floating row cover? Is the seed or seedling a variety that is naturally resistant to Verticillium or Fusarium wilt or tobacco mosaic virus? The tag or label will tell you.

I hope this book will be a major help to you in your gardening adventure and one that you refer to often in answering those kinds of questions. But still, keep those plant tags handy as backup.

When you put the right plant in the right place, and especially if you don't, the plant will let you know about it.

Locate veggies that love lots of sun sun, such as these beans, in a site that receives full sun. The plants will be healthier and more productive.

RIGHT PLANT, RIGHT PLACE

If there is such a thing as a golden rule of gardening, this is it. You'll hear gardeners everywhere repeat it like a mantra that supersedes everything else. Even if you understand all there is to know about a plant's primary nutrient needs and basic requirements for sun, soil, and water, all of the botany basics essentially boil down to "right plant, right place."

Many edible crops share similar location requirements which means that as long as you site your garden in the "right place," whatever you choose to grow there will do well. But there are quirks from crop to crop that you need to keep in mind. Most vegetable crops prefer full sun. Some, though, such as spinach, lettuce, and arugula do quite well in light shade, since they don't have the extra duty of producing fruit (like tomatoes or corn). So that corner of your garden that sits in dappled shade most of the day isn't the "right place" for your prized tomato plant if you want maximum results, but your spinach crop may like it just fine.

No matter how meticulous you are in your gardening practices, I've found that there's almost nothing you can do to outsmart this rule. If

Mother Nature doesn't want it to grow where you put it, it's probably not happening. Start with "right plant, right place," and everything that comes after will be much easier.

SOME COMMON TERMS, DEFINED

Any activity comes with its own specialized language, the abbreviations and shorthand lingo that help communicate the details that are specific to it. But those same terms can often present an obstacle to those coming to the hobby for the first time or just starting out.

Gardening is definitely one of those pastimes with our own language. Even if all you're trying to do is grow a few tomatoes in the backyard, it won't take you long to run into enough Latin botanical names, scientific terms, and five-dollar words to make you wonder if you need a dictionary just to make your garden grow.

So, to make sure we're all on the same page as you continue on in this book (or just for reference whenever you may need it), this section covers a handful of key terms and phrases that you're sure to encounter as you get into vegetable gardening.

Most traditional vegetable crops are annuals, completing their entire life cycle in a single growing season.

Beets are a good example of a biennial, a plant that requires two growing seasons to complete its lifecycle. They develop roots, stems, and leaves in the first season. Then flower and set seeds in the second season.

Asparagus is the classic perennial vegetable, able to come back and keep producing year after year.

Annuals vs. biennials vs. perennials

These terms all refer to the lifespan of a given plant.

Annuals complete their entire life cycle (germinate, grow, flower, set fruit, and then die) all within a single growing season. There's no point in trying to keep the plant alive or even in the ground until the following season. It's one season and done. Plant a new one next year. Many cold-season annuals can tolerate light frost or cold weather. Their growing season is simply on a different schedule than warm-season annuals. Most traditional vegetable crops are considered annuals.

Biennials, as the name suggests, require two growing seasons to complete their lifecycle. They develop roots, stems, and leaves in the first season. Then flower and set seeds in the second season before finally dying. Some weather conditions, though, like cold spells or drought, can trick the plant into compressing both seasons into one. There are more biennials in the vegetable gardening than you might think. Beets, brussels sprouts, cabbage, carrots, lettuce, onions, and parsley are all examples of biennials.

Perennials come back year after year. The top foliage may die back in winter, but the roots will survive if left undisturbed, and the plant will regrow when temperatures warm again in spring. Asparagus is the classic example of a vegetable garden perennial. Garlic is a perennial, too. Blueberry plants aren't vegetables, but they are perennials that are always in my garden, providing visual interest for multiple growing seasons.

Open-pollinated vs. heirloom vs. hybrid vs. GMO

These terms are used when differentiating groups of plants or seeds.

Open-pollinated varieties are those which have simply pollinated freely in the field, isolated from other varieties of the same species. Just one variety of these plants, left entirely to its own devices, will produce seed that's "true to type," meaning a new plant from that seed will be virtually identical to the parent crop.

Heirloom plants are open-pollinated varieties that have been handed down by gardeners and farmers over many years (or even centuries). Most gardeners consider plants heirlooms if they were being grown roughly before World War II. For decades upon decades, these plants thrived without artificial fertilizers and pesticides, with only the best and strongest plants surviving to produce seed. This makes heirlooms exceptionally popular with organic gardeners. Best of all, heirlooms often produce uniquely shaped and unusually colored fruit in far superior flavors, which make them so sought-after by chefs and gourmets.

Hybrid plants were developed starting in the 1930s and 1940s to grow produce that could be transported long distances and last longer in the sales bin at the supermarket. To create a hybrid, two open-pollinated plant varieties of the same species are maintained separately from one another and then intentionally cross-pollinated. Seed saved from a hybridized plant will produce a plant that has some characteristics of each parent plant. By pairing open-pollinated plants that each had a certain desirable quality, for instance, fruit from the new plant would take on the aspects of both. In the world of vegetable hybrids, flavor often takes a backseat to other traits like higher yield, longer shelf life, improved disease resistance, thicker skin, consistent size, and blemish-free appearance.

Be aware, though, that seed saved from the fruit of a first-generation hybridized plant will not produce identical fruit in the second generation. And contrary to surprisingly popular opinion, the term *hybrid* is **not** synonymous with *genetically modified*, as explained next.

GMO stands for *genetically modified organism*. A GMO variety takes the concept of hybridization and introduces human manipulation on a genetic level by inserting DNA that is not from the same species into a plant to create the desired blend of characteristics.

There is no lack of vigorous debate in the gardening community about GMOs, and the topic alone opens a Pandora's box of ethical and political issues that I won't go into here. Suffice it to say that GMO seed and GMO crops have revolutionized commercial agriculture and large-scale farming. Whether that's a good thing or not may depend on your personal perspective. And whatever your stance, GMO seeds are currently unavailable to home gardeners anyway.

Heirloom plants have been handed down by gardeners over several generations. They often feature superior flavor and striking shapes and colors.

'Sungold' tomatoes are a good example of a hybrid crop that most people are familiar with. Hybrids have been intentionally crossbred to display certain characteristics of two parent plants.

Determinate vs. indeterminate

These two terms can help differentiate varieties of potatoes, soybeans, and some other crops. But for most home gardeners, they apply to the fruiting habit of tomato plants.

Determinate varieties (usually the bush varieties) grow to a certain height and then stop growing. They put on all of their fruit in one relatively short explosion, and then they're done. They're less common than indeterminate varieties. 'Roma' is by far the most popular determinate tomato, so plant an adequate number if you have plans to make batches of sauce, because you get just one harvest per plant.

Determinate tomatoes, like 'Roma', grow to a certain size and produce all their fruit in one big blast. Then they're done. Indeterminate varieties like 'Black Krim', keep getting bigger and putting on new fruit throughout the season.

Indeterminate varieties are generally more vinelike in their growth habit, and they put on fruit continuously throughout the season. The plants themselves can get huge and unruly, and they often produce more tomatoes than an unprepared gardener knows what to do with. (You'll find much more about growing tomatoes of both types in the Grow Guides that begin after Chapter 12.)

WHEN IN DOUBT, THINK LIKE A PLANT

This chapter has thrown a lot of science and some new vocabulary at you. But for my last piece of advice when it comes to plant basics, I encourage you to set aside the hard and fast rules every once in a while and engage in a little bit of anthropomorphic role-playing.

Whenever I'm troubleshooting a problem in the garden, I often take a step back and try to get out of my own head for a moment. Forget the books, never mind what the seed packet says or what worked well last year or what I *think* I know beyond a shadow of a doubt. Instead, I try to, quite simply, think like a plant.

I'll put myself in that plant's place and ask myself, "What's wrong?" "Why am I not growing well?" "Why am I not living up to potential?" "What else is happening around me that's having an impact?" "Is this where I'd really be happiest?" "Am I getting everything I need?" It may sound a little silly, but nearly every time I go through this self-assessment exercise, I find that I notice things about the situation at hand that provide helpful answers.

Maybe a plant is wilting, even though it's getting consistent water. But when I put myself in the plant's place, I might observe that the soil is too sandy or there's more of a slope than I ever noticed before and water is draining away too quickly. Or maybe a plant just doesn't seem to be healthy, even though other plants of the same variety are doing quite well. It's then that I look around through the plant's "eyes" and realize that I'd probably prefer more light or air circulation coming into my interior branches. And it might dawn on me that what I need is some selective pruning, or that a neighboring shrub or tree is blocking vital sunlight.

Spending time in your garden and putting yourself in the plant's place is often the best way to troubleshoot a problem in the garden.

Educating yourself as a gardener is a lifelong pursuit. There's so much to learn about how to grow plants. But remember that it's really the plants themselves that teach us how to grow them. The plants will tell you what they need to thrive. Oftentimes, your most important job as the gardener is to learn how to listen to them. Don't be afraid to turn off your own brain from time to time and just think like a plant.

YOU'VE COMPLETED BASIC TRAINING

Well, that's it. Not exactly a comprehensive master class in botany, but I hope these few pages helped you better understand the basics behind your plants. I've found that getting at least a rudimentary grasp on what plants need to thrive helps me do a better job of providing it. Throw in a reliable cheat sheet, remember the golden rule of "right plant, right place," never forget that no two years are the same, and keep a few important vocabulary terms in mind, and you're well on your way to being a better, smarter, more confident vegetable gardener. Now it's time to start pulling all that knowledge out of your head and putting it into the garden.

4

WHERE TO GROW YOUR FOOD

WHERE YOUR GARDEN GROWS is important, but so is what your garden grows in. Generally, where you grow your food will be determined by things you may have a lot of control over. These include sun exposure, easy access to water, a convenient spot on your property, the surrounding environment, local predators, and more. These things help you site your garden, and they're dealt with in detail in Chapter 1, along with other factors about starting a new vegetable garden.

But let's get more specific, because what your garden grows in matters, too. What physically holds the garden? Are your edibles planted directly in the earth? Should you build or buy raised planting beds? What material should those beds be made out of? Would some alternative to big, boxy, constructed beds (and there are many) be more effective for your unique situation?

Gardening is a creative endeavor with endless options and interpretations, depending on the gardener, and is limited only by imagination. In this chapter, I'll help you think outside the box when it comes to growing your vegetables, but just in case, I'll share some keys on how to build the best box, too.

IN-GROUND BEDS

Obviously, this original gardening option requires the least amount of set-up. You could put this book down right now and be planting vegetables in the earth in the time it takes you to find a shovel. And in-ground gardening couldn't be any less expensive to start. People have been planting crops directly in their native soil for all of recorded history, and for millions of today's gardeners, it's still the preferred method. If it's not broken, why fix it?

In-ground beds aren't fancy, but they're still an excellent way to garden for millions.

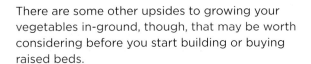

All it takes to effectively kill off a section of lawn for planting a new garden is newspaper or cardboard. And a fair amount of time.

Many gardeners have turned their back on tilling, as it destroys soil structure, kills organisms residing there, and brings weed seeds to the surface (where they'll germinate and grow).

There are some other upsides to growing your vegetables in-ground, though, that may be worth considering before you start building or buying raised beds.

In-ground soil is generally better insulated from both heat and cold than soil in a raised bed. This can mean your earthen garden plot is a few degrees cooler in the spring and your crops can go just a bit longer as fall turns to winter.

As we'll discuss in Chapter 9, one tenet of good watering practice is to help your soil hang onto moisture. In-ground beds tend to retain moisture better than raised beds.

RAISED BEDS

My personal preference is always to grow edibles in raised garden beds. When I was starting my own backyard garden (the one I would use as homebase for a national television show), I didn't have much of a choice in the matter. The plot of land I had to work with sat on top of a septic drainage field, so in-ground planting was out of the question. But as the years and growing seasons have passed, I've come to believe that raised beds simply offer overwhelmingly obvious benefits to in-ground gardens.

Make Your Bed Before You Plant In It

Unless you just happen to have the perfect patch of bare earth waiting for you and your garden, you'll likely have to put in a little elbow grease to reclaim the site from turf or shrubs or weeds.

To remove lawn, rent a sod cutter and dig up the grass (roots and all) with a flat-bladed shovel or spade, or smother the grass and turn it into compost. This involves covering the grass with several layers of newspaper or cardboard and then topping it with a layer of organic material like rotted leaves, straw, compost, or manure. Top it off with shredded wood chips and perhaps add some extra nutrients like an organic nitrogen source. The whole mound should be about 6 inches (15 cm) deep. Keep it consistently moist, and in a few months, the area will be grass-free, easy to work, and loaded with organic matter for your plants.

For a weed-infested area, solarize it. This process uses the sun to kill off weeds, so it's best done in the hottest part of the summer. Mow as low as possible, then wet down the area until thoroughly soaked. Then cover the area with clear plastic sheeting, burying or otherwise securing the edges to get a tight seal and trap the moisture underneath. Check the plastic edges periodically and repair any tears or holes with duct tape. Remove the plastic after eight weeks (longer than this and you risk killing off too many beneficial microorganisms) and recycle it. All the weeds down to a depth of 3 inches (7 cm) or so should be dead, but don't dig in it pulling up deeper weed seeds.

It may be tempting, or even necessary, to till the area before trying to establish a vegetable garden, but tilling comes with drawbacks. Tilling wastes nutrients stored in the soil, kicks up dormant weed seeds, ruins the soil's structure, and destroys much of the microscopic soil food web that makes growing possible. (Much more on this in Chapter 2.)

No matter what is in your future garden spot now, reaching for a topical lawn- or weed-killing product is not the answer. Yes, herbicides are a time-saver. But the chemicals in that product can linger in the soil and affect your vegetable beds, possibly introducing things you would never want anywhere near food that you're eating or serving your family.

Raised garden beds offer easily accessible and fully customizable growing areas and can be placed even over native ground that would make gardening impossible.

Raised beds offer complete flexibility. You decide the size, shape, and orientation of your garden.

First, as I just mentioned, is location. You can build a raised bed pretty much anywhere. I've seen incredibly productive raised-bed vegetable gardens that were plopped down on wooden decks, balconies, rough gravel fields, or even paved parking lots! Plan your raised beds to hold enough growing medium, and you don't even need native soil underneath!

As for soil, your site could be hardpack dirt, heavy red clay, or fine-grained sand. It could be severely lacking in one or more of the nutrients essential for plant growth. A soil test that also screens for metals could show lead or other dangerous contaminants in the soil where you live. In a raised bed, you can custom engineer your own ideal soil because you're starting from scratch.

Also, consider accessibility. Gardening in your native soil means a lot of bending, stooping, and hunching over. Crawling around on your knees can take a lot of the fun out of growing food for many folks, myself included. Raised beds put your plants at a better level for planting, maintenance,

watering, observation, and harvesting. The more convenient your garden is, the more time you're likely to devote to it.

Raised beds can be built in just about any size or shape to suit your available space. I designed the sixteen beds in my own garden with a few key parameters in mind.

Height: I find a bed that sits 12 to 18 inches (30 to 45 cm) off the ground to be ideal. It allows plenty of depth for roots to grow, puts most of your vegetables at eye level, and gives you a great seat while you garden! A raised bed as low as 6 inches (15 cm) can be plenty productive, but growing root crops like potatoes, carrots, parsnips, and the like may be tricky.

Width: Four feet (1.2 m) is perfect. It allows you to space rows adequately within the bed, but you'll still be able to reach the center of the growing space from either side without stepping on the soil and compressing it. For this reason, I don't recommend making your beds any wider.

Length: This one is up to you, your site, and your budget.

Shape: Squares and rectangles are most common, but I've seen triangles, circles, ovals, and T-shaped beds that were designed to maximize every square foot of space.

Materials for raised beds

As for the material that comprises your raised beds, the options are plentiful. Find what works best for you and your budget. If it's built right, a raised bed can last for years and years—but remember that it doesn't have to be permanent at all!

Untreated wood: I'll start with my top choice for raised beds. Redwood, cedar, cypress, oak, walnut, and others can last a very long time in any weather conditions. Best of all, you don't have to worry if the roots, foliage, or produce comes in direct contact with these natural and untreated woods. Just be sure it comes from a sustainable source before purchasing.

Treated wood: Lumber such as pressure-treated pine is certainly easy to find and work with. It is very cost-effective and can last for years. But it has been treated with chemicals that protect it from rot. Those chemicals may leach into the soil and could affect the plants growing in it. While the likelihood and risk of this is pretty low, many gardeners are hesitant.

Composite lumber: Made from recycled materials, this has become a trendy option. It often has a fake, plastic appearance, though, and long pieces of it can have more bend than you may want. Composite lumber can be quite heavy and is sometimes very expensive, but it is usually guaranteed to last for many years.

Concrete or cinder blocks: They're a snap to stack, cheap to buy, and easy to obtain. Plus, they last a lifetime. But be aware that some masonry products (especially older blocks) contain fly ash, a petroleum byproduct that contains heavy metals. These hazardous metals are only released if the block breaks and the dust mixes with the soil.

Treated lumber is easy to obtain and withstands the elements, but some gardeners prefer not to introduce the chemicals used to their gardens.

You can have raised beds without building walls. Mounded soil beds are a great no-fuss option in many gardens.

Galvanized metal: Large feeding or watering tubs from farm supply stores are showing up in more and more gardens as raised beds. Make sure the metal beds have adequate drainage. The metal surface will heat up in sunlight and raise your soil temperature, so some vegetables may need to be placed in the center of the beds, where the soil is cooler.

Mounded soil only: I include this option to show that a raised bed doesn't have to have walls at all. Shape your planting soil over the existing grade in a long mound, with the edges tapered out roughly at a 45-degree angle.

Quirky and cool, but think about the materials and chemicals used to manufacture tires, not to mention where they've been previously. This is not a planting container for edibles that I can recommend.

Simple brackets can turn boards into a raised bed of whatever size and shape you like in no time.

Ties and Tires: Raised Bed No-Nos

You've no doubt seen them, but don't be tempted to create raised vegetable beds out of old railroad ties or tires. The repurposing notion behind both materials is commendable, but both present a very real hazard.

Though they last a long time, railroad ties are made from creosote, an oil distilled from coal tar. The Environmental Protection Agency labels it as a probable human carcinogen and says it is not approved to treat wood for residential use, specifically citing the dangers of using it in landscape timbers or garden borders.

Tires are a petroleum-based product. They will leach chemicals into the soil as they age, and the rubber breaks down. As cute and quirky as a tire garden can look, don't use them for growing edibles.

Raised bed kits

For all the upside of a raised bed, minus all the DIY drama, you can purchase full kits in a variety of sizes that have everything you need. Or simply buy corner brackets for the wood or composite lumber of your choice and you have an instant garden bed of any size you choose. If you use boards that are already cut to your preferred size, you may not even need tools! An added bonus—these kits are stackable to give your beds extra height.

Containers

Whether you're talking about fancy glazed ceramic planters, inexpensive terra cotta pots, or handmade window boxes, container gardening expands your growing options significantly. When you think about it, a container is just a raised bed on a more miniature scale. Lots of edibles do particularly well in containers too. If you're an apartment dweller or are otherwise deprived of natural growing space, containers may be the only way you can grow your own food. Containers can dress up a balcony, deck, or patio nicely.

Size definitely matters when it comes to containers, so match your crops to containers carefully. You still need to provide your container vegetables with the proper depth of soil and room to grow. And just like conventional garden beds, don't overcrowd your pots.

Your choices are endless when it comes to materials. Ceramic, clay, metal, wood, fiberglass, plastic, or Styrofoam—containers are out there in any size, shape, color, and style you want. Generally, you get what you pay for. A cheap plastic pot won't last nearly as long as a heavy-duty ceramic planter that costs more. Be aware that some materials will crack in cold weather. And don't ignore the kitschy appeal of planting in non-traditional objects. I've seen everything from antique wheelbarrows to old work boots used as very effective (and very memorable) planters.

I love to use containers as a way to squeeze in extra growing space. Options range from expensive ceramic urns to simple terra cotta pots.

Check the label on any bagged mix you intend to use in a container. It should be clearly marked as designed for that purpose. Ordinary garden soil is far too dense for containers.

A good growing container must have drainage holes to prevent your plant roots from drowning. And the container may need to be elevated off the ground to allow water to seep out. As for the long-standing practice of adding gravel or Styrofoam peanuts to the bottom of a container below the soil, ostensibly to help drainage, research actually shows it does more harm than good.

Soil for a container needs to be less dense than what you'd want in your garden beds. Look for bagged soil labeled as "potting" or "container" mix. They're ideal. Alternatively, you can lighten ordinary garden soil by adding vermiculite, perlite, and finely ground wood fines, all together or separately. (You can play with the ratios to get what you like best.) A slow-release fertilizer can also be added. I use compost when planting, but you may choose to supplement throughout the season according to the crop. I stay away from any water-retentive polymers or soil mix-ins that promise to hold water for your container plants. Those products don't know when a plant is too wet, and they can do their job too well during rainy periods. Water as normal by whatever method you like (See Chapter 9) but know that container soil often dries out faster than in-ground beds.

Just Bag It!

This specialty container deserves its own mention. Grow bags are a very inexpensive, and downright utilitarian, option for growing edibles just about *anywhere* you want. These bags, usually made of felt or polypropylene fabric, hold anywhere from 5 to 15 gallons (23 to 58 L) or more of soil and are plenty deep enough for any crop you have in mind. The bags drain well and sit perfectly flat when filled. Some even have a flap along the bottom for harvesting root crops! They could be black or white or any number of decorative colors. Granted, they may not exactly give you that traditional garden look. But they are very convenient and unquestionably effective. I have a friend who grows over 200 of the biggest, healthiest, prettiest tomato plants you've ever seen using these bags every season *in his driveway*!

Grow bags are an easy and inexpensive way to put your favorite edible plants almost anywhere at all.

I was skeptical the first time I heard about growing food in a straw bale. But it works wonderfully, and now I'm a believer.

Straw bales

What started out as an experiment for a budget-minded gardener who had grown up on a farm has turned into a popular method for gardeners everywhere who love the no-muss, no-fuss, low-cost, temporary flexibility that growing food in straw bales offers.

Start with a straw bale (hay bales break down before a single growing season is over) from a reputable source so you know it's pesticide-free. Place it with the cut side up (it will be prickly to the touch) to aid in water and nutrient penetration. Condition the bale for planting by wetting it and adding a nitrogen source to speed up the decomposition of the straw. I use blood meal as an organic nitrogen source, but synthetic lawn fertilizer is an inexpensive and fast-acting option too. Apply water and nitrogen every

other day for about 18 days to grow beneficial bacteria inside the bale. You'll know when it's working. The straw should feel warm to the touch and look like it's starting to break down and soften.

Plant seedlings directly into the straw bale by separating the straw with your hands and inserting the root ball directly into the cavity. If you're sowing seeds, mound a thin layer of soil mix over the top of the bale.

For seeded crops, follow the packet instructions for spacing, but use a checkerboard pattern to get the most production from the bale's planting surface. Allow proper spacing for transplanted crops and don't overcrowd the bale. One indeterminate tomato plant, for example, may need an entire straw bale to itself.

Straw bale gardening takes soil out of the equation, but you'll still have to do a little digging to get the bale ready for plants.

One great bonus to the straw bale method is that you can plant small plants into the sides. Herbs do especially well planted this way.

A straw bale will hold 3 to 5 gallons (14 to 23 L) of water. Early in the growing season, aim for 1 gallon (4.5 L) per day, increasing the amount as the season progresses. You can set up a drip irrigation system over straw bales, use a soaker hose, or water by hand.

Straw bale gardening may not be for everyone. It's certainly an untraditional look. But you'll have minimal weeds and no soilborne diseases to remedy, you can start planting earlier in the season thanks to warmer temperatures down in the straw, and you can grow an incredible amount of food anywhere you can stick a bale. What's not to love about that?

ONE SIZE DEFINITELY DOESN'T FIT ALL

There is no one "right kind" of vegetable garden. And the ideal garden for you could even be a combination of in-ground beds and raised beds and grow bags and containers. They can all give excellent results and bountiful harvests and make the absolute most of all the growing space you have to work with. And once you start to get a little bit creative with asking yourself, "Where can I grow food?" you may soon find yourself wondering instead, "Where can't I grow food?" It's all fair game, limited only by the number of crops you can keep alive and healthy with sunlight, water, and those all-important nutrients, which just so happens to be the subject of our next chapter.

Just when I thought I had no room in my vegetable garden, I got turned on to straw bale growing.

FEEDING YOUR PLANTS

I'LL ADMIT THIS chapter's title is a little misleading, at least within my own gardening philosophy. That's because when I think about "feeding my plants," what I actually mean is "feeding my soil."

I know what you may be thinking. *I don't want to eat my soil; why does it need nutrients? It's my vegetable plants that need the nutrients*! As discussed in Chapter 2, the soil food web is a fascinating world that's a little bit foreign to most gardeners. In ideal conditions, according to scientists, a tablespoon of soil is teeming with billions of beneficial microorganisms that provide plants with what they need to naturally grow and prosper.

So, the goal is to feed the soil and let the soil feed your plants.

Of course, *what* you feed the soil will have massive ramifications on how your plants grow (or, in some cases, don't).

Generous and frequent helpings of organically rich compost are the absolute best way to feed the soil and, in turn, let the soil feed the plants, and there's plenty to say about compost in Chapter 2.

This chapter, however, deals specifically with garden fertilizer, which can be defined as any material of natural or synthetic origin that is applied to soil or to plant tissues to supply one or more nutrients that are essential to plant growth.

But which nutrients your fertilizer provides, as well as *how* and *when* you provide them, can make a significant difference in the overall health and production of your vegetable garden.

Nitrogen is responsible for the plant growth that you can see above ground.

PRIMARY NUTRIENTS AND WHAT THEY DO

For all plants, there are three primary nutrients required for growth: nitrogen, phosphorus, and potassium. They're abbreviated as N, P, and K, respectively.

Gardeners always refer to them in that specific order, N-P-K. And a simple mnemonic phrase, *up, down, and all around*, will help you remember what purpose each nutrient serves in the garden.

Nitrogen aids in plant growth above ground (the "up" in our little rhyme). It promotes the green, leafy growth of foliage.

Phosphorus helps establish growth below ground (or "down") in the form of healthy root systems. It's also the component most responsible for flower blooms and fruit production.

Potassium provides for "all-around" plant health by building strong cells within plant tissue. That allows the plant to withstand stressors like heat, cold, pests, and disease.

These aren't the only ingredients that factor into good plant growth. In fact, there are twelve other elements that are considered essential, too. Organic soil amendments are ideal for providing all of them. You can find my perfect soil recipe that includes them all in Chapter 2.

Understanding the numbers on fertilizer labels

Keeping that N-P-K abbreviation in mind as you shop at your local big box store or garden center will help you decode the strings of numbers prominently displayed on most fertilizer packaging.

One common type of fertilizer is labelled as 10-10-10. Those numbers represent the percentage, by weight, of each of the big three nutrients. In a 50-pound (23 kg) bag of 10-10-10, then 10% (5 pounds or 2.25 kg) of it is nitrogen, 10% (5 pounds or 2.25 kg) is phosphorus, and 10% (5 pounds or 2.25 kg) of it is potassium. The remaining 70% is filler (inert ingredients), which is there mostly to help disperse the chemicals upon application.

Sometimes Ten Doesn't Really Mean Ten

Generally, those fertilizer N-P-K numbers are sufficient to go on for most gardeners in most situations. But it's important to note that not all the percentages listed on the bag are mathematically correct. Only the nitrogen count is completely accurate—10 really does mean 10 percent by weight. But the actual levels of the other two nutrients are lower than the number indicates. That's because neither phosphorus nor potassium are present in their pure molecular forms.

The phosphorus in fertilizer is represented chemically as P^2O^5, meaning much of it is actually oxygen molecules. Technically, only 44 percent of the number on the bag is pure phosphorus. Similarly, the potassium number represents K^2O, a compound that's also part oxygen molecules. The true potassium content is 83 percent of the number printed on the label.

Again, though, the ratio on the packaging is close enough for most gardeners' needs. If you do require precise measurements, perhaps to meet a soil test recommendation to the letter, keep these exact measurements in mind and do the math accordingly.

Understanding the numbers on that bag of fertilizer is key to knowing what it will do to your garden plants. I promise there won't be (much) math involved.

Understanding the chemical makeup of the 10-10-10 example makes it clear why it's considered a good all-purpose fertilizer. It is a **balanced** fertilizer that provides all three major nutrients in equal parts, helping the plant grow "up, down, and all around" in equal measure.

A fertilizer with a higher first number contains more nitrogen, so it's meant to encourage lush, green foliage. One with a high middle number will boost root growth and fruit production.

The results of a soil test might recommend that you add a specific fertilizer ratio, 1:1:3, for example. Mathematically speaking, that could be 5-5-15 or 10-10-30 or 20-20-60 fertilizer. The ratios, or relative percentage of the total nutrients, are the same for all three, but the higher numbers always indicate a higher quantity of nutrients by volume. But you still may not be able to find a fertilizer for sale with that exact ratio. Don't sweat it. As long as you choose one with a higher third number, like a 10-5-15 or a 10-10-20, you can rest assured you're heading in the right direction.

As for what form your fertilizer takes, granular or pelletized fertilizers are easiest to distribute evenly, and the nutrients are taken up more slowly by plant roots. Liquid fertilizers offer a quicker delivery method for nutrients, but they do have a higher leaching rate and are more prone to washing away (more on that momentarily). Stay away from those fertilizer spikes you stick in the soil. They don't provide an even distribution of nutrients.

Food for thought

My life as an organic gardener began by accident—literally. One day years ago, I spilled fertilizer on my lawn. It was expensive, so I was careful to pick up as much of the granulated material as I could. I thought I did a pretty good job, leaving what seemed to be only the thinnest layer behind.

I was stunned when I returned days later to see that where I had spilled, the grass had died. Not only did I have to reseed the entire area, but it took a surprisingly long time for the new grass to reestablish. It bothered me that a product designed to benefit my lawn had, instead, done considerable harm and caused lasting damage. I started researching. And the more I learned, the more organic practices I began incorporating into my own gardening routines. Over time, I found that natural materials and methods created healthier and longer-lasting results, made my work in the garden easier, and left me feeling better about the choices I was making.

Eventually, I came to think of fertilizer in the garden the way I think of the food we put in our bodies. If you're hungry, you can fill up on something that was produced in a factory like junk food loaded with empty calories. Sure, it may satisfy that hunger craving, but it doesn't do anything at all for your body's long-term health. It works the same way in the garden. Synthetic fertilizers will get some nutrients to your plants quickly, just like sugary candy will quiet a growling stomach. But it's certainly not best in the long run.

Organic vs. synthetic nutrients

Plain and simple, plants don't care where their nutrients come from. In fact, plants can't even tell the difference between natural and synthetic nutrients—the chemical makeup is exactly the same.

Synthetically manufactured fertilizers are engineered for "quick-release." They deliver nutrients rapidly. While that may sound great, think about that junk food analogy. Plant roots will binge away, taking up all the nutrients they can as quickly as possible. But too much too soon damages the plant's systems, often manifesting as browning foliage referred to as "fertilizer burn." Nutrient overdose can even kill vegetable plants. That quick-release feature of synthetics often forces a plant to put out an excess of top growth before the roots can catch up. This overabundance of foliage often results in weaker plants that are more disease-prone and less productive when it comes to fruiting.

For me, organic fertilizers created healthier and longer-lasting results. They also help me feel good about the impact I'm having (or not) on the environment when I use them in the garden.

Worms, my most trusted garden helpers, and other organisms contribute mightily to the intricate ecosystem at work under the soil's surface in a healthy garden.

Synthetic fertilizers may feed your plants, but they do nothing to feed the soil. Whatever nutrients aren't taken up by the plant typically leach out of beds as water moves across and through the soil. Synthetics are often a water-soluble product. If the plant roots don't take it, it's gone just the same. And when it goes, it often leaves the garden entirely, finding its way into watersheds and aquifers, where it can do damage downstream to other plants, wildlife, humans, and our environment as a whole.

Organic, or natural, fertilizers are derived from plant, animal, microbe, or mineral sources. While many organic nutrients are generally not in a form that can immediately be taken up by plant roots, that's actually a good thing. They require organisms in the soil—bacteria, fungi, protozoa, earthworms, etc.—to digest them and break them down into a form that the plants can work with. They feed the soil, and the soil feeds the plants.

The nutrient content in the soil will build up slowly over time, created as microbes continue to digest organic matter. As the microbes eventually die off at the end of their life cycle, they release more of the nutrients consumed during their lifetime. The circle of life goes on, and your soil's structure and organic content is the beneficiary.

This process takes longer, but that's okay, because organic nutrients bind to soil particles and stay there. Unlike synthetics—foreigners in a natural ecosystem—organic fertilizers make themselves at home in the soil until they're utilized, with very little risk of burning plant roots.

It's important to remember that natural fertilizers can be notably slower to take effect in winter, since the microorganisms doing the breaking down are less active in cold weather. That's not to say you shouldn't still have an eye toward feeding your soil all year long, just allow extra time for things to happen!

Here are a few of my favorite organic nutrients and their release rates, so you can see just how long-lasting the benefits can be.

Blood meal and many types of manure can be available to plant roots within 2-6 weeks.

Alfalfa, clover, rye can be available to plant roots within 2-6 months.

Fish emulsion and other soluble or liquid concentrates can be available to plant roots very quickly.

Obviously, for gardeners seeking a quick-fix approach to a garden problem, organic nutrients may not seem very appealing. Weeks or months is a long time to wait for results if vegetable plants are looking unhealthy or not producing. That's why it's important to think of organic fertilizer not as a "bandage" to be reactively applied when there's evidence of trouble, but instead, as a proactive input to be incorporated regularly, continually feeding and improving the soil and making it better and better over time.

Fish emulsion and blood meal are fantastic products for giving your soil an organic boost of nitrogen.

Organic granular fertilizers are easy to apply and provide long-lasting nutrition to your plants.

That said, you can deliver organic nutrients to your soil to be taken up by plant roots quickly using liquid concentrates (such as the fish emulsion example above) or soluble organic options (dry granular products that quickly dissolve in water). These products can offer that quick feed that many of the traditional dry organic products don't.

When and how to feed your plants

While organic N-P-K ratios aren't always as clearly spelled out as they are on synthetic fertilizer packaging, organics supply the same valuable nutrients to the soil. And each type of organic fertilizer has its own specialty when it comes to providing "up, down, and all around" benefits.

Nitrogen providers: Blood, cottonseed meal, fish emulsion, seaweed extract.

These are my go-to fertilizers for early in the season, when I want that blast of nitrogen to get the top growth off to a good start. Fish emulsion, with a 5-1-1 ratio, is my first choice. Worm effluent (liquid waste from my vermicompost bin, as discussed in Chapter 2) also delivers supplemental nitrogen (as well as phosphorus and potassium) when diluted with 10 to 20 parts of water.

Phosphorus providers: Bone meal, rock phosphate.

Several weeks into the season, once the plants are coming along and strong enough to put on fruit, I switch to a liquid fish concentrate with a ratio of 2-3-1. The higher phosphorus level stimulates root, flower, and fruit growth as the season really kicks in, while backing off on the nitrogen that promotes vegetative growth.

Potassium providers: Greensand, sulfate of potash.

For me, providing a potassium-heavy feeding during the growing season isn't something I think much about. That's because anytime I supplement my beds or soil with additional fertilizer, there's always a natural inclusion of potassium. It doesn't take much, especially if you're building healthy soil over time with plenty of compost and organic matter. That's how I incorporate this nutrient—slowly and steadily—to keep my plants' overall health strong and vigorous all the time (not in occasional spurts). Soil tests confirm that's the right way to do it, and the tangible proof is apparent every day when I walk out into the garden. As a general rule, I apply a bit of organic fertilizer (whichever one is most appropriate) in my vegetable garden about every two weeks during the active growing season for my heavy summer feeders. But just as with any product, follow the label's instructions for proper usage, application instructions, and coverage rates. And don't overdo it, because too much is never a good thing—even with organic fertilizer.

FEED YOUR GARDEN LESS, SO IT CAN FEED YOU MORE

For the incredible variety that our vegetable gardens provide to us, it's sometimes staggering to think, for the most part, that the plants themselves all require the same core menu of three nutrients. Fertilizer is a topic that can often be overcomplicated by even the best-intentioned gardener, but it shouldn't be difficult. Stick with a simple approach and give your plants only the bare minimum of what they need to survive. Let Mother Nature do the rest. You'll be amazed at how she transforms simple seeds and tiny seedlings into a bountiful harvest.

The Challenge of Chicken Manure

A quick word of warning here about one organic source that gets talked about often. Chicken manure is thought by some who have a backyard flock to be a wonderful source of all-natural nitrogen for the garden. And it can be, but only after it's been allowed a month or longer to properly mellow. Too much of it while it's still raw, or "hot," can burn tender plants.

6

SEEDS AND SEEDLINGS

FINALLY, THE STARS of the show, the seeds and seedlings. After all of the planning and prep work, all of the soil analysis and amendments, all of the research in choosing what you'll grow and where you'll grow it and how you'll feed it throughout the season, it all comes down to the plants themselves.

As the gardener, you have a big decision to make. That's whether you'll grow your crops from seeds or from *seedlings*, young plants that have been started and are already growing for you.

Think of it like two friends taking a cross-country road-trip. One has done all the planning, packed a bag, washed and tuned up the car, bought the snacks, even made a special playlist of songs. The other friend gets picked up on the morning of departure.

From that moment on, they have the exact same vacation. They both end up in the same destination. They took the same route and have the same souvenirs after the trip is over. But one of them had a big head start on the whole adventure and played a much more hands-on role in how it all came together. And neither friend is in the wrong.

That's the difference between growing plants from seed versus growing plants from seedlings. It's about options and control and how involved you want to be in the entire process. You can be there from the very beginning, or you can hop in right when the main event is about to get underway.

So, buckle up. This chapter is all about how to work with seeds, either starting them indoors or sowing them directly in the garden, and how to plant out your garden with seedlings.

Whether you start your crop from seed or plant a seedling of the same variety, you'll end up in the same place in the end.

Starting seeds indoors is a gardening practice that gives me total control over my plants from day one and is an annual ritual that I find to be incredibly rewarding.

IT'S NOT AN EITHER/OR PROPOSITION

It's not entirely fair or accurate to talk about "seeds versus seedlings" as if it were a competition with a winner and a loser. Both are perfectly acceptable and commendable ways to enjoy vegetable gardening.

One thing you'll want to remember is that, whether you start your plants from seed or simply plant seedlings that have already been started, you don't treat them any differently in the garden. There aren't two separate sets of rules. You water, feed, maintain, and harvest crops that were started from seed the same way you do plants that you purchased as seedlings.

Even for the most experienced gardener, there's a time and a place for both seeds and seedlings. There are distinct advantages with each.

Seeds

If you hadn't guessed after my road-trip analogy up front, I'm a planner. I'm an unapologetic control freak, especially when it comes to my vegetable garden. As a result, growing from seed, and more specifically, *starting seeds indoors*, is my choice the majority of the time.

And there are a lot of reasons why.

Unlimited options

The most obvious benefit of growing from seed is selection. Go to your favorite nursery (or even your local big box store's gardening center) on the busiest weekend of spring and count how many ready-to-plant seedlings they have for sale. You might end up with a total number of a couple dozen or so. Now walk over to the racks of seed packets. There's hundreds.

With pre-grown seedlings, you are at the mercy of whatever the garden center chooses to sell. They're generally hybrid varieties (as discussed in Chapter 3), so they're considered the most foolproof for your area and can have a certain amount of inbred resistance to various diseases or exhibit other particular growing traits, but they're the standard go-to varieties of the most common crops year after year. They are proven sellers with mass appeal and you should get excellent results at season's end.

When you start your plants from seed, though, anything goes. Want to grow exotic varieties from overseas? Looking to be the only gardener on the block growing a certain crop? Interested in unusual shapes or crazy colors? All of this is on the table when you grow from seed.

You can find a good number of seedlings at your favorite nursery, but the options when you start your crops from seed are literally endless.

If you have ambitions of harvesting fresh food well into fall and even winter, starting seeds throughout the year is the only practical way to get there.

More control over timing

Most retail garden centers assume that you're starting a vegetable garden in spring once the weather breaks and that you'll be shutting your garden down with the late summer or early fall harvest. That's why they devote so much floor space to all those seedlings in spring. But by autumn, that same aisle of the store may be filled with Halloween decorations and snowblowers! Fall seedlings are incredibly hard to find. Growing food year-round would be next to impossible if you were dependent on store-bought seedlings. If you grow from seed, your favorite cool-season crops are ready to be planted whenever you (and the weather) are.

The stakes are low

This is a simple matter of dollars and cents. When you buy seedlings, someone else has done the work to grow the plants to a certain stage, then they've been packaged, shipped, and stored (maybe multiple times). Finally, at your local retailer, store employees water and take care of them until they're purchased. So each seedling you buy for your vegetable garden is likely going to cost several dollars apiece. Not a huge investment but compare it to a packet of seeds that may cost two bucks for fifty seeds, each of which has the potential to grow into its own plant!

More educational

So much of how a plant develops happens in the first eight weeks, long before those seedlings are even ordered by your local store. You'll learn more about plants and their fascinating growth cycle from one season of starting your own seeds than you will in years of raising plants that someone else started. If you're into gardening for the long haul and truly want to learn how to do it well, I can say with absolute certainty that starting plants from seed will make you a better, smarter, more confident gardener.

Allows an earlier start

Even if you grow cool-season crops, the time you spend outside gardening likely takes a serious dip for several months out of the year. Starting plants from seeds, though, means you're kicking off your new growing season indoors, when there's nothing happening outside, getting your hands dirty weeks or even months before the box-store shoppers are catching spring fever.

Sometimes a Head Start is the Only Way

Depending on where you live and what you want to grow, starting seeds indoors may be your only option. Some tomato varieties, let's say, take three months or more from the seedling stage to produce ripe fruit, and it takes six to eight weeks for the seed to get to that point. So in reality, that tomato plant needs as long as five months to fully mature if grown from seed! And there are plenty of areas where the weather just doesn't allow a growing season that long. When you start seeds indoors, the first six to eight weeks of growth happen in a controlled environment while conditions outside are still less than ideal. That head start can make all the difference in growing the variety you want so you won't have to settle for something else entirely.

Seedlings

I know, that was quite a sales pitch for seeds. But there is absolutely a place for seedlings in almost every vegetable garden and for almost every gardener. Even though I am a fanatical seed starter, I still purchase the occasional seedling from my local nursery, usually to take advantage of one or two main benefits.

Convenience

As wondrous as growing a plant from seed is, it is time-consuming. And not every gardener can always be proactive enough to start seeds for all the crops they want in time for spring planting. If you want to grow edibles with minimum upfront effort and on little advance notice, seedlings are the way to go. You can wake up on a gorgeous spring Saturday, decide you want to grow cucumbers, and have established plants in the ground within hours.

For me, I sometimes supplement the plants I started from seed with a few seedlings. Maybe it's a variety I didn't get the seed for, maybe I have more room in my beds than I thought, maybe a crop jumps out to me at the store that I just hadn't considered or simply want to try on impulse. Nothing wrong with using store-bought seedlings to fill a gap like that.

Because you have a front-row seat for the entire life cycle from germination to finally transplanting your seedlings outdoors, starting seeds will make you a better and smarter gardener almost immediately.

I still buy certain edible crops as seedlings every year, as some plants simply don't do well for home gardeners when started from seed.

Inexpensive wire racks provide lots of horizontal shelf space for indoor seed starting.

Reliability with certain crops

There are certain edible crops that are, to be blunt, a real challenge for the home gardener to grow from seed. No matter how methodical and dedicated you are, things like cauliflower and spinach, for example, are just extremely difficult for some to raise from seed in a home setting. If you want to enjoy those crops, you may be better off buying them as seedlings. There's nothing wrong with paying a little bit more for the big commercial operation to do the heavy lifting, so you can take the crop across the finish line and literally reap the reward.

Timing and The Eight-Week Rule

Generally, a store-bought warm-season seedling is ready to go in the ground as soon as you are past the last risk of frost for your area. Let's say that date (planting day) is May 1st for you. You could go to the nursery and buy seedlings that morning and plant them that afternoon.

If you started your plants from seed, you will have to have started that process much earlier. Seed-starting is basically making your own seedlings in preparation for that same planting day. My rule of thumb is eight weeks in advance. If my planting day is May 1st, the calendar says I need to start those seeds indoors the first week of March.

Learn what your first and last frost dates are for where you live. And remember that if you want to start seeds, you need to backtrack about eight weeks in order to get the timing right.

Save those containers from the kitchen! Yogurt cups, milk jugs, plastic cups, and takeout tubs make wonderful trays for seed starting.

Starting seeds: The process

The goal of seed starting is to create your own seedlings, to get them to the point that they're healthy enough to be planted outside in your vegetable garden. It's just a six-week process (roughly), but what happens in those first six weeks is critical to the plant's life and the ultimate success of your crop.

Just like when you bring a new baby home from the hospital or introduce a puppy to the household as a permanent member of the family, there are specialized things you'll need to have in order to make that starting-out process easier and certain practices you'll have to adopt that are unique to that short starting period of growth.

The set-up

When you take on seed starting, there is a bit of upfront expense for the materials you'll need. First-timers are often intimidated by the amount of "stuff" that they assume is required to start seeds, but it's all actually pretty straightforward and shouldn't be a prohibitive factor.

Racks and shelves: Whether your seeds will be housed in your basement, a spare room, a warm garage, or an actual greenhouse, you'll need horizontal surfaces. Lots of them. I like to use wire rolling racks. They're inexpensive, lightweight, sturdy, and I can wheel them around as needed.

Containers: What are you going to physically plant your seeds into? Black plastic flats divided into multiple "cells" are popular and easy to obtain, but I know plenty of gardeners who repurpose plastic cups, yogurt tubs, kitchen containers, takeout packaging, and milk jugs for seeds. Just poke a few holes in the bottom to allow for drainage, and you're good. Keep in mind that you'll likely need two sizes: small ones to start the seeds in, and then larger containers to move the seedlings to as they grow larger.

Domes and covers: Trapping warmth and moisture is essential for seeds to germinate. Covering your containers keeps your seeds from drying out in the early days. Plastic domes or covers should be clear to allow sufficient light to reach the plants. Even clear plastic wrap from the kitchen does the job. Once the seeds germinate, you're done with the covers.

The soil

Gardeners work hard to make sure the soil in their beds is ideally suited for growing edibles. But even perfect outdoor garden soil is too heavy for starting delicate seeds. You need a specialized lightweight seed starting mix as your growing medium for this critical period.

Also called "soilless mix," it doesn't technically contain any true soil at all (so is considered sterile). It's often peat moss and/or coconut coir fiber mixed with a little bit of perlite to aid with drainage and to create some air space within the mix.

The stuff

There are a few other recommended accessories that can help your seed-starting adventure go more smoothly.

Wicking mats: These absorbent mats sit in a shallow reservoir underneath your seed trays. Moisture is absorbed by the soilless mix through the holes in the trays. You can, of course, handle watering manually, but it's important that you don't let your seed cells dry out. I'll often make my own mat out of an old T-shirt, hand towel, or piece of felt from the craft store.

Grow lights: Seeds need a lot more light than they'll get on a shelf in your basement in the dead of winter. Hang "shop light" fixtures outfitted with regular 40-watt fluorescent bulbs (or specialized bulbs that use less energy and produce more beneficial light). I'm always experimenting. Whatever bulbs I'm using, I run my grow lights on a timer to match Mother Nature—16 hours on, 8 hours off.

Be aware of how high your lights hang over your seed trays. The closer the bulbs are to the tops of the plants, the better (generally). The purpose of "grow" lights is not to produce tall seedlings. Leggy plants are usually weak plants. The real goal is to encourage the seedlings to stay dense and compact, building their strength as they grow at a proper, sustainable, healthy rate. I move my lights up gradually as the seedlings grow taller, until it's time to plant outside. And I have great success every single season.

Plastic domes or covers come in handy for trapping warmth and moisture over just-planted seeds. Even clear plastic wrap will work.

Soilless mix is the ideal growing medium for seeds, providing everything they need while not harboring potential pathogens.

Wicking mats, grow lights, germination mats, and a fan can all help with your seed-starting adventure.

Whether you use ordinary shop lights or specialized grow bulbs, artificial light is a key to starting seeds indoors.

Germination mats: For every seed, there's a preferred range of temperatures at which it will germinate. A germination mat plugs in and holds a set temperature through a built-in thermostat. Once your seeds germinate, you're done with the mat. It's certainly not a must-have, but it's a minor investment that eliminates guesswork, helps safeguard against mistakes, and lasts season after season.

Fans: After a seed germinates, I like to use a small fan to keep air moving gently across the soil level, mainly to help reduce the risk of a disease called damping off. It's the number one killer of seedlings, and it's caused by a fungus, most likely to impact young seedlings in soil that is too wet. A little moving air cuts way down on the chances of that happening. But it also helps toughen up my growing seedlings, getting them ready to handle actual breezes once I move them into the garden.

Planting seeds

When it comes to actually planting your seeds, follow the instructions on the seed packet. That's not a cop-out. It's the advice I still follow religiously every time I plant. Each crop has its own set of guidelines of when to plant relative to moving the seedling outdoors, how deep to plant the seed, how many seeds per cell, the ideal germination temperature, how many days germination should take—it's all different for every crop. And it's all printed right there on the packet. Even after I empty that packet of seeds, I keep it as a user's manual of sorts that I can refer to, giving me a good idea of what to expect as the growing season progresses.

As the seed grows

Once your tiny seeds have germinated and you can see sprouts, you have a front-row seat for the most fascinating show you'll ever see. Over the next several weeks, your seedlings (that's what they are now) will develop and get taller, strengthen, and even start to produce leaves. And your job is to keep them doing exactly that, by continuing to meet their water, light, and temperature requirements.

Every seed prefers slightly different growing conditions. Part of the fun for me is meticulously following the directions to give each crop exactly what it wants most.

Thinning seedlings to keep just the strongest one per cell is always difficult, but it's necessary for your crops' vitality. Only the best of the best are planted in the garden.

Pay attention, jot down notes, take photos. And don't discount your gut instinct, even if this is your first-time starting seeds. If something doesn't look right, there's a good chance it isn't. Do those tender seedlings look more wilted than they did yesterday? More often than not, it's a sign they need water. Do the tips of your sprouts seem discolored? Your grow lights could be a little too close, causing burn. Make a slight adjustment and just watch. Seedlings at this young stage tend to respond quickly to changes in their environment. Now that you have miniature plants, there will be a few added duties for you to take on.

Scout for pests: Generally, pests aren't much of an issue for indoor seedlings. Chapter 11 deals with what to be on the lookout for *outside* in the garden, but at this early stage, in a controlled indoor environment, fungus gnats are likely your biggest worry. They tend to hitchhike into your home as eggs in your seed starting mix. They're more a nuisance than anything. Control them with yellow sticky-card traps available at most plant stores.

Thinning: Most of the time, your seed packet will have instructed you to plant more than one seed per cell in your plant tray. After the seeds have germinated and small plants have sprouted, you typically need to thin them to one seedling per cell.

Yanking out perfectly healthy seedlings can be extremely difficult. The natural inclination is to keep every seedling that has sprouted. But thinning to leave the strongest and healthiest seedling (one per cell) means the best of the best are going into your garden. The seedlings you leave intact will grow healthier and stronger without competition for water and light and nutrients in the tray cell. You can thin by pulling out the unwanted seedlings with your fingers, but I like to use a pair of microsnips just to make sure I don't accidentally disturb or stress the roots of the one I'm keeping.

My Perfect Potting Bench

For every plant or seedling or seed that goes into your garden beds, there is very likely a need for a place to stage tools or gather supplies. Often, you'll want a flat worksurface on which to sow those seeds or harden off seedlings, etc. Enter the potting bench. Over the years, I've learned what I need a potting bench to do for me and have provisioned mine accordingly. Here's a sample of how I set mine up.

The top surface of all my potting benches is as clear and mess-free as possible whenever they're not in use. So, Rule No. 1: Keep the clutter off the worksurface. To help with this, my main potting bench has a mailbox mounted on the far edge. It's perhaps not the most aesthetic addition to my garden, but what it lacks in refined looks, it makes up for in function. I keep all my quick-access, most-used items in there, where they're out of the elements, safe, and dry.

My Rule No. 2 is to keep the bottom shelf occupied with only what I use the most. On one side, I have a big storage tub with a locking lid. This is where I store my organic fertilizers, pest and insect controls, tank sprayer, and measuring spoons and cups. The rest of that shelf is usually filled with stacks of pots of various sizes, seed trays, potting soil, and compost.

But I make use of the vertical space, too. Just beneath the top surface, I mounted a series of hooks to store an assortment of hand tools for digging and weeding. Those handy soil scoops and trowels are always at the ready.

The perfect potting bench may vary by gardener, but there are few things I've learned that my ideal workspace has to have.

Bumping up: It's common for your indoor seedlings to outgrow their first cells in just a few weeks. The top growth has likely gotten too big for the relatively small mass of roots contained in the tiny original cell. About midway to your outdoor-planting date, you'll likely need to move your rapidly growing seedlings to a larger container, a specific transplanting process I call "bumping up." It's still too early to plant these seedlings outdoors, so the goal is to give them a larger home indoors.

One indication that your seedlings are ready to be bumped up is when the roots start growing out of the drainage holes in the bottom of their cell. Carefully loosen the seedling, roots and all, from the original cell and replant in a slightly larger container (25 percent to 50 percent bigger only) filled with the same soilless mix used to start the seeds.

Seedlings will quickly outgrow their original containers and will need to be "bumped up" to larger ones before planting day.

To Fertilize or Not to Fertilize Seeds, That Is the Question (And This Is the Answer)

You may have noticed that feeding your newly planted seeds or indoor seedlings is not on the to-do list. While it may seem like a no-brainer way to help your young seedlings get off to the best start possible, I find fertilizer to be unnecessary (and often counterproductive) when seed starting. As far as nutrients go, the seed has everything already built into it that it needs to germinate and get through its earliest stages of life. You can, in fact, get big, fat seedlings pretty easily by using some supplemental fertilizer. But in the indoors environment, under artificial light that's not as intense as the sun, fertilizer pushes the plant's growth in an unnatural way. It may become extra tall and leafy, but it's not as strong. And now it's actually stressed because it's outgrown its growing environment. It needs to be outside, but it's abnormally early and likely too cold for it to survive outdoors.

For my money, it's just too easy to go overboard with fertilizing seed-started plants without meaning to. The goal, once again, is just to get those plants healthy enough to get them outside, then Mother Nature can take over. You won't get bonus points for bigger, fatter seedlings on planting day. You'll often get weaker plants in the long run.

Hardening off

Planting day will be a massive adjustment for your seedlings. It's a great big garden bed out there, with full-bore sunlight and stiff spring winds and torrential rain. It's important that you gradually prepare them for life on the outside. This is the conditioning process known as "hardening off."

You'll need 7 to 10 days, so time your hardening off period to end just before your planting date. On the first day, move your potted seedlings outdoors into a full-sunlight environment and leave them there for just 30 minutes before bringing them back inside. (If you have as many seedlings as I typically do, time's up on the first ones I placed before I'm even done bringing them all out!) The next day, increase their time outside to 60 minutes. Add 30 minutes more each day until you get to Day Four. Then you can start to increase the exposure time a little bit more per day with an extra 45 minutes, an extra hour, etc. The goal is to let your seedlings spend the final day of the process in full sun for the entire day.

Don't be tempted to take a shortcut and, say, jump from 2 hours to 6 hours of sun the very next day. Too much sunlight all at once can burn your tender young seedlings in a hurry. You will likely lose a couple weeks of growing time while your plants recover.

Hardening off can be a time-consuming and repetitive process, to be sure, but at the end of the cycle your seedlings are toughened up for final transplanting. My method here is just one of many. The key is to not rush this stage of the process. You've gotten them this far. Don't blow it now.

Don't underestimate the power of observation. Pay attention to your seeds and check on them often. You'll start to get a real feel for how they're doing and what they need based on the clues they provide.

Getting your seedlings acclimated to life in the great outdoors takes time. "Harden off" your tender baby plants by exposing them to a little more sunlight every day until they're ready for a full day in the garden.

You've worked hard to raise your seedlings to this point, so getting them into their new home in the vegetable garden is a big day.

Planting Day

Once you've hardened off your warm-season seedlings, the risk of that last frost where you live has passed, and your soil temperature is warm enough—it's graduation day. Cool-season plants, of course, follow a different schedule. You've done the advance work through the summer. Planting day is determined by checking first frost dates or desired harvest dates and working backward on the calendar. More on this in Chapter 7.

Congratulations! Your raised-from-seed plants are ready to go in the ground.

Your soil should be properly amended ahead of time so that your seedlings will be able to take immediate advantage of the rich organic matter in their new garden home. (Chapter 2 is all about soil and the year-round work that should go into constantly improving it.)

As I remove my seedlings from their containers, I like to untangle the roots just a bit before placing the root ball in its planting hole. This may seem destructive, but a gentle untangling with your fingers encourages them to spread out once they hit the new soil.

Most seedlings should be planted in the ground so the seedling sits at the same depth that it did in its container. That is, the top of the rootball sits flush with the garden soil level. If the seedling seems a little too floppy, it's usually safe to plant them a bit deeper, to bury more of the stem underground just to make them sturdier.

You need good contact between your seedling roots and the garden soil. Fill in around the rootball with garden soil, but don't push down as you plant! It may seem like this would help, but it only compacts the soil and makes it harder for your seedling roots to get to nutrients and water.

Water your seedlings right away. A good drink helps your seedlings deal with the stress and shock that comes with planting, but it also does a better job of settling the soil around the roots.

Some gardeners like to give their seedlings a light dose of fertilizer upon planting. I prefer to wait about a week to let the plants get acclimated to their new growing environment on their own. And when I do that first feeding, I back off even from the amount printed on the label. More is never better, and for me, I'd rather go light and let the plants do a little more of the work of getting stronger on their own at this early stage.

The last step, as always, is mulching. There's a whole chapter (Chapter 8) devoted to it and why it's so essential to gardening success. But suffice it to say here that a top layer of organic mulch around your new vegetable plants is just as vital to their growth as anything you've done up to this point.

Even if the weather seems nice enough to plant outdoors, double-check the soil temperature to be sure.

A light layer of mulch serves many purposes, all of them designed to get your new plantings off to the best possible start.

Express-Lane Gardening with Seedlings

Obviously, if you're bringing home seedlings that someone else has grown to that point, all of the early work has been done for you. You can jump right in with the instructions as spelled out in the "Planting Day" section above. But there are just a few things you may want to keep in mind as you work with store-bought seedlings.

It starts at the store

Just as you would when choosing fresh produce at the market, be picky as you shop. Go through that rack of young tomato plants to find the ones that look healthiest. The ones in the back may have been there for a while, getting leggy in the shade. Yellowing leaves? Don't take that one home. Same with plants that already have indications of pest or disease damage. If it has problems at the store, it may not get any better once you plant it at home.

If you start your own plants from seeds, be sure to make a tag for each plant or tray at least. If you don't do it right away, you may never know what variety of plants is in that container or tray.

Some crops are still best planted the old-fashioned way, by dropping seeds directly into the soil when the weather is just right.

Take the tag seriously

Make sure your store-bought seedling actually has a plant tag. That's not just to make things easier for the cashier; that tag contains valuable information for you. It's your user's manual for the rest of the season. On planting day, it tells you when to plant, how to plant, where to plant, how to space your plants, and how deep to plant. But beyond that, a photo on the tag might remind you of what the plant should look like. The tag should tell you how many days it will take for fruit to mature. It may offer helpful advice on harvesting. There are few things more maddening than having a massive success (or an utter disaster) with a plant late in the season and not being able to identify what variety it is because you didn't save (or never had) the little plastic tag.

Direct-Sowing Seeds Outdoors

There is, of course, one more option for growing certain vegetables—simply planting seeds directly in the ground on planting day. Not every seed does well in an indoor setting, and for many crops, it's not recommended that you even try. It may be, in the case of carrots, beets, radishes, among others, that they don't like to have their roots disturbed in the way that transplanting always does. For other crops like beans, melons, or squash, they're exceptionally fast growers. There just isn't much advantage to starting them indoors.

Direct-sowing seeds means giving up on the head start that an indoor controlled environment provides. But there are still some measures you can take to help your seeds germinate properly once they're in the ground.

Amended soil: This is just a blanket rule, no matter how you plant. Organically rich, well-draining soil is the ultimate key to gardening success. Test your soil, amend it accordingly, and you're more than halfway there when it comes to giving your direct-sown seeds a good start.

Seed prep: Certain seeds need a little extra TLC before they're sown. Check your seed packet for instructions. Stratify (expose to cold), scarify (nick the seed coat), or soak your seeds as necessary (depending on the crop) prior to planting day.

Hills and mounds: A seed packet may instruct you to hill or mound your soil at planting to help create ideal growing conditions (for, say, squash or melons). The idea is to eliminate the chances of standing water around the seed (and later, the plant roots). Hills and mounds can also provide added warmth in the soil, which is helpful for some seeds to germinate.

The Cheapest Planting Tool You Won't Want to Garden Without

As you might imagine, I have an entire barn full of gardening tools. But for all the fancy, pricey, whiz-bang gadgets I have, the tool I use more than any other is one I made myself for free out of a piece of scrap lumber. Allow me to introduce you to the planting board. I think you'll find it as indispensable as I do in the garden.

It's a 1×4 (20 x 90 mm) piece of wood. That's it. Really. It can be any length you prefer, but I find six feet (1.8 m) to be a good size that serves my needs and is easy to wield. Using a tape measure, mark the board every 3 inches (8 cm) along one edge. Now use a speed square to make a V-shape at every mark. I like to make shallow ½ inch (1 cm) "Vs" at 3 inches (8 cm) and 9 inches (23 cm), slightly deeper 1 inch (3 cm) Vs at the 6-inch (15 cm) marks, and big 1½ inch (4 cm) Vs at the 12-inch (30 cm) intervals. That helps differentiate the measurements at a quick glance. Cut those V-shaped notches with a circular saw, jigsaw, or hand saw. I label the notches with a permanent marker for extra reference.

The uncut edge of the planting board itself makes a perfectly straight furrow when pressed lightly into the soil. I can even gently scoop an entire line of soil away for a deeper planting trough without touching a shovel. The uncut edge also makes a convenient leveling and grading tool when scraped across the surface of the soil.

When I'm instructed to plant seeds or seedlings at, say, 3-inch (8 cm) intervals, I place the board with the notches facing the furrow, and it shows me exactly where to plant, and in record time. I use the notches again when it's time to thin seedlings. The measurements offer an instant guide to achieve consistent spacing for the plants left to grow. And should I ever need to quickly measure a plant's vertical growth in the middle of the season, I simply turn the planting board on its end and use it as a giant yardstick to check height.

You probably have a scrap piece of 1×4 (20 x 90 mm) lumber sitting in your garage or basement right now. You're just thirty minutes away from creating the handiest tool you'll ever want to have in the garden.

A piece of 1x4 (20 x 90 mm) lumber that was destined for the scrap pile has truly become one of my most valuable and versatile gardening tools. A few minutes of work transformed it into my trusty planting board.

FROM THESE SEEDS (OR SEEDLINGS), A THRIVING GARDEN

I hope that this chapter has taken away some of what many beginning gardeners view as the intimidating mystique behind starting seeds. It's not nearly as daunting a process as it may seem. Most gardeners who try it fall in love and never look back. But I also hope I've made a case for how and when using purchased seedlings can be the way to go. Starting seeds shouldn't be scary, and choosing to grow seedlings shouldn't be considered cheating. Whether you grow your garden from seed or from seedlings (or a mix of both), I hope you've also come to the end of this chapter with some solid techniques that will help whatever you grow get off to the very best start possible. Speaking of the start, that's the next thing to learn. Knowing *what* to grow and *how* to grow it only produces great results if you understand *when* it's the best time to put all of that knowledge to use.

Whether you start your garden from seeds or transplants, or a combination of both, a thriving, productive garden is in your future!

GETTING THE TIMING RIGHT

TIMING, AS THEY SAY, is everything. And that old adage definitely holds true for gardeners. You can have beautiful and textbook-healthy baby plants that you've meticulously nursed along from seed, and you may have a perfectly sited garden bed that you've filled with rich, fertile soil. But if you put the two things together at the wrong time of year for that crop, or rush things by planting before frosty mornings in your area are over for the season, or don't give your crop enough time to mature before winter weather kills it prior to harvesting, then all that work was in vain.

It can be a real juggling act. The successful gardener constantly strives to understand, anticipate, and coordinate his or her to-do list around both the climatological cues of the seasons and the natural life cycle of the plants they're growing. It takes research and homework, it takes a keen observational eye, and it takes a whole lot of good old-fashioned first-hand experience. And even lifelong growers find themselves reevaluating what they *thought* they knew as they continually work to get the timing just right.

No one ever truly masters it. Even the best gardeners I know occasionally get blindsided by a surprise cold snap or accidentally stumble across a new way to think about the sequencing of their gardens. It's all about following Mother Nature's schedule and knowing that, just like our own personal schedules, hers is subject to change. But the more you know, the better prepared you'll be for staying in sync with the vegetable crops you choose to grow.

WARM-SEASON VS. COOL-SEASON CROPS

I'm a beach guy. Given a choice, I like it hot and humid and downright tropical. But I know plenty of people who gravitate toward snow-kissed mountains and cold-weather adventures. If I went on vacation with them, I'd tend to stay inside and cozy up to a roaring fire, and vice versa. They likely wouldn't do as well with day after day of the "island time" I enjoy so much.

Vegetables are the same way. We tend to think of growing vegetables as a classic summer pursuit, but there are both "warm-season" and "cool-season" crops, and a plant's classification as one or the other will tell you when it prefers to grow.

Gardeners often preach "the right plant in the right place," but "the right plant in the right season" is just as critical. Warm-season crops just won't perform in winter, and cool-season crops can't be magically coaxed to grow their best in the heat of summer. Start your garden by matching up what you want to grow with when those plants will grow, and you'll make your efforts more successful right out of the gate.

Popular warm-season crops include (but are certainly not limited to) tomatoes, peppers, cucumbers, melons, beans, corn, squash, eggplant, and potatoes. Generally, they're planted outside after the risk of frost has passed, though many gardeners get a jump on things by starting at least some of their warm-season vegetables indoors from seed, well in advance.

Most cool-season vegetables are planted (or started) in late summer, and can, depending on the crop, be harvested in fall or even well into winter. I can tell you that gardening without the heat, humidity, gnats, bugs, sunburn, and sweat of summer can be a real treat. And you might be surprised at the variety of fresh vegetables you can pull out of your garden even when it's blanketed in snow! (Some are even improved, taste-wise, by a bracing frost.) Cool-season crops include lettuce, onions, brussels sprouts, broccoli, carrots, beets, radishes, cauliflower, and spinach.

If you're really on top of your timing, some cool-season crops can be planted as soon as outdoor soil is workable, grow to full maturity, and be harvested—all before your warm-season crops truly get going. It's like a bonus mini-season every year!

The two most important dates to know

There are a lot of dates to keep track of when you garden. You need to remember when you planted each plant, and you should be counting the days for each crop to reach maturity, so you know when to be ready to harvest.

Frost doesn't have to mean the gardening season is over. Learn which crops can take (or even embrace) the winter weather!

Cool-season crops are often planted when it's still warm out, but are harvested in fall or even winter.

Warm-season crops like tomatoes get their start outdoors after the risk of frost has passed for the year.

In my own garden, I can have as many as twenty different kinds of edible plants at any one time, and each has its own growing time. And you think it's hard keeping your family's various birthdays and anniversaries straight! This is just one reason why keeping notes of some kind, whether it's in a journal or on an app, can be so helpful.

But when it comes to the gardening calendar, there are two dates that rank as most important of all—the first frost and last frost for your geographical area. "But, Joe," I hear you saying, "my own local TV meteorologist can't get the forecast right. How can I possibly be expected to know when the first frost or last frost of the year will come?"

Fair point. But we're talking about the *average* frost dates. Using historical records that can date back over a century, many almanacs, websites, and your local governmental or university-based agricultural service can tell you the average date to expect the last frost in spring as well as the first frost of autumn. These dates are considered the safe start and finish lines for the traditional growing season. Work backward from, or count down to them to determine your planting and harvesting dates for either warm-season or cool-season crops.

Let's Compare Calendars

It's not enough to say simply, "This crop should be planted in early spring," or even, "Be sure to harvest that crop by mid-November." Frost dates can, as you would expect, vary dramatically based on where you garden. In my area, for instance, the first frost date is listed as October 27th. But my friend who lives much farther north has a first frost date of September 22nd. That's over a month earlier! Obviously, she and I can't follow the same planting or harvesting calendar, even if we're talking about the exact same crop!

Do we all get faked out once in a while with an unseasonably warm winter or a cold snap that hits earlier than expected? Of course. But the average first and last frost dates are the most reliable information that gardeners have, and they're pretty close to right far more often than they're wrong.

How to know when to plant what

Well, this is the million-dollar question. And there's no one-size-fits-all answer, as evidenced by everything you've just read in this chapter. But if you're looking for very loose parameters to use as a starting point for your own garden, here's my suggested timeline, with all the appropriate asterisks and fine-print footnotes about how your particular circumstances could warrant something different.

Let's start with warm-season crops. As a rule, don't plant seedlings before the average last frost date. Or if a frost is imminent, cover them overnight to protect the tender young foliage from the cold.

If you're starting warm-season crop seeds indoors, aim to get them into soilless potting mix about 6 to 8 weeks before the last frost date. They should be sturdy enough to plant outdoors by the time that date passes. Don't start seeds too soon. Holding them too long before planting them outdoors can weaken the seedlings.

Wait to plant warm-season crops like these eggplants until the danger of frost as passed.

Don't feel you need to limit yourself to planting warm-season crops just once per season. You can keep starting new seeds and transplanting the seedlings through much of the summer. For example, I plant my first tomatoes outdoors around mid-spring. I tend to pick my first ripe fruit in mid-summer. I also plant a second batch of tomato seedlings in mid-summer. By the time the first plants have faded, this second set is putting on their harvest of amazing homegrown tomatoes!

For cool-season crops to be harvested in fall, target mid- to late summer or early fall for getting seedlings in the ground. But again, these dates will vary as well depending on where you live. In colder climates, you may be planting your cool-season crops in early to mid-summer so that they have enough time to mature before things come to a halt in fall. But no matter where you live, many cool-season crops don't mind the heat during the early stage of their growing cycle. The key is having them maturing for harvest close to (or after) the first frost date of fall. Again, for indoor seed starting, backtrack about 8 weeks before the date you want to transplant outdoors.

As mentioned earlier, many cool-season crops can be planted before and harvested while the warm season crops are growing. Try planting these seedlings about a month before your last frost date—as long as your soil is workable. But be ready for these crops to fade quickly as temperatures warm in the spring.

Succession planting: what it is and why to do it

All of this attention to frost dates and the exact number of days to maturity is predicated on the notion that you as a gardener want to get as much of a harvest as you can out of every vegetable you plant.

But for all of the working *with* Mother Nature that gardeners do, there's also a fair bit of *manipulating* going on, too. If you could create slightly warmer temperatures earlier, or push the first frost date just a little later, you could get even more out of what you grow. Chapter 10 is full of time-tested techniques that many gardeners use to extend the growing season.

Bush beans are the perfect plant for succession planting, so I've got fresh beans ready to enjoy for a longer period of time.

Interplanting, or companion planting, takes advantage of every square foot of your growing space to get the most out of your garden.

While most of them involve adding some physical apparatus to alter the temperature immediately surrounding a given crop, there's also a so-simple-it's-brilliant method to maximize your garden's production using nothing but timing.

Succession planting, in a nutshell, refers to simply planting one crop after another with the maturity dates as the driving force. The end goal is always to get more fresh produce out of a set period of time or space—a nonstop harvest, basically. Staggering my tomatoes for a longer harvest, as mentioned above, is one version of succession planting. I could also plant multiple tomato varieties, one with a short maturity date and one that takes longer, to spread out my tomato harvest over a longer period of time.

But for many gardeners, true succession planting involves planting two or more crops in the same space, either at the same time or one right after the other.

The first of these multi-cropping techniques is called *intercropping, interplanting,* or *companion planting*. Consider cabbage, which can take several months to reach full size and certain radishes that are ready to pick in just 30 days, start to finish. If you plant radishes in the gaps between your young cabbage plants, the radishes can be harvested and enjoyed before the cabbages need the room to grow.

Be aware, though, that it's *interplanting*, not *overplanting*. The method doesn't work for just any two vegetables you want to squeeze into a single space. Research growing times as well as plant size and spacing before experimenting with this practice.

The second succession planting trick is to plant new vegetables frequently, whenever you have open space in the garden. That open space around the bottom of your tall, mature tomato canopies? It's perfect for a new crop of basil. Ready to pull out your spent cucumber plants after the summer harvest? Have a row of cool-season seedlings ready to transplant that same day.

Turn your soil around with crop rotation

Getting the timing right also includes knowing when your garden beds need a rest period. We often tend to grow the same things season after season. But if you grow the same things *in the same spot* every year, it can deplete the soil of plant-specific nutrients and allow pests and diseases particular to that crop to build up in the soil over time, often to levels that will impact subsequent plantings.

This is where *crop rotation* comes in. The term simply means mixing up the placement of what you plant from year to year. The soilborne pests that attack tomatoes, for example, will stay as long as you keep feeding them new tomato plants every year. What's worse, it's not just tomatoes; anything in the nightshade family (peppers, eggplant, potatoes) will just exacerbate the problems if they're planted in that spot.

Break the cycle by moving, or rotating, your tomatoes to a different garden bed the next year, eliminating the pests' or pathogens' food source. This may be difficult to do in small home gardens, but even moving your tomatoes to the opposite side of the same bed can help. Or try growing them in containers or grow bags for a year.

The more seasons you can rotate your crops to a new location, the better. Four is a magic number of sorts that seems to kill off many of the pests and diseases that impact a particular crop family. But let's face it, many backyard gardens don't have the space to rotate all of their plants to a whole new bed every four years.

Crop rotation is a good practice if you have room. If you just don't have the space, though, it's not something to worry too much about. It's not a garden requirement, just another tool in your arsenal to use (or not use).

If you want to try your hand at crop rotation, the chart on the facing page offers a quick look at the most common plant families. Treat all plants in each family as the same and rotate your crops accordingly.

If you have the space, practicing crop rotation in your beds by moving plants to a new bed every season helps break the cycle of soilborne pests or pathogens.

LEARN YOUR GARDEN'S TIMING, SO YOU CAN STOP THINKING ABOUT IT

Getting the timing of a vegetable garden right is ultimately a delicate dance between you and Mother Nature. She'll provide the cues on when conditions are right for the magic of gardening to occur. It's your job to pay attention and follow her lead. But the savvy gardener also knows a host of clever ways to get the most out of every moment.

Understanding the optimal timing for what goes on in the garden frees you up to give more thought to how things are growing and what you can do to help your crops along throughout the season. And one of the most beneficial things you can do just happens to also be one of the easiest. Let's talk about that next.

Vegetable Plant Families

Plant family	Other names	Crops & cover crops
Amaranthaceae	Amaranth family	Beets, spinach, sugar beets, swiss chard
Amaryllidaceae	Amaryllis family, alliums	Chives, garlic, leeks, onions, shallots
Apiaceae	Carrot family, umbelliferae, umbellifers	Carrots, celery, chervil, cilantro, dill, fennel, parsley, parsnips
Asparagaceae	Asparagus family	Asparagus
Asteraceae	Sunflower family, aster family	Artichoke, chamomile, chicory, endive, escarole, Jerusalem artichoke, lettuce, radicchio, safflower, tarragon
Brassicaceae	Cabbage family, mustard family, brassicas, cruciferae, cruciferous crops, cole crops	Arugula, broccoli, bok choy, brussels sprouts, cabbage, cauliflower, Chinese cabbage, collards, horseradish, kale, kohlrabi, mustard, pak choi, radish, rutabaga, turnips, watercress
Convolvulaceae	Morning glory family	Sweet potatoes
Cucurbitaceae	Cucumber family, squash family, cucurbits	Cucumber, melons, pumpkin, summer squash, watermelon, winter squash, zucchini
Ericaceae	Heather family, blueberry family	Blueberries, cranberries
Fabaceae	Pea family, bean family, leguminosae, legumes, leguminous crops	Alfalfa, beans, cowpeas, clovers, edamame, fava beans, lentils, peanuts, peas, soybeans, vetch
Lamiaceae	Mint family, labiatae	Basil, catnip, lavender, marjoram, mints, oregano, rosemary, sage, thyme
Malvaceae	Hibiscus family, mallows	Okra
Poaceae	Grass family, gramineae	Barley, corn, fescue, millet, oats, rice, rye, sorghum, timothy, wheat
Polygonaceae	Knotweed family	Buckwheat, rhubarb
Rosaceae	Rose family, rosaceous plants	Almonds, apricots, apples, blackberries, cherries, nectarines, peaches, pears, plums, quince, raspberries, strawberries
Solanaceae	Nightshade family, tomato family, potato family, nightshades, solanaceous crops	Eggplant, peppers, potatoes, tomatillos, tomatoes, tobacco

MULCH MATTERS

WHEN IT COMES TO the health of your plants, mulch is as important above the ground as the soil is below the ground. Some gardeners call mulch "the icing on the cake." To me, though, mulch isn't an extra or a bonus. It's a nonnegotiable ingredient, critical to the overall success of the garden. I don't eat cake without icing. And I never plant a garden without adding mulch.

At its most basic, mulch is just a layer of material that covers exposed soil. But that top-dressing mulch serves many very important functions:

- Moisture retention
- Temperature management
- Compaction prevention
- Runoff and erosion control
- Disease suppression
- Soil improvement
- Weed control
- Beautification

That's a lot of important boxes to be checked for something that some gardeners consider to be just a bonus feature! Here's a bit more on what makes mulch such a critical multi-tasker in every successful vegetable garden.

Moisture retention

One of mulch's main jobs is to hold moisture in the soil. It's an insulating barrier that keeps rainfall or irrigation in the soil longer. Without it, heat and wind would force much of that life-giving moisture to evaporate before it ever reaches your plants' roots.

Proper mulching lets you cut down on both the frequency and duration of your supplemental watering. (Take a deeper dive into watering in Chapter 9.) Less watering from you means your plants become more naturally drought-tolerant, and that can be the difference between life and death when summer arrives.

Temperature management

Extreme temperatures can damage or kill plants' tender feeder roots, which mostly lie in the first few inches of soil. During a hard frost or sustained freeze, mulch is like a warm jacket for those roots, protecting them from the cold. Then in summer, mulch goes into sunblock mode, preventing the intense heat from baking exposed soil and creating a hard crust that moisture will have a harder time penetrating.

Compaction prevention

Loose, well-aerated soil is the ideal medium for plant growth. Anything that compacts the soil around plants does long-term harm to the delicate soil structure. A mulch layer helps to soften the blows that walking and working in the garden invariably bring, helping the soil retain its beneficial structure for longer.

Runoff and erosion control

Directly exposed to enough rain or irrigation, that rich soil you've worked so hard to create can literally wash away before your eyes. Wind can also carry your soil off a few precious particles at a time. A protective layer of mulch, quite simply, keeps your garden soil in your garden.

Disease suppression

Many plant diseases come from pathogens that live in the soil and infect a plant only when they contact its foliage. Rainfall or irrigation can splash these soilborne pathogens directly onto lower leaves, transmitting the disease. Mulch shields your vegetables from these pathogens and reduces the spread of soilborne disease.

Soil improvement

Healthy garden soil contains around 5 percent organic matter. While that should mainly come from lots and lots of compost (as discussed earlier in Chapter 2) mulch can also contribute. The best mulch materials break down naturally over time and feed the soil as they biodegrade.

Weed control

Many garden weeds pop up from seeds lurking just below the soil surface. With a little water and sunlight, they will germinate just like any other plant. A thick layer of mulch cuts off that sunlight and keeps many weed seeds from germinating in the first place. That's the good news.

The bad news is that it's not absolute. Weeds are inevitable, and no amount of mulch will smother them all. But proper mulching will drastically cut down on the number of weeds you have to pull while tending to your vegetables.

Beautification

Mulch gives your beds a neat and finished appearance. But since it does all the other things listed here *and also* adds the beauty of a thriving vegetable garden, maybe *that's* the real icing on the cake.

A layer of mulch helps protect your vegetable plants from soilborne pathogens that can splash up onto foliage.

Mulched pathways help keep the garden walkways weed-free.

What Makes a Good Mulch

The best mulches break down naturally. The smaller or finer the material, the faster it decomposes, and that's generally a good thing. In my vegetable beds, I want the mulch I apply in spring to be just about gone by the end of the growing season, already starting to mix in with the soil itself.

I always encourage using mulch that's readily available where you live. Not only will it look more natural, it will also be easier and cheaper to obtain when you need more of it.

Wood mulch

This is hardwood that used to be part of an actual tree, that has been shredded, finely chipped, ground-up, or left as large chunks of bark. It will break down and greatly improve your soil quality as organic matter.

Different kinds of hardwood mulch are always easy to find (usually in bags) at your big-box store or garden center. Larger landscape supply companies deal in bulk quantities, either filling up your vehicle or delivering mulch to you in a truck.

But here's my favorite way to get all the hardwood mulch I need. Whenever I see a tree crew working near my home, I always let them know I'm happy to take the tons of arborist wood chips that they generate off their hands for them. As long as I provide them safe access onto my property and a suitable spot to dump, they can often end their day early by offloading their freshly-ground wood chips without even leaving the neighborhood! And I get a truckload of beautiful garden mulch for free.

Hay/straw

The terms hay and straw are often used interchangeably by people who have never spent time on a farm or around horses. While there are differences between the two, both are readily available and make good mulch. Both are easy to spread, finely textured, and very lightweight.

What, Me Worry About Wood Chips?

There are two myths about arborist wood chips I'd like to dispel here. First, according to most studies, chips that come from a diseased tree will not magically spread that disease to garden plants. That's something I simply don't worry about, and you shouldn't either.

Second, I've had gardeners ask about certain hardwood mulch types, especially pine bark, throwing their soil pH levels out of whack. The thinking is that the bark's natural acidity will rob your soil of valuable nitrogen or lower the soil pH to the point of adversely affecting plant growth. But when used above ground as mulch, there just isn't enough contact with soil to have those unwanted effects.

Local tree companies are usually happy to unload the arborist wood chips they produce for gardeners to use as mulch.

Hay comes from grass crops like fescue and bluegrass. It typically contains seed heads, so if you use it as mulch, be prepared for a few seeds to germinate and turn into the occasional stray weed.

The bigger concern is herbicides. If the grass crop had previously been treated with a persistent herbicide, the residue can be transferred to your vegetable beds. There, it can dissipate into the soil, killing many of your plants (some, such as tomatoes and beans, are especially sensitive) and tainting the soil for years. Buy from a reliable source who can verify the absence of herbicides.

Straw comes from grain crops and is just the stalk of the plant. That means you shouldn't have to worry about seeds. Also, straw breaks down more slowly than hay, so it will last longer in your garden beds. While there are instances of straw being tainted with persistent herbicides, it's not nearly as common.

Grass clippings

You can use grass from your own yard as mulch! It's free, and for most of the year, your lawn will just keep making more of it for you.

If you own a mulching mower with a bagging attachment, it's easy to dump the clippings directly into your garden beds.

And resist the temptation to use grass clippings from any other source unless you know they are free of chemicals. Residential lawn services are notorious for applying herbicides and pesticides and you don't want those going onto your garden beds.

Leaves

If you've ever spent a Saturday in the fall raking and blowing your leaves into a huge pile only to then bag them up and set them out on the curb with your trash cans, I hope I can convince you to try turning that yard debris into the best mulch you'll ever use.

Grass clippings make an excellent, and easy-to-replenish, mulch material for vegetable gardens.

A leaf shredder makes quick work of a pile of fallen leaves, producing my favorite mulch material of all.

The easiest way to do it is to simply run over the leaves with a mulching lawn mower and collect them in the bagging attachment. They'll be diced up into pieces small enough to spread immediately in your garden beds. Chippers and leaf vacs work, too.

However you process your leaves, you'll be left with finely shredded debris that quickly decomposes into the more humus-like leaf mold. It is, to me, the perfect mulching material, full of calcium and micronutrients, easy to work with, and quick to return to the soil as pure decomposed organic matter. Shredded leaves protect my garden beds all growing season and reach a soil-like consistency just in time for my fall compost amendment, which goes right on top.

Pine straw

Where I live, pine straw is abundant. The brown, dead needles rain out of the trees every fall and blanket everything. It's lightweight and can be easily shaped, so it makes a fantastic mulch in landscape beds. It's not, however, a great option for vegetable gardens. It can be prickly and cumbersome to work with, it stacks high around tender vegetable seedlings and plants, and it doesn't break down as quickly as I'd like.

Shredded paper

It's not pretty, but shredded paper from your home office is biodegradable, so it does make an effective mulch material. Because it becomes a soggy mess when wet, you may find it more useful in enclosed situations like a hoop house or a low tunnel (where the look doesn't matter) or buried underneath a layer of some other mulch. And don't worry about printed paper. Most inks now are soy-based! Personally, though, I prefer to use shredded office paper in my compost heap.

Compost

Some people use compost as mulch. Yes, it adds to the organic makeup of the soil in your beds (that's the whole point of compost), but compost doesn't really protect the soil the way a true top layer of mulch does. The nutrient-rich compost that I've worked so hard to create is part of what I want my mulch to protect!

How Much Mulch?

Whatever material you use, the rule of thumb is a 2-inch (5 cm) layer throughout the vegetable bed. This depth is enough to provide the protection benefits outlined earlier, but not so deep that plants are smothered, or water can't pass through.

If I need to purchase mulch and I need more than a little I prefer to buy it in bulk.

Mulch is sold in bags or bulk. If you're filling a small bed or topping off an area, bagged mulch may be easiest. Still, I buy in bulk whenever I can. Bulk mulch is usually locally sourced, so there's less environmental impact than from bagged mulch, which has been processed and shipped from afar. And of course, every bag of mulch you buy just puts more plastic into the landfill.

Finally, I've found that when I buy mulch in bags, it's easy to guess too low and not get enough. That results in either extra trips to the garden center or a too-thin layer of mulch. If the worst thing that happens when I buy in bulk is ending up with more than I need, that's far preferable. Because it does so many things to encourage a healthy and thriving garden, it seems there's always a need for more mulch.

MAKE MULCH MANDATORY

Mulch serves so many important functions for the plants in your vegetable garden, and the benefits couldn't be easier to implement. It's literally the last step in planting out your crops, but it may make the biggest difference of all in your garden's success. If you've looked at mulch in the past as an optional last step, try just one season following the tips laid out in this chapter. See if it makes a difference for you. From weed suppression to disease protection, feeding your soil to conserving the precious resource of water, something we'll dive into in the next chapter, mulch helps you do it all.

GETTING THE WATERING RIGHT

WATER EQUALS LIFE. For our planet, for our bodies, and for our gardens, water is one of the few truly nonnegotiable essentials. But it's absolutely possible to have too much of a good thing, and the same holds true for water. Just as with so many other things in life, finding the right balance is the key to the precious resource of water.

It might seem strange that so much attention is given to the idea of conserving a substance that covers more than two-thirds of the Earth's surface. Every drop of water that exists now has been here for 4.4 billion years—not a drop more, not a drop less. Water doesn't disappear, and new water can't be created. It just changes forms and location. The amount we have is the amount we've always had, and it's the amount we'll always have. So, what's all the fuss about saving it?

It comes down to basic math. That finite amount of water across the globe has

to serve a population that is constantly increasing. During the past century, according to Charles Fishman's book *The Big Thirst: The Secret Life and Turbulent Future of Water*, the number of people inhabiting this planet has grown by a factor of four. But the rate of human water consumption has gone up in that time by a factor of seven. It doesn't take an ecologist to see that's a recipe for trouble.

Again, it's about balance—having the water we need without wasting too much of it unnecessarily. In the vegetable garden, your harvest depends on the life-giving sustenance that water provides. But more water isn't automatically better. A greater number of plants die from overwatering than underwatering.

The goal is to be like Goldilocks when it comes to watering in the garden. Not too wet, not too dry. You want your watering to be just right.

As vegetable gardeners, it's up to us to find that sweet spot in the middle. This chapter is devoted to using the resource of water wisely in the vegetable garden and helping your plants get the ideal amount that they need—not a drop more, not a drop less.

HOW OFTEN IS OFTEN ENOUGH?

Obviously, there is no blanket rule when it comes to watering your vegetable garden. Some vegetable crops are notoriously thirsty and demand heavy watering, while others actually prefer to be quite a bit drier. And for many home gardeners, those examples might be planted right next to each other, making a one-size-fits-all approach to watering the garden impossible.

One guideline that does hold true pretty much across the board is that it's better to let your soil get too dry than remain too wet.

All plant root systems require oxygen to remain healthy. Proper soil drainage and moisture levels allow oxygen molecules to reach the roots. If garden soil becomes too soggy, the oxygen is pushed out, literally suffocating and drowning your plants.

Your plants will usually tell you when they're having a moisture problem. Limp and dull foliage is a telltale sign. But pay attention to the coloring and feel to really diagnose the issue. If the leaves are dry or starting to turn brown and crispy, that's generally a case of a plant needing more water. If the foliage doesn't feel crispy but is trending toward shades of yellow or a dull, pale tone where leaves are beginning to droop, you may be overwatering.

Generally, the depth of your watering is more important than the frequency. Roots are opportunistic. They go where the water is. Water that's always near the surface encourages the roots to remain near to the surface, too. This means your plants may look robust for a while, but that shallow watering doesn't set them up well for times of drought.

Watering for a longer period once or twice per week lets the water soak more deeply into the soil. This encourages the roots to grow more deeply to follow the water. Watering less often also trains the plant to better sustain itself during periods of drought.

Finding the sweet spot of just the right amount

Of course, your soil's ability to hold moisture for the proper amount of time depends greatly on your soil's structure. As you now know, healthy soil contains lots of organic matter. Organic materials act like a sponge to hold water, so it

Wilting plants is a telltale sign that you have a moisture problem in the garden.

Healthy soil with plentiful organic matter will help your plants make the most of every drop of water.

can be accessible to plant roots as needed. At the same time, those particles also create better drainage, so excess water is able to seep away from roots more quickly.

As you improve your soil with organic amendments like compost, you'll achieve that moisture-maintenance sweet spot, which will help your plants weather the storm (or drought). And don't forget that a healthy layer of mulch will help retain moisture in the soil longer.

You can test your soil's ability to hold moisture by grabbing a fistful of it and squeezing. If it binds together in your hand but still breaks apart easily when you run your fingers through it, you've got a good level of organic matter for proper water retention.

Let Your Fingers Do The Water Testing

For a hands-on method of testing your soil's actual moisture levels, try the finger test. Stick your finger into the garden bed down to the second knuckle. If your finger comes up dirty, there's enough water in the soil. However, if it comes up dry and relatively clean, the soil is too dry, and it's time to water. Simple, right?

If you're looking for a rule of thumb to employ, 1 inch (2.5 cm) of water per week, in the absence of rain, is a nearly universal guideline. An easy way to gauge this is with an empty tuna can. Strategically place one (or several) in your garden beds and do your supplemental watering as normal. Once the can is full, you've reached roughly 1 inch (2.5 cm).

However, that 1 inch (2.5 cm) per week is just a starting point. And while it's generally a safe place to land, common sense and your own gardening judgement should be used, too. If your tomato plants look thirsty in the heat of summer, don't hold back on watering them merely because they got their weekly allotment five days ago.

You have the perfect tool for checking your soil's moisture level attached to the end of your hand.

One inch (2.5 cm) of water per week is a good rule of thumb. An empty tuna can make a simple gauge.

Early morning is the best time to water your vegetable plants, so the moisture soaks in as the temperature rises.

Apply your own observational skills to help you determine when it's okay (and necessary) to color outside the lines. Ultimately, watering is about feel. Paying attention to weather and temperature, and noting how your plants are reacting to the water they've gotten, will go a long way in helping you instinctively know what to do, even if it breaks some rule you read in a book.

Watering methods

While your vegetables will be happy to get their water however it's delivered to them, the method you use will determine how efficiently you're using this precious resource, not to mention how much of a chore watering is for you.

Whichever method, it's almost always best to water plants early in the morning. Watering during the heat of the day tends to result in a lot of moisture being lost to evaporation, and watering at night leaves your plants too wet for too long, inviting disease and rot. Early morning is ideal— so the water can soak in as the sun comes up and temperatures rise.

Around dinner time, after the heat of the day has dissipated, is a great alternative to mornings, so long as you keep the water right at the soil surface. This gives your plants some relief after a hot day, and an evening watering has a chance to soak in and be available to the plants even longer before the next day's heat arrives.

As you might expect, each method outlined here has benefits and drawbacks you'll want to consider.

Overhead watering

For gardeners like me who remember summer days running through the sprinkler, there is a certain nostalgia that comes with dragging out the garden hose and hooking up a big sprinkler.

At first glance, this method is the one that closely resembles a big soaking rain shower, so it might seem perfect. But once you turn on the spigot, you're watering not just your vegetable garden, but also the driveway, the sidewalk, the lawn, and everything else within the sprinkler's overhead

Overhead watering can cover a large area quickly, but you usually waste a lot of water in the process.

pattern. An overhead sprinkler is effective in dousing everything equally, so it might make sense for a lawn. But it's inefficient in directing the right amount of water just to the roots of your vegetable plants.

Overhead watering means you'll lose a good bit of water to overspray and evaporation. In a vegetable garden where every drop of water matters, I find almost any other method of watering to be more efficient than overhead sprinklers.

Soaker hose

For vegetable gardens with long rows of densely packed plants like lettuce or carrots, I love soaker hoses. Lay one of these down in your beds, stake it to the ground in any configuration that gives you good coverage, and let the water seep out of the hose. It gently puts the water right at the base of the plants and covers a large area with very little wasted water.

The original soaker hoses were made from recycled rubber tires. It's a great way to reuse discarded material, but many gardeners are leery about having water seep through recycled tires. Some manufacturers have responded by making soaker hoses out of food-grade polyurethane. They're more expensive, but they may provide added peace of mind if you're concerned about using their traditional rubber counterparts around your vegetables.

Soaker hoses are especially effective for long rows of plants that are packed in tightly.

A drip irrigation system can put an exact amount of water directly on each individual plant's root zone.

A drip irrigation system can be customized with emitters that water in various quantities, giving each plant the perfect amount.

Drip irrigation

A drip irrigation system allows for pinpoint accuracy, both in placing the water directly on the individual plant that you're feeding and in the amount of water you use.

The typical system uses flexible piping that branches off a standard garden hose or irrigation line. The tubing extends through the garden bed, with optional smaller spaghetti-like tubes running from it. Along the pipe or at the ends of each spaghetti tube are small plastic emitters. Water drips out of the emitter at a specified flow rate (set by the size of the emitter). Some emit ½ gallon (2.3 L) of water per hour, others might emit 1-2 gallons (4.5 to 9 L) per hour. By placing the correct emitter at the base of each plant in your bed, you can put the appropriate amount of water directly over the roots of each plant. Of all the watering methods described here, a drip system uses the least amount of water for the greatest benefit.

Most gardening retailers will have a whole aisle full of parts and pieces and tools designed for drip irrigation systems. It's easy stuff to work with, and it can be quite fun to configure your own irrigation system right down to a plant-by-plant basis.

Think Small for Big Results

If the thought of individual emitters at the base of each plant sounds like overkill for your garden, you can use the same flexible piping and spaghetti tubing to supply miniature sprinklers called micro drip emitters and micro-bubblers. Instead of an emitter cap that releases water one drop at a time, these small fixtures put out adjustable sprays of water just a few inches across and in several different patterns, from quarter-circles to half-moons and full 360-degree umbrellas. These small-scale sprayers can be centrally placed among your vegetables to water several plants at once while keeping the water off the plants' foliage and close to the root zone.

Hand watering

Call me a purist but watering my vegetable garden by hand is a method I will always employ, even with more automated drip systems and hands-off soaker hoses. The reason is simple. You should ideally be checking on your plants every day, doing a thorough visual inspection for signs of things like pests and diseases. This is what allows you to see what in the garden is doing well, and which plants might need a little extra attention. If you're spending several minutes watering each plant individually, you can cross two items off your to-do list simultaneously.

I use a wand attachment for my garden hose so I don't have to stoop down in order to get the water right at the base of the plants. It saves my back, and that dedicated time I spend with each plant gives me ample opportunity to look over new growth and keep an eye out for potential problems.

Accessories to make watering easier

You have to water your vegetable garden plants, but no one said you can't find ways to make the watering job easier and more efficient. Accessories help you do just that. Here are a few of my favorites.

Timers

Timers are the best thing to ever happen to irrigation. While I do enjoy watering my plants by hand, my schedule sometimes makes it neither feasible nor practical. Whether you use a timer that attaches at the spigot or an in-line version that controls one irrigation fixture, a battery-powered timer lets you set a watering schedule that fits your garden's needs. You decide which days to water and what time to start and stop, and it's done. Your plants get the water they need, even if you're away.

Shutoff valves

It's a pain to walk all the way back to the house to turn off the water or adjust the flow every time you need to do so. For a few dollars, a shutoff valve gives you that same control right at the business end of the hose.

A timer takes care of your watering schedule for you, even if you're away doing other things.

Quick-connect couplers

Screwing and unscrewing anything to the end of a garden hose can be frustrating, especially if you have to do it over and over. Maybe your hands are wet, maybe the hose threads are dirty and grimy, maybe the fittings don't seal all that tightly anymore after years of use. A quick-connect coupler can help you switch out compatible fixtures, nozzles, or other hoses and attachments with a snap.

Watering wand

The best watering wands have a shut-off valve at the handle and allow you to adjust the spray. The long neck makes it easy to reach under mature foliage and direct the water right at the base of a plant.

Rain barrels

Funneling rain from the gutters on your home or garden shed into a barrel is a great way to harvest water that's already falling onto your property in the form of rain. You'll be surprised how quickly even a minor rain shower can fill a 55-gallon (250 L) barrel! Most barrels have a standard hose fitting built into them. If your barrel is elevated on some sort of stand, gravity will do the rest once you hook up a hose, allowing you to redirect that water to your garden beds. You won't have any real water pressure, but you can fill watering cans all day long.

MASTERING YOUR OWN WATER REALM

Water may be the most basic and abundant natural resource on the planet, but the plants in your vegetable garden are relying on you to administer it to them in the appropriate amounts, at the optimal times, in the most beneficial places, and by the most efficient methods. Too little, and your crops could die. Too much, and your crops could die. It's suddenly a bigger responsibility than just hoping that it rains, now, isn't it? The good news is that plants are highly adaptable, and you can easily master the ins and outs as you go throughout the season. For many gardeners, the real fun comes when they start learning how to control the growing season itself. How? By extending the season, of course. Which brings us to the topic of the next chapter.

Rain barrels can hold a huge quantity of water that would otherwise be lost and save it for your garden needs on a non-rainy day.

A watering wand helps you navigate mature plant foliage and direct moisture right at the base of your plants.

10

EXTENDING THE SEASON

GARDENERS, PERHAPS MORE than any other group I can think of, love to find ways to defy nature, either by getting an early jump on the start of the growing season, or by attempting to push their plants to keep on thriving long after the calendar says time's up. And I love that about us.

"For everything there is a season," goes the classic verse. And whether you're talking about the Bible or the hit '60s song, "a time to plant, and a time to reap" is right there in the very next line.

From coaxing a little more life out of your most productive plants to encouraging entirely new crops coming into their prime in the dead of winter, the techniques for extending your growing season are surprisingly easy, and make gardening much more fun by turning it into a year-round endeavor.

TECHNIQUES FOR EXTENDING THE SEASON

There's a good chance the first thing that popped into your head when you read the title of this chapter is a greenhouse. A romantic Victorian-style greenhouse, is the ultimate season-extender for most. It's also a luxury that many gardeners, myself included, just don't have, for any number of reasons.

But the basic concept of manipulating climate in an enclosed growing space can take on many forms besides a greenhouse. And with a little creativity and ingenuity, any gardener can put that same idea to work on a much smaller (but no less effective) scale in their own garden.

A greenhouse is the ultimate season-extender, but it's also the ultimate luxury wish-list item for many gardeners.

Cold frames

A cold frame is a box with an open bottom and a transparent or translucent lid that acts like a miniature greenhouse in the garden. Placed over a growing bed, it creates a micro-environment inside the box that is 5°F to 10°F (3°C to 6°C) warmer than the outside temperature. That may not seem like much, but it's just enough to keep slow-growing root crops like carrots and beets and greens like kale, spinach, arugula, lettuce, and mustard going strong well after the first frost date.

The cold frame box can be made with wood, metal, plastic, cinder blocks or bales of hay. The lid of the box, typically angled slightly with the low end facing south to capture more sunlight and heat, can be made of glass (like an old

A simple cold frame puts the greenhouse concept to work on a smaller, movable, and more attainable scale.

window sash) or an acrylic material like plexiglass. But my favorite is plastic sheeting because it can be easily cut to fit any size cold frame you want to build. Affixing the lid with hinges allows you to open the cold frame for gardening access or venting the cold frame on warmer days.

Even in winter, several hours of direct sunlight can heat up the interior of a cold frame significantly. So prop open the lid any day when the temperature outside is, say, warmer than 40°F (5°C) to allow excess warmth to escape. Close it back up at sundown to protect plants from frigid nights.

Depending on what you're growing inside your cold frame, your local climate, and what your cold frame is made out of, you may choose to insulate your cold frame further with additional materials.

Need to give a greenhouse-type boost to just one plant? Cloche it!

Many gardeners double up the inside walls of their cold frame with pieces of rigid foam insulation or mound mulch around the outside to keep even more heat in.

Cloches

If a cold frame is the downsized version of a greenhouse, then think of a cloche as a miniature cold frame. Instead of covering all or a portion of a bed, a cloche typically houses just a single plant.

Elaborate and ornate glass cloches were all the rage centuries ago. Thomas Jefferson used them in his gardens at Monticello. But in today's garden, there's no better way to reuse plastic 2-liter bottles.

Make your own by cutting off the bottom of the bottle, allowing for the height of the plant you want to protect. Stick the bottle into the soil around the plant. You can anchor it to the ground with a thin (bamboo) stake through the top opening. Some gardeners prefer to leave the cap in place overnight when temperatures are chilliest, but be sure to unscrew it in the morning to keep from cooking the plant inside.

Row covers and frost blankets

Physical barriers can be an effective way to capture and retain a few precious degrees of warmth while keeping deadly frost from hitting your plants. Floating row cover is a polypropylene-spunbonded, polyester, or nylon material sold in long rolls and generally lightweight enough that it can be laid directly on top of plants.

Even though floating row cover won't weigh down growing plants, when able, I choose to support mine with short pieces of PVC pipe to hold it off the foliage. Just be sure to secure the edges to the ground to keep it in place.

Row cover material allows light, water, and air to pass through, but also provides a few degrees of warmth around the plants that can be the difference in survival for marginally hardy plants. It's also an effective physical barrier that keeps many garden pests from attacking your plants. (More on pests and insects in Chapter 11.)

Row covers and frost blankets may not look like they offer much in the way of warmth, but just a few degrees can often be the difference in helping your plants survive a chill.

A frost blanket is very much the same as a floating row cover, but typically is a slightly heavier material. Be aware that a heavier material that protects to a lower temperature may also block more sunlight from reaching the plants underneath. Check the manufacturer's recommendations and consider your local weather conditions when selecting a floating row cover or frost blanket.

Low tunnels and hoop houses

I mentioned above that I generally prefer to elevate my floating row cover just off the plants' foliage. Low tunnels and hoop houses take that idea and give it more structure.

A low tunnel uses a series of small arches over a garden bed as a framework to support the fabric. The arches are most often made from flexible PVC pipe, thin and workable metal rods or wickets, or lengths of electrical conduit shaped with a bending tool. The cover fabric can be fastened to the arches (or not) and secured to the ground along the edges. The result is a low, inexpensive tunnel of fabric that contains plants in a warmer environment. It can be deconstructed, moved, and reassembled as needed based on weather or location.

It's easy to create your own low tunnel over a garden bed using readily available supplies. Just break it down and relocate it as needed.

A hoop house (or *polytunnel* or *high tunnel*), made from heavy plastic sheeting that creates the walls and roof, usually refers to a structure tall enough for the gardener to walk into. The arches are therefore much bigger, and more are required so they can support more weight (in both material and snow load in colder climates). Whereas a low tunnel's covering might be removed and replaced frequently, a hoop house is left standing as a permanent structure. There's often a full-size door in at least one end and built-in ventilation (a motorized fan).

If a hoop house sounds a lot like the prototypical greenhouse that we started this conversation with, you're right. The two structures are similar in most regards. A hoop house, though, is far less costly to construct than a traditional greenhouse, albeit a little less pretty to look at. For the gardener looking to dramatically extend their growing season, it's what's happening inside the hoop house that matters far more than what it looks like.

A hoop tunnel can be a more economical, if slightly utilitarian, approach to creating a greenhouse environment for your plants.

Even Extending the Season Has Its Limits

Eliot Coleman, the well-known market gardener known for his successful four-season growing techniques in the harsh winters of Maine, uses a fascinating combination of low tunnels *inside* a hoop house! On one visit, he told me that using a hoop house for certain crops was like moving those plants 500 miles (800 km) to the south. By adding a second layer over it in the form of a low tunnel, it improves the climate by another 500 miles! It might be tempting, then, to keep adding layer upon layer to try growing tropical produce in New England in the middle of winter. But the clever Coleman has also figured out that each layer also cuts down on a significant percentage of sunlight. So freely use the techniques here to help extend your growing season, but understand that there is a point at which you're probably going too far.

Winter sowing outside

Another effective way to get a jump on the growing season is to start cool-season seeds in containers in late winter. The goal? Give cool-season seeds exposure, but still within a controlled environment, to their local winter conditions to help trigger germination. It's a "tough love" approach, you could say, to seed starting, but it's really just mimicking the natural process with a method that's as low-tech and low-cost as it gets. And you'll love the results.

Start by collecting containers to grow in. You probably already have some of the best choices lying around right now: plastic milk jugs and plastic takeout containers are my favorites.

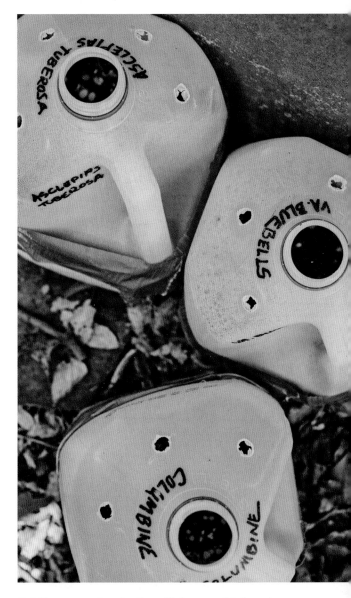

Put those empty plastic milk jugs and takeout containers to work by starting cool-season seeds like broccoli, cabbage, or lettuce in them in late winter.

Next, gather your seeds. Look for terms on the seed packet like *self-sowing, direct-sowing, cold-hardy,* or *sown when cool*. These seeds will do well with this technique. Broccoli, cauliflower, cabbage, lettuce, kale, bok choy, sage, oregano, dill, and mint are all excellent candidates. Summer edibles like tomatoes, eggplant, squash, and peppers need much warmer temperatures and likely won't take well to winter sowing, no matter how careful you are.

Create drainage holes and venting holes in the top and bottom of your containers. I like to heat the tip of a Phillips-head screwdriver and touch it to the plastic. It melts a perfectly sized hole easily, without crushing or denting the container.

With a milk jug or soda bottle, slice around the circumference, 5 to 6 inches (12 to 15 cm) from the bottom, but don't cut it off completely. Leave 1 inch (3 cm) or so attached. Now you have a planting tray, a well-fitting lid, and even a hinge that keeps them together.

Winter is Coming...Wait for It

Don't start this technique too soon. My magic date for winter sowing is the winter solstice, December 21. But since that's usually one of the busiest times of year for my family, I'll often wait until the holidays are over. There's still plenty of cold weather to come for the seeds.

Add approximately 4 inches (10 cm) of regular potting soil, then sprinkle your seeds over the surface and lightly tamp them down with your hand. Top it off with a very light layer of more soil (too little is better than too much) and water the seeds in.

Now pop the lid down over the tray and use duct tape to seal it up all the way around the seam. Use a marker or paint pen to label the container with what's growing inside. Place the containers in a sunny spot with access to natural moisture. Once they germinate, the seedlings will benefit from the sun's warmth. Keep your containers away from places where they may get knocked around or buffeted by wind. Check on the seedlings regularly and keep the soil from drying out.

Once seedlings begin to develop and temperatures start to warm, cut new openings in the containers to allow more sunlight and air circulation to reach the plants. On warm days, you may want to remove the duct tape and open the entire top. Seedlings that reach the top of their tray and have a root system sturdy enough to hold together are fully acclimated to your conditions and ready for planting in the garden, right about the time that you're getting eager to start the spring growing season!

IT'S WHATEVER SEASON YOU SAY IT IS

Gardening is all about working with a specific set of conditions to get a desired result. But no one said you had to be content with the conditions that nature gives you. Not when there are numerous ways to manipulate the environment necessary for growing your own food. Whether it's getting an early start on the gardening year by starting seeds indoors in the dead of winter or allowing certain crops to survive outdoors under a low tunnel or cold frame in temperatures that would normally kill them, gardening is also about creating your own conditions to extend the growing season and showing Mother Nature who's boss (within reason, of course). Of course, Mother Nature will hit back with two issues that every gardener will inevitably face, the subjects of our next two chapters.

11

INSECTS AND BUGS: FRIEND OR FOE?

INEVITABLY, WITHOUT DOUBT, every gardener will face many battles with insects and diseases in the garden. But are you ready for me to blow your mind? As we start this chapter, I'm going to share with you something that rocked my world when I first heard it years ago. I've never forgotten it, and I am confident it's made me a better gardener—and having fewer pest battles.

One of my very good friends is a well-respected figure in the world of entomology, the study of insects. And she told me something that totally changed the way I think about garden pests.

If you want to *increase* your pest problem in the garden, the number one way to do it is to *spray for pests*.

It sounds completely counterintuitive, I know. But once she explained the thinking behind her statement, it started to sink in for me.

Most insecticides or pesticides are considered broad-spectrum, or non-selective. That means they don't differentiate between good insects, harmful insects, or neutral insects. They simply kill everything, either through direct contact or being ingested. After the population in an area is wiped out like that, things start to come back slowly. And the first and fastest to recover are usually the insects we would consider "bad," the ones we were spraying to eliminate in the first place. That's because they're the ones who have evolved to develop a tolerance or a resistance to these insecticides. As they return, there are no natural predators around anymore since they, too, were killed by the insecticide. So the numbers of harmful insects grow even faster, and your pest problem just increased exponentially.

As counterintuitive as it may seem, spraying to kill garden pests frequently results in an even bigger population of harmful insects in the long run.

If, instead of spraying, you had done nothing at all, Mother Nature would have likely stepped in and provided a better solution. There are entire armies of predatory insects out there that live off garden pests at all different stages of their life cycles. If you promote an environment that lets that ecosystem flourish, natural balance will be restored. The "good" insects will come in response to a plentiful food source, the "bad" insects that came in response to your squash plants, let's say, and things take care of themselves.

This chapter will help you better understand the insects that will inevitably find your vegetable garden, show why being patient when it comes to pests is almost always the best strategy, and give you ways to effectively deal with a genuine pest problem—but in a responsible way.

MOST INSECTS ARE GOOD

If you were on a game show and the jackpot question was to estimate the percentage of all insects that are actual pests doing damage to garden plants, what would your guess be? Did you guess 3 percent? Because that's the right answer. (And some experts suggest it's even lower.)

Simple math says that if only 3 percent are "bad," meaning harmful or destructive, then 97 percent aren't. Some are neutral as far as the gardener is concerned, and many are actually *helpful* to a thriving garden. Mother Nature has tipped the scale—heavily—in favor of the "good" insects. If 97 percent of all insects won't do any damage whatsoever to your crops, why would you spray anything that eliminates 100 percent of them?

What's in a Name? Bugs vs. Insects

A quick word about the terms I'm using here. Most of us use the words *bug* and *insect* interchangeably in conversation. But the fact is, the two terms are not the same. At least not to entomologists.

All bugs are a type of insect, but not all insects are bugs. *Bugs* are a smaller subset of the larger all-encompassing category of *insects*.

"True bugs" (that's how entomologists refer to them) are about 75,000 species strong and are the only insects that warrant the term bug. They have a piercing, sucking, needle-like mouthpart called a *stylet*. It's what they use like a straw to take in juices from tissue. True bugs you may know include aphids, squash bugs, stink bugs, and whiteflies.

To make the nomenclature even more confusing, many insects with the word bug right in their common name aren't really true bugs at all. Ladybugs and lightning bugs, for example, are technically beetles (and therefore insects)—but not true bugs.

Even when you know which is which, insect or true bug, that doesn't tell you definitively whether it's beneficial in the garden. The assassin bug, for example, is a wonderful garden helper, despite its less-than-honorable name and terrifying appearance. It hunts down and feeds on a whole slew of common garden pests, sometimes carrying around carcasses of their prey like body armor or camouflage. But it's a true bug, just like the aphid—which is a certified garden menace for numerous crops.

The point is, all bugs are insects, but not all insects are bugs, and not even getting their names right will tell you with certainty whether it's beneficial or a garden pest.

A diverse vegetable garden, with a wide variety of edibles and flowers, attracts many insects, most of them beneficial because they'll help control the population of problem pests.

Ignorance is not bliss

For a long time, garden professionals like me were asked very frequently, "What can I spray to kill (*insert any type of insect here*)?" The blank was always filled by the name of a different insect (or sometimes just a vague physical description), but what these well-intentioned gardeners wanted was for me to simply spit out the name of a chemical they should let loose in their prized garden to kill all the bugs. Often, they didn't even know what insects they were actually dealing with. They simply assumed that all insects are bad.

Thankfully, I get that question a lot less often now. Most of us have become aware of the important role that beneficial insects play, both in the garden and in the greater scheme of the environment as a whole.

At the risk of being blunt, if you don't even know which insect is causing damage in your garden, you have no business spraying anything at all out there. Your chances of successfully solving your problem are incredibly small. Your chances of doing more harm than good are all but guaranteed.

Getting to know who's visiting

Before you can solve a pest problem, you need to be able to identify the pest. That means getting at least marginally familiar with the entire life cycle of the insects who show up in your garden.

Consider the lady beetle, commonly called a ladybug. It's one of the true garden heroes and one of the best friends gardeners have. But at the larval stage, the youngest stage of its life, the darling little lady beetle looks like a miniature crocodile or some alien creature from a sci-fi flick. And if you don't know what it is, you may react to its scary appearance alone and reach for some nonselective chemical to spray.

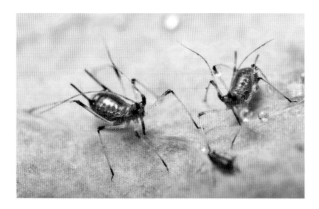

True bugs are characterized by a piercing needle-like mouth part called a stylet that they use like a straw to suck juices out of plant tissue.

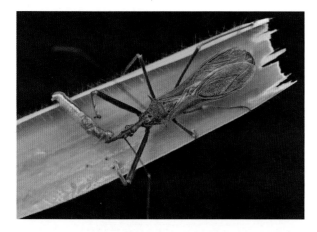

The assassin bug sounds and looks like a nasty fellow, but only if you're one of the numerous garden pests that this beneficial true bug will hunt down for you.

This tiny insect looks like the stuff of nightmares, but don't spray it! It will grow up to be the universally loved ladybug, one of the best friends your vegetable garden can have.

Let's take it even further. Let's say you do choose to spray because you found scary little dinosaurs on your crops during a mid-morning stroll through the garden. Again, if you don't understand the life cycles of the insects at work, you're compounding your issues.

That's because mid-morning is the worst time of day to apply any sort of product. It's when honeybees and other pollinators are most active, doing their work as the day just starts to heat up. And that broad-spectrum chemical you just sprayed everywhere has doomed the beneficials who were trying to pollinate your blooming vegetable plants.

All because you saw a baby ladybug.

Gardening involves a lot of detective work about plants, about soil, and about the environmental conditions in your garden. The same goes for insects. Knowledge is power, and the more you know, the better your results almost always are.

Warning: "Organic" Doesn't Automatically Mean "Safe"

In addition to understanding the insects in your garden, the responsible gardener also needs to have a working comprehension of any products under consideration for applying there. Some controls are only effective when they come in direct contact with the pest. Some are meant to be applied to the plant so that they're ingested internally as the insect feeds.

And just because you found an organic control, that doesn't mean you should douse the garden in it. Pyrethrum pyrethrin is a great example. It's a naturally derived product, made from the extract of chrysanthemum daisies. It's often marketed as a natural way to treat backyards for mosquitoes. But pyrethrum pyrethrin is incredibly lethal—to nearly all insects. It's organic, yes, but it's also nonselective. You're not doing the overwhelming majority of insects who are beneficial any favors by using it.

As my friend Dr. Jeff Gillman, the director of a large university botanical garden and a former associate professor of horticultural science who also holds degrees in entomology and horticulture, is fond of saying on the subject, "Snake venom is organic, too…but you wouldn't really want to drink it." (Didn't I tell you we gardeners are a blast at parties?)

Bumblebees and other pollinators are at their most active in the morning hours, before temperatures get too hot.

Managing pests responsibly

I hope the previous sections have started to turn you around and convinced you that not all insects you encounter in the garden are a problem.

But make no mistake, some of them are. If you have a member of that destructive 3 percent club among your crops, you definitely want to take action. But there's a whole host of steps you can (and should) be taking to manage legitimate garden pests in a responsible way.

Inspection and manual control

I talk about this topic a lot, for good reason. It's often the easiest method for controlling pests. Throughout this book, I've encouraged you to get out in your garden on a regular basis. If, on my morning stroll, I spy an insect I know to be a troublemaker hanging out on the leaves of one of my tomato plants, I simply pick it up and toss it out of the garden (where a neighboring bird or one of my chickens can find it). Yes, it was just one insect, but if I caught it before it had a chance to lay a few hundred eggs, then I may have just saved myself, and my entire crop, from a major infestation. No need to even think about coming back later with an extreme-measure remedy, and I did it with a literal flick of my wrist.

Barriers

Physical barriers are my personal favorite pest control method. Things like floating row covers, a lightweight mesh fabric that gets draped over a row of plants, keep many insects from landing on your plants. If they can't land on the plant, they can't feed or lay eggs on the plant—voila, problem solved.

Taking a regular walk through my garden is still my preferred way of monitoring for pests and proactively preventing large-scale problems.

A good floating row cover still allows sunlight, air, and water to pass through, and it's light enough that it doesn't impede the plants' growth. It can usually be installed over a row immediately upon planting but do remember that if the crop you're protecting requires pollination, you'll need to remove the cover once you see flowers starting so pollinators can get in there and do their thing. (You may find yourself uncovering the plants for the morning hours when pollinators are most active and then replacing the cover by midday.) If you're willing to manually pollinate your crops with a cotton swab or artist's brush, the protective row cover can stay on full-time.

Physical barriers have the added benefit of safe-guarding your crops from hungry noninsect garden pests like rabbits, raccoons, squirrels, or deer.

A simple floating row cover can prevent many pest infestations by blocking insects from access to your crops.

Trap crops

Whether it's in your vegetable garden or somewhere else, insects have to eat to survive, too. And just like humans, insects have a definite preference for certain foods. Trap crops work on the premise that you can lure pests away from certain plants by giving them something that is more attractive to them than the crop you want to protect. It's basically sacrificing one crop to save another.

Squash is a classic example. Let's say you have your heart set on a big, beautiful bounty of summer squash like zucchini. Nasty pests like the squash vine borer can be a huge threat. If they get to your crop, it's basically game over before you even realize you have a problem. But that insect (as well as the squash bug and cucumber beetle) happens to love the 'Blue Hubbard' squash variety even more than they love zucchini. Strategically plant a few 'Blue Hubbard' plants in and around your garden, and they become sacrificial bodyguards for the zucchini. The squash borers gorge themselves on the 'Blue Hubbard', and it's like they don't even know your zucchini plants exist. You should destroy the trap crop once you know the trap is full, so the pest doesn't get the chance to increase its population in your garden.

Radishes are another commonly used trap crop that's effective for a variety of pests. For the cost of a few extra seed packets or additional plants, you may find that planting a crop to *feed* garden pests may be the best way to *fight* them.

Diversity

This technique builds off that same idea. The more types of plants you have in your garden, the more types of insects you'll also attract. And because, as we've already learned, the majority of insects are beneficial (or at least neutral), a larger overall insect population means a greater chance that you're bringing in the good ones who will take out the bad ones. Plain and simple, a greater diversity of plants equals a greater diversity of good insects.

Diversity in the vegetable garden is also a nice insurance policy against disease (which is discussed in the next chapter). If potatoes are the only thing you plant, you've basically got a monoculture. One pest problem, and you're done. Even if you protect your potatoes all season long, a single potato pathogen that takes hold will wipe out all of your efforts and leave you with nothing. Mother Nature doesn't do monocultures. That's a hint that gardeners shouldn't, either.

Repellents

Controlling insects doesn't have to mean *killing* them. Using a simple repellent is often quite effective in persuading pests to find another food source. Homemade concoctions are an organic warning shot that I have no qualms about using in the garden.

Here's my favorite repellent recipe. Blend 2 cups (473 ml) water with 2 cups (473 ml) hot peppers. Wear gloves, as the capsaicin in the peppers (depending on the variety) can burn your skin. Use a cheesecloth strainer to remove the pulp, and pour the liquid into a spray bottle. You can replace the peppers with 2 cloves of garlic instead, or use both for a double whammy. Adding a few drops of dish soap will help the spray stick to plants but isn't required. The spray will mask the scent, or alter the taste of the plants, enough to encourage your pests to find greener pastures.

Remember, a diverse garden attracts a wide variety of insects, and the good guys will outnumber the bad guys.

Integrated Pest Management

Start doing some research on dealing with garden pests, and it won't take long for you to run across the abbreviation IPM. It stands for Integrated Pest Management, and while it's a very formal, quite official-sounding entity, it's actually a very common-sense system, an eco-friendly philosophy. IPM uses knowledge, science, and data to control pest damage in a sustainable way that minimizes cost and risk to humans and the environment. It encompasses many of the practices I've detailed throughout this book.

The IPM approach starts with the least environmentally damaging tactic first and then escalates things one predetermined step at a time, only if necessary. IPM is a big topic that warrants further exploration by gardeners. Here's a very simplified version of what it entails:

Step 1: Use cultural methods. Change the conditions the pest needs to survive, like water, shelter, or food. This includes putting the right plant in the right place and maintaining strong plants that are less likely to fall victim to pests.

Step 2: Turn to physical methods. Simply prevent pest access with barriers, traps, or hand-picking.

Step 3: Employ genetic methods. Plant pest-resistant varieties or hybrids that have been crossbred to have resistance built into them.

Step 4: Utilize biological methods. Use predators to target pests. This can include leaving the naturally occurring population of good insects alone as well as purposely introducing new beneficial insects to go after pests. Biological options can also include *Bacillus thuringiensis* (Bt), a soil bacterium, that targets many destructive caterpillars.

Step 5: Last resort chemical methods. These can be either *biorational* controls like diatomaceous earth (DE) that target a specific part of a pest's biology in an organic way, or *conventional* synthetic insecticides. Both are highly lethal and some can last a long time in the environment. That's why they're treated in IPM as a last resort and used only in carefully controlled circumstances.

Beneficial insects, like this lacewing, are often purposely introduced to gardens to gang up on problem pests.

Diatomaceous earth is organic, but it's still highly lethal to insects. In Integrated Pest Management (IPM), it's treated as the last resort for a pest problem and used only in controlled circumstances.

DON'T BUG OUT ABOUT INSECTS

I hope this chapter has started to challenge some of your preconceptions about insects. When you grasp the notion that only 3 percent of the insects you'll ever see in the garden pose a problem for your crops, it changes the way you interact with them. From getting to know the other 97 percent to finding responsible ways to control the occasional true garden pest, learning how to successfully grow vegetables is largely about learning how to successfully coexist with the millions of insect species that also inhabit our world.

So chill out a little bit the next time you see a tiny visitor crawling on your tomato plants. The plant profiles found later in this book include notes about the specific insects you'll need to watch out for, along with some tactics for managing them. It's important to realize, though, that insects just aren't the dealbreaker that many new gardeners make them out to be. Diseases, on the other hand can be very problematic. Let's cover those next.

12

DISEASES: MANAGING THE INEVITABLE

DEATH, TAXES, Mariah Carey songs at Christmastime, and plant diseases in the vegetable garden—these are the things that are inevitable in life. I can't help you completely avoid any of them, I'm afraid. With a little patience and knowledge, though, I can help you manage the last item from that list to make it a little less intrusive.

Disease management takes some effort, and (spoiler alert!) it's a battle you'll never fully win. But disease in the garden is typically more of a nuisance that you can work through than an all-or-nothing proposition that leaves you empty-handed at the end of the growing season. Every year brings different circumstances, which means a fresh chance to improve your skills of observation, diagnosis, and containment. And growing your way through those experiences will make you an exponentially better gardener.

Having to deal with disease in the garden does not mean you've failed, by any means. It just means you're a gardener. It's *how* you deal with disease in the garden that matters.

PLAYING DOCTOR: BACTERIA, FUNGUS, OR VIRUS?

No one expects you to get a degree in plant pathology just to grow backyard tomatoes. But a basic understanding of what causes the most common plant diseases can go a long way in helping you correctly diagnose and appropriately treat the problem (and maybe even prevent it from happening again in future growing seasons).

When a plant is diseased, it's because of a bacteria, fungus, or virus.

Bacteria

Just as is the case for humans, not all bacteria are bad for plants and soil. By far, most of the millions of types of bacteria are beneficial for your garden, and many are even necessary for true growing success. (See Chapter 2 for more on the soil food web and what's happening down there on a microscopic level.) There are, however, approximately 200 types of bacteria that cause diseases in plants.

Among the most common bacterial infection is leaf spot. In this case, bacteria attack the plant and produce a toxic chemical that begins killing plant cells. The plant goes into defense mode and kills off its own surrounding healthy plant cells as a way to isolate the infection. In some instances, the dead cell areas even drop from the plant, creating "shot holes" in affected leaves.

Wilting and drooping can often be a sign of a moisture deficiency (as discussed in Chapter 9). But if your watering is on target, wilting can also be from certain types of bacteria stopping a plant's ability to deliver water and nutrients to the rest of the plant. This process can occur quite rapidly, often resulting in a dramatic decline in the plant's appearance—sometimes within a single day!

Other bacterial infections produce cankers and soft rot, sunken areas that are left behind by dead and dying plant tissue. But sometimes, bacteria can trigger abnormal growth in an infected plant.

Bacterial leaf spot is easy to identify. The plant's defense mechanisms kill off healthy plant cells to isolate the infection. Ultimately the dead cell areas fall away.

A plant may respond to certain bacteria types by rapidly producing clusters of new cells, called galls, that appear as unusually large and misshapen growths anywhere on the plant.

Bacteria spread in several ways. Insects, splashing water, other diseased plants, and even garden tools can help spread bacteria around among your crops. They enter plants through tiny openings from cuts, injury, or just natural openings on the plants themselves.

Once a plant is infected by bacteria, it can be difficult to control, as options are limited. Copper-based sprays can provide some help but are not a cure. Your best bet is to remove affected plants (or portions of plants) from the garden, immediately destroying them. They shouldn't be added to your compost pile.

Bacteria is best controlled preventatively, treating plants before damage is even present. That includes good cultural practices like sanitizing garden equipment and tools, refraining from overhead watering to help keep foliage dry, and removing plant debris from the garden.

Fungi
Like bacteria, most fungi are actually good for the garden. But the odds start to work against the gardener. There are *thousands* of harmful fungi that can cause problems for your edible crops. Most problems—when they're true diseases and not simply misdiagnosis—are fungal in nature.

When a Disease Isn't a Disease at All

It's easy to look at any plant that's not performing as expected and assume you have a disease issue. But remember that the most common culprit of garden problems and damaged plants isn't a disease at all. Plants can take on a less-than-healthy appearance because of drought, sunscald, leaf scorch, or too much water or fertilizer. Environmental conditions and gardener error aren't the same as diseases, so make sure you know what you're dealing with before you start blindly treating plants or taking drastic measures.

Do you see rotting or dead roots? Swelling on buried roots? Seedling stems that are rotting or flopping over at soil level? Leaves that display spots, rusts, wilts, or powdery patches of mildew? If so, a fungus may be among us.

Fungal spores are incredibly small and light-weight, so they can be transported great distances through the air. They're also easily spread by water, animals, insects, and people.

Infected plants or plant parts should be removed to help minimize an outbreak in the garden. Fungicides are available, with copper, sulfur, and sodium bicarbonate (baking soda) being common organic options. Keep in mind, though, that these treatments are best at preventing the germination of *new* fungal spores and stopping future outbreaks. They're less effective at reversing an existing issue.

Prevention is the best medicine when it comes to fungi. Buying disease-resistant plants is an easy step to take. Careful watering at the soil level and adding a mulch layer will minimize the amount of moisture contacting the foliage, thereby reducing the possible pathways for fungi to reach your plants. Water early in the day to allow any wet foliage to dry out quickly. Space plants properly and keep plants pruned to allow good air circulation.

Viruses

As you might have guessed, you want no part of any viruses in your garden. They can persist for years, even before presenting any problems. And when they do show themselves, things tend to go bad in a hurry, since they attack the entire plant system.

Plant foliage may start off turning yellow or displaying mosaic patches of yellow, light green, or white. Then the plant may start to look stunted. Plants can appear misshapen or mal-formed. Leaves may be rolled, swollen, puckered, or abnormally narrow. The specifics can vary depending on the virus, but it's generally pretty obvious that something is very wrong.

Fungal spores can be transported great distances through the air, water, or on living things, spreading disease where they land.

Watering only at the soil level and mulching around your plants is a simple way to reduce a common fungal pathway to your crops.

Yellow-tinted mosaic patches on a plant's foliage can be a sign that a virus has taken hold.

My Super-Simple Seven-Step Maintenance Routine

The sad fact is that a lot of would-be gardeners give up because the maintenance gets the better of them. And it's true. If you let all those nitpicky tasks and basic chores pile up over time, you can easily be left with a daunting day in the garden that's sure to leave you overwhelmed and frustrated by the time you finally finish.

So don't save it all for a sunup-to-sundown Saturday work session. (Unless that's your idea of a good time. No judgment.) Here are seven ways I try to streamline my time when I do my daily disease check in the garden. A few minutes here, a few minutes there, and it can start to feel like your vegetable garden is taking care of itself.

1. **Take time to look around.** Make note of things to do and changes you see (both good and not-so-good). Use a phone app that allows you to dictate your observations and add photos. Keep those notes handy for later.
2. **Come equipped for recurring tasks.** I store my most-used tools in an old mailbox right in the garden to save steps. And I always come to the garden with my pruning sheath on my hip. It holds my trusty pruners and a soil (hori hori) knife so they're with me if I need them.
3. **Wear gloves.** You spot something that needs attention, but your garden gloves are back in the house. There's a good chance you'll find a reason to not come back right away or just "save it for next time." So just have them on when you're in the garden.
4. **Tie up loose ends.** It seems there's always something in the garden that needs to be tied up or staked. Keep a well-stocked selection of twine, Velcro tape, and bamboo stakes of different sizes; you'll save countless hours rummaging for supplies or running to the store.
5. **Be ready for bulk.** Some small jobs turn into a big one without warning. I keep a stack of flexible tub trugs (10-gallon (45 L) flexible rubber totes with handles) right inside my garden fence. You'll find hundreds of uses for them, in addition to collecting weeds, harvesting fruit, and hauling a quick load of mulch or compost.
6. **Sanitizing spray.** I keep a spray bottle of alcohol with me whenever I'm in the garden. Anytime I snip off a diseased branch or funky-looking foliage, I hit the blades of my pruners with the spray to make sure I don't spread any pathogens from a sick plant to a healthy one.
7. **Keep your hose handy.** There was a time when my garden hose didn't live in the garden because I didn't like the long, tangled mess strewn all over my neat pathways. I still don't, so I installed a new spigot in an out-of-the-way corner. The hose stays connected and within easy reach, without all the laborious coiling and uncoiling every time I need it.

I hope these tips make your time in the garden more efficient, so you can spend more time enjoying your vegetables and less time keeping up with them.

Plant viruses cannot be spread by wind or water. They must physically enter the plant, often from insects who feed on an infected plant and then transmit the virus to a healthy plant upon feeding again. But viruses can also be spread by plant propagation, infected seed, and human contact. Once you have a virus in your garden, there's unfortunately nothing you can do to treat it. It may seem drastic, but your most effective course of action is to remove all suspected infected plants to stop the spread. Cutting out foliage alone won't save the plant.

Preventing a virus is difficult. Buy virus-resistant varieties, use physical barriers like floating row covers to protect plants from virus-carrying pests, and be active in repelling and removing harmful insects from the garden (as explored in Chapter 11).

An old mailbox serves as a convenient storage box in the garden, keeping gardening tools and supplies dry and at the ready for when I need them.

A plant that looks iffy at the nursery won't get better when you bring it home. It could even be diseased and spread the problem to other plants.

Plant tags and seed packets will specify disease resistance with coded letters.

Early detection is key

The best way to prevent any disease issues from taking over in your garden is to stay on top of them from the start. Look your plants over thoroughly and on a regular basis. You'll get good at spotting something that doesn't look quite right. And when you do, it's time to start doing your homework. Take pictures, research online, and ask other gardeners. The earlier you can identify a disease issue proactively, the better you'll be able to deal with it reactively.

Often, early detection means paying close attention at the nursery. Only put the best of the best in the ground. If it looks suspect at the garden center with spotted leaves or discolored foliage or a floppy stem, it could be due to disease. And a diseased plant won't get any better once you get the plant home. It could even spread the disease to the rest of your garden. The same goes for seedlings you raised from seed. Start enough seeds that you can pick and choose only the strongest and healthiest-looking seedlings on planting day.

Resistant varieties

Many seed and seedling varieties have been bred over time to be resistant to certain diseases. To be clear, that does not make it "genetically modified" or anything scary. It's actually plant science at work, where the best and healthiest traits are combined to produce hybrid varieties (there's more on some of this terminology in Chapter 3) that are naturally more adept at warding off diseases that target that crop.

You'll often see this noted on a plant's tag or the seed packet with various letters, and alongside will be a key to tell you which letter stands for which disease. An F tells you the plant is especially resistant to Fusarium wilt; a V denotes resistance to Verticillium wilt; BW notes resistance to bacterial wilt; and so forth. Be aware that "disease-resistant" doesn't translate to "bulletproof" against disease. It just means the plant will put up a stronger fight against that particular pathogen than other varieties.

Keeping my tools clean is one way I cut down on disease in the garden. A quick spray of rubbing alcohol kills pathogens like fungal spores that could be transferred from one plant to another on the blades of my pruners.

Sanitation: Keeping it clean equals keeping it green

I catch a lot of heat for how meticulous I am about keeping my garden tools and supplies as clean as possible. But it's not because I'm super persnickety. Okay, it's not *just* because I'm super persnickety (because I totally *am* super persnickety).

The fact is clean implements, like shovels, trowels, and pruners reduce the spread of pathogens in the garden. As I pointed out earlier, many diseases are transmitted from one plant to another through direct contact. It could be from an army of aphids or it could easily be from a pair of pruners carrying the disease to the next plant you unwittingly give a little trim.

I keep a spray bottle of rubbing alcohol nearby when I work in the garden. (A homemade solution of 10 percent bleach to 90 percent water is effective, too.) After every few cuts and between every plant, I give the tools I'm working with a quick spritz.

This concern for contamination even extends to garden helpers like tomato stakes and trellises. If they're made of wood, they can harbor pathogens from one season to the next. It's even suggested to clean metal cages and supports before reusing them the following season.

Good sanitation in the garden also means not handling plants when they're wet, since your hands can pass disease from plant to plant just as easily as infected tools.

When you remove foliage, don't just cut out that one leaf that looks suspect. Trace back to the branch and remove the whole thing. This generally saves you from having to do it again the next day to remove more leaves. After pruning, remove those questionable branches entirely. Don't leave them lying in your garden beds where, if they are diseased, they can pass those pathogens to the soil, mulch, or any healthy plants they happen to come in contact with. The compost pile is no place for diseased plant material, either. Most backyard piles don't get hot enough to reliably kill off all fungal spores. Put it in a bag, tie it up, and get it off your property.

I keep my garden pathways free of weeds, but not just because I'm a neatnik. Fewer weeds means fewer plant diseases among your crops.

Keeping your garden weed-free is also a good sanitary practice. Besides being unsightly, weeds can provide a safe haven for insects that may carry disease, or be the actual disease source that insects transfer to other garden plants.

Grab bag: Other good practices

Many of the other gardening techniques I espouse throughout this book also have a sneaky disease-suppression element to them. Because plant disease is a prevalent issue, preventing disease any way I can is something that creeps into every decision I make in the garden.

- How you water (Chapter 9) matters. Overhead watering soaks the entire plant, and water can be an effective vector for disease. You can't do anything about rainfall, but supplemental watering should always be done at the base of your plants, either by hand or with soaker hoses or a drip irrigation system. And water in the morning so any excess on the foliage can dry off quickly.

- A good layer of mulch (Chapter 8) can keep many soilborne pathogens from splashing up onto plants. Can mulch harbor pathogens? Yes, but most natural mulch materials will break down over the course of a year or so. An annual layer of new mulch on top keeps any pathogens from contacting your plants.
- Rotating your crops (Chapter 7) breaks the reproductive cycle of many soil pathogens that can infect one crop, overwinter in the soil, and return the next spring to affect the same crop the following season.
- Raised beds and well-composted soil helps with drainage. Soggy soil causes root rot and allows moisture-loving diseases to flourish.
- Proper spacing of plants doesn't just give your crops ample room to grow, the air circulation between plants helps make it harder for pathogens to transfer from one plant to another. And keeping fruit and vegetation off the ground by trellising helps prevent rot and keeps plants dry.

The Disease Triangle

Calling plant diseases "inevitable" can make it seem like you'll be fighting a continuous battle in the garden, like there's nothing you can do but sit and wait to have your crops wiped out by some invisible and unbeatable foe. But there's a way to boil it all down to one simple image that helps me keep disease (and my options for tackling it) in perspective. It's called the Disease Triangle.

Three things have to exist in order for disease problem to develop: the pathogen itself, a host plant, and a conducive environment. Take away any one of them, and you don't have a triangle. Eliminate just one of those elements from the equation in your garden, and you no longer have a disease problem.

You can obviously eliminate the pathogen by not introducing diseased plants into the garden in the first place, or removing the diseased plant.

Most disease pathogens are host-specific to a certain plant species or plant family. Avoid that plant or at least choose varieties of it that are disease-resistant, and you eliminate the second point of the triangle.

Or change the environment to make it less hospitable to pathogens. More sunlight and air circulation through a little selective pruning could make all the difference in knocking out that third point of the triangle.

The point is, you don't have to fix *everything* to get a foothold against disease in the garden. You just have to ask yourself which *one* of the three points of the Disease Triangle you can most readily change. That, for me, always makes the fight a little less daunting.

The Disease Triangle is made up of three points. Eliminate any one of them, and you no longer have a triangle—or a disease problem.

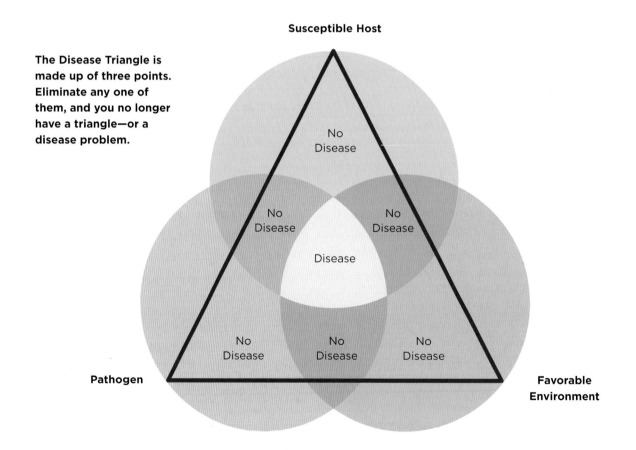

Getting (some) control over disease

The main thing to know here is that treatments may not prevent an infection from occurring, but at least they slow down the spread of a pathogen. The best you can do is remove as much diseased plant material from the area as possible to remove pathogen propagules and minimize the impact on your current and subsequent crops.

As hard as it is, we simply must learn to tolerate some diseased spots and damaged leaves here and there. I'll use early blight on tomatoes as a personal example. I deal with this fungal disease pretty much every year in the hot and humid Southern United States. It tends to affect the lowest foliage first. As soon as a leaf branch starts to show symptoms, I prune the entire branch out. That doesn't remove the pathogen (the whole plant is infected), but this maintenance does slow the spread throughout the rest of the plant, and especially to other plants. Photosynthesis continues in the upper foliage, so the plant continues to set perfectly good fruit, even as more and more of the lower branches succumb to the blight and get removed.

Keep in mind that, for many of the diseases that your vegetable plants may get, it's not a death sentence. There's no need to panic. But proactively removing what you can usually helps reduce the spread—just like with early blight.

Diagnosing the particular disease you're dealing with is often no easy feat. Many plant diseases look the same. Even the experts sometimes struggle with visual identification alone. There's plenty of bad information on the internet, so consult a reliable source before taking action in the garden, and always follow directions to the letter, as improper application of a treatment may end up being worse than the disease you're battling! In the plant profiles later in this book I'll tell you which common diseases to be on the lookout for, along with some helpful tips for their control.

As gardeners, we need to learn to live with some degree of imperfection. I can't completely remove the early blight from this tomato plant, but I can slow the spread by taking out the affected branches. The upper part of the plant will still put out perfectly good fruit.

DO WHAT YOU CAN DO... AND NOTHING MORE

For me, I've learned to be patient when it comes to disease. I practice good habits, like not handling my garden plants in the morning when they're wet with dew or after a rain. I'll often proactively apply a copper fungicide before a forecasted heavy rain to try to minimize the risk of a problem afterward. I use seeds, plants, soil, compost, and mulch from trusted sources. I keep my tools clean. I take notes and try to determine if there's something I could do better. I rotate my crops so that nothing from one plant family is in the same bed for a few years. I police the garden regularly and remove infected foliage or even whole plants. If the damage is minor or won't affect my harvest or other crops, sometimes I just do nothing. And if I have to replace a tomato plant or two during the season, I consider it a small price to pay to prevent a serious disease from spreading.

Remember, disease is a given in the garden. How you choose to deal with disease is the variable that can ultimately decide the overall success of all your crops, no matter what you're growing.

GROW GUIDES

THE FAB 40 FOR FILLING YOUR VEGETABLE GARDEN

I hope the previous 12 chapters have inspired you to expand your existing vegetable garden, to make some improvements to what you have now, to try some new techniques, or maybe to start growing edibles for the very first time.

But I know that talking about vegetable gardening in theory only goes so far. At some point, you just want to get out there and plant things in the ground. Well, it's time to get into the nuts and bolts of the individual crops that will make up your vegetable garden.

I'll admit that there are dozens of wonderful crops that aren't included in the following pages and hundreds of unique varieties that I simply don't have room to name. I had to draw the line somewhere, so I picked a nice round number of forty crops to discuss.

There's a good mix of warm-season and cool-season crops, crops that are easy to grow, and crops that are notoriously challenging. There are some I couldn't grow a garden without, and a few that even I typically don't bother with. I've snuck a few fruits into the vegetable garden too and I took the liberty of compiling all of the culinary herbs into one guide entry (because if you can grow parsley, you can grow cilantro). The big favorites get some extra attention, but I also tried to include at least a few lesser-known veggies that are worth seeking out and growing, too. I know I've missed a few crops. So if you were really counting on in-depth instructions for growing your own award-winning cucamelons, my apologies. I'm hoping I've covered enough of the basics throughout the rest of the book to give you the fundamentals needed to tackle that on your own and have great success.

The information for each crop is broken down under headings that should cover most of what you need to know. I loved collecting baseball cards as a kid. So to start, I give you the pertinent stats in an easy-to-digest format: the sun and soil requirements, seed-starting info, transplanting details, and how long you'll have to wait to harvest your bounty. Then I offer my own thoughts and experiences with each crop, as well as some nerdy plant trivia. I even list my favorite varieties of each to help you get started picking out what's best for you.

Then I'll take you through planting day, special mid-season maintenance, identify pests and diseases to watch for, and guide you through harvesting the fruits of your labor, all with an eye toward the best possible flavor. If there are special considerations when selecting your varieties or extra steps you can take for long-term storage, these earn their own sections in the grow guide. Let's get growing with forty edible crops you should have in your vegetable garden.

ARTICHOKE

Cynara cardunculus
(Scolymus Group),
Sunflower family

The Down and Dirty

Preferred climate	**Mild**
Sun	**Full sun to partial shade**
Soil	**Sandy loam, compost-rich**
pH range	**6.5–8.0**
Sow seeds	**Indoors, 10–12 weeks before last frost date**
Sowing depth	**¼ inch (6 mm)**
Days to germination	**10–21, then thin to one seed per cell**
Germination temperature	**60°F–80°F (16°C–27°C)**
Note	**Crowns are easier to grow than seeds. Grow as an annual in colder climates.**
Plant crowns	**6–8 inches (15-20 cm) deep, 2 weeks after last frost date**
Spacing	**4 feet (1.2 m) apart in all directions**

Notes from the garden

On the dinner table, artichokes are delicious roasted, grilled, steamed, or fried. In the garden, they provide incredible ornamental value with their structural form, silver-green foliage, and blazing neon purple color when allowed to bloom. While they're a member of the sunflower family, artichokes can prove to be needier than their flower garden relatives. But for the patient gardener who's willing to cater to the artichoke's particular climate demands, they'll be rewarded with beautiful, showy buds that can be even more of a showstopper in the kitchen.

My favorite varieties

- 'Colorado Star' A newer variety, think of this early-maturing annual as the purple version of 'Imperial Star'. It can become a perennial if grown in warm climates.
- 'Green Globe' A reliable cold-weather producer that's hardy in warm regions, it's meant to be grown as a perennial and flowers in early summer.
- 'Imperial Star' Developed to mature faster than other varieties, this is the choice for growing artichokes as an annual. Transplant to harvest is 85 days.
- 'Violetto' This Italian classic is known for its striking purple heads. It matures later than 'Green Globe', but produces greater yields.

Choosing what to grow

Artichoke divisions, called crowns (or root divisions), are far easier to grow than seeds. Unfortunately, they're only really easy to come by at nurseries in coastal, central California when in-season. That's where nearly all commercial artichokes are grown, thanks to the region's mild winters and foggy summers. Crowns are identical to the parent plant, so you know exactly what you're getting when you plant them.

Life is Like a Packet of Artichoke Seeds

Even from reputable seed companies, artichoke seeds can be a hit-or-miss proposition in that they don't always grow true to the variety listed on the packet. That's just a quirk of artichokes and how they reproduce. But outside of areas that almost never freeze (where they are perennials) growing artichokes as annuals from seed (and living with whatever variation you get) may be your only option.

Pay attention to your growing climate, as artichoke is not cold-hardy. Where winter temperatures can go below 14°F (-10°C), artichokes should be grown as annuals. They'll need exposure to cool temperatures to induce budding (called *vernalization*). Subject seedlings to ten straight days of 40°F to 50°F (5°C to 10°C) temperatures before transplanting, or they won't go to flower until the following year. In colder climates, they won't survive to the second year.

Planting

Most artichokes fail because either the soil's too dry in summer or too waterlogged in winter. Soil should retain moisture but also drain well. The best soil is a sandy loam generously amended with compost. Plant on mounds or in raised rows to help with drainage.

Artichokes prefer a site where they do not have to compete with trees for water and nutrients or in planting beds where frequent turnover may disturb the roots. Transplants need to have their roots loosened upon planting in a hole twice as wide as the root ball.

Mid-season care

Plan on giving artichokes about 1 inch (2.5 cm) of water per week during the growing season. Supplemental watering may be required if rainfall provides less than that, but be prepared to pull back if the soil becomes heavy and fails to drain. Artichokes are heavy feeders. While compost-rich soil provides a good range of nutrients early, a balanced all-purpose organic fertilizer will be needed to supplement monthly throughout the season.

Pests & disease

Slugs and snails are the biggest pest concern, leaving holes at night. For a minor infestation, remove slugs by hand. Organic slug and snail baits with iron phosphate as the active ingredient may be used for more difficult populations.

Perennial artichokes may be susceptible to the artichoke plume moth. The larvae feed on bud stalks, eating the plants from the inside. Affected buds should be removed and destroyed. Check under leaves and on stalks for single, tiny, green-yellow or orange-yellow eggs and scrape them off.

Artichoke crowns, if you can find them, are easier to grow than seeds.

Curly dwarf is a virus that stunts the growth and vigor of artichoke plants. Be on the lookout for curled leaves and buds that are fewer in number, misshapen, and undersized. Remove infected plants and do not use divisions from them.

Blight sometimes affects the older leaves of artichoke plants. Remove leaves at the first sign of blight, disposing of them outside the garden.

Harvesting

Healthy plants will yield tall stems and multiple flower buds, usually starting in early summer.

Cut buds when they're firm and still closed, about 3 inches (8 cm) in diameter. Leave 2 inches (5 cm) of stalk below the bud to make handling easier, being careful not to bruise the bud leaves. Use buds upon harvesting or refrigerate them for up to 2 weeks.

Once a bud begins to open, its taste diminishes rapidly. Leave opened buds to become flowers. If all buds have been harvested from a stalk, it can be cut back to the ground.

If frost is rare, artichokes can give a first crop in fall and continue producing throughout winter until peak production in spring. Cut stalks down after spring harvest so new stalks grow for fall. Artichoke plants produce more with age, so over-wintering is recommended. In areas where winter temperatures don't drop below 10°F (-12°C), cut back plants to ground level after the fall harvest. Cover with 3 to 4 inches (8 to 10 cm) of mulch to protect from severe frost.

Gardeners in regions where it dips to -10°F (-23°C) can try cutting back plants to about 12 inches (30 cm). Bury the exposed stalk with compost and mulch, cover the pile with an overturned basket or box, and add more mulch. Secure a rainproof cover over the covered pile. Once the ground thaws in spring, uncover and add a new layer of compost around the plant to encourage top growth.

Tall stems and multiple flower buds are the signs of healthy artichoke plants ready for harvest.

In cold climates, artichokes need exposure to winter temperatures in order to induce budding.

ARUGULA

Eruca vesicaria,
Cabbage family

The Down and Dirty

Preferred climate	Cool, frost-hardy
Sun	Full sun to light shade
Soil	Nutrient-rich, well-draining, evenly moist, and mixed with several inches of compost
pH range	6.0–7.0
Sow seeds	Not traditionally sown indoors since it germinates quickly and easily when sown directly outdoors. If sowing indoors, start seeds in late winter or early fall.
Sowing depth	¼ inch (6 mm)
Days to germination	4–10
Germination temperature	65°F–85°F (18°C–30°C)
Note	Seeds prefer warmer soil to germinate. But once they're out of the ground, arugula prefers cooler temperatures and has a reputation of bolting in hot weather.
Transplant seedlings	As soon as the ground can be worked in spring and in fall once the temperatures start to cool
Spacing	6–10 inches (15–25 cm) between plants and 10 inches (25 cm) between rows
Days to maturity	Any time after germination, but more typically 4–8 weeks after sowing.

Notes from the garden

Arugula is also known by other names: rocket and roquette, among them. But whatever name you use, it's a joy to grow, and I find its fresh peppery flavor hard to pass up. If you've ever bought mesclun mix from the grocery store, those small leaves with the loped edges and tangy taste are arugula. It's also delicious when picked fresh to add to pasta, top a pizza, or layer in a sandwich—although I've been known to eat my share straight from the bed anytime I pass by.

If you're looking for a carefree crop that grows quickly in the cooler months, arugula is a must. It's easy to direct-sow and germinates in a few short days. For that reason, I never start it indoors. I love sprinkling a row of seeds down a vacant space, knowing it will fill in quickly. It's so undemanding, I don't even supplement with any fertilizer. It always seems to grow quite happily wherever I plant it.

You can grow a lot of arugula from a single packet of seeds, so consider sowing a new round of seeds at periodic intervals, approximately every 2 to 3 weeks during cool weather, for a more continuous harvest.

My favorite varieties

- 'Esmee' Quick-growing and very cold-tolerant, this dark green variety has a flavor that is more nutty than spicy.
- 'Rocket' The easiest to find off the rack and in catalogs, it's known for spicy flavor and finely lobed leaves.
- 'Runway' If bigger is better for you, this fast-growing variety with large lobed leaves will hit the mark.
- 'Sylvetta' In warmer regions, this variety tends to be slower to bolt than most.

Planting

Direct-sow or plant seedlings once the ground can be worked in early spring, or in fall as days start to cool. Thin to 6 inches (15 cm) between plants and keep the soil evenly moist.

Mid-season care

Arugula is a carefree plant, so monitoring soil moisture and scouting for flea beetles should be all it requires. As a light feeder when it comes to nutrient demands, supplemental fertilization is not necessary when planted in rich soil. Consider this

to be one of the most hands-off plants you will grow in your garden.

Pests & disease

Flea beetle is the most common pest of arugula, so a floating row cover is the most effective control. Install it after seeding or immediately after transplanting.

Harvesting

Arugula can be harvested as a microgreen as soon as leaves are present. Otherwise, anytime during the season, harvest by cutting leaves from the outside for continual plant growth.

Arugula's recognizable shape and peppery bite make it stand out within the other young salad greens contained in your favorite mesclun mix.

Quick-growing arugula always gets tucked in and around my crops that take longer to mature. It'll be harvested and enjoyed long before crowding becomes an issue.

ASPARAGUS

Asparagus officinalis,
Asparagus family

The Down and Dirty

Preferred climate	Cool to warm (preferably not hot)
Sun	Full sun to part shade
Soil	Well-drained, rich in organic matter
pH range	6.5–7.5
Sow seeds	Indoors, 12–14 weeks before the last risk of frost
Sowing depth	½–¾ inch (1.3–2 cm)
Days to germination	8–12
Germination temperature	60°F–85°F (16°C–29°C)
Note	Although asparagus can be started from seed, the standard practice is to plant crowns (1-year old roots with buds). Crowns will produce a harvest one year earlier than seed-started asparagus.
Transplant seedlings	After last frost
Spacing	8–14 inches (20–36 cm) between seedlings or crowns, 3–6 feet (0.9–1.8 m) between rows.
Days to maturity	For crowns, two springs after planting. For seed-started plants, three springs after planting.

Crowns, the root systems of asparagus plants, develop two springs after planting. This is how most home gardeners plant asparagus.

Notes from the garden

I admit to being a latecomer to planting a dedicated asparagus bed. Even though I have a large garden, I never felt comfortable committing to the long-term obligation that asparagus demands. But as I became older and much wiser, I realized I had been missing out on one of nature's greatest gifts. Not only is asparagus unsurpassed in flavor and sweetness when you grow it at home, it's downright beautiful, too. The tall, ferny foliage acts as a backdrop to your other plants—especially if you have female asparagus plants, which will produce red berries like little ornaments to light up the bed. What's not to like?

And as long as we're talking color, there are purple and white asparagus varieties in addition to the textbook green. But no matter the color, you plant this crop once and get twenty years of return on your investment.

Choosing what to grow

Asparagus plants are either male or female. The females produce red berries late in the season. While they are attractive, they do pull energy away from productivity. So plant breeders have developed varieties that produce mostly male plants that are far more productive.

Planting 25 male crowns (which is how most crowns are sold these days) will result in a harvest of about 20 pounds (9 kg) of spears per year once the plants are fully established.

My favorite varieties

- 'Jersey Giant' An all-male variety with medium to large green spears and attractive purplish bracts. This variety is cold-tolerant and resistant to rust disease.
- 'Jersey Knight' Another all-male variety with large green spears and uniform size, this one grows well in most climates and is highly resistant to rust. More tolerant to Fusarium than other varieties.
- 'Jersey Supreme' This all-male variety has slim but high-yielding green spears. A good variety for cool and warm regions, it's also resistant to rust.
- 'Purple Passion' Its large-diameter purple spears are sweeter and more tender than green varieties. It emerges later than green varieties, which can be an advantage in avoiding early frost damage. The purple spears fade in color when cooked.

Planting

Pick your planting location carefully. Asparagus is a perennial crop that can remain productive for twenty years or more. They produce tall fern-like foliage as the year progresses, so site it in a location where the tall, ferny growth won't shade out other plants. The north side of the garden or in a dedicated space where they can grow undisturbed for years is ideal.

Female asparagus plants produce attractive red berries, but that takes away from their production of edible spears.

Asparagus crowns should be planted in furrows that are about five to eight inches (13-20 cm) deep.

Plant seedlings after the last frost. Plant crowns in early spring, unless you live in very warm regions (in which case, plant from fall through winter). In all cases, plant crowns in furrows that are 5 to 8 inches (13 to 20 cm) deep, bud-side up and with the roots spread out. Hedge your planting depth towards the shallower side for heavy soil, deeper for colder climates. Allow 8 to 14 inches (20 to 36 cm) between crowns and 3 to 6 feet (0.9 to 1.8 m) between rows.

Don't backfill furrows to the soil surface immediately after planting. Instead, cover with just 2 to 3 inches (5 to 8 cm) of soil at planting time, and then gradually add soil to fill the furrow as the spears continue to lengthen.

Mid-season care

All things considered, asparagus is an unfussy plant. But providing consistent moisture and a good layer of mulch during the growing period will help retain it and keep invading weeds from competing for water and nutrients. Speaking of nutrients, asparagus appreciates a steady supply of nutrients from well-rotted manure, compost, fish emulsion, or a balanced organic fertilizer.

As perennials, make sure key resources are available throughout their active growing time to ensure productive plants from season to season. At the end of each growing season, cut back the ferny growth that will become brown and stiff by fall. You could leave the cut growth in place as mulch, but it's a good time to check the soil pH and add compost or other soil amendments. In all cases, cover the bare soil with straw or shredded leaf mulch.

Pests & disease

Asparagus aphids cause deformity and stunted growth, damaging the spear tips with their feeding.

The asparagus beetle can be found in both common and spotted varieties. The common asparagus beetle is the greater threat because it lays its eggs and feeds on spears, causing them to become deformed and damaged. The spotted asparagus beetle also feeds on spears, but lays its eggs on fern foliage.

Cutworms cause bent or crooked stems from these caterpillars feeding at ground level.

Japanese beetles can cause heavy foliage damage, which results in a lack of photosynthesis. That leads to lower plant vigor and reduced productivity.

Fusarium is a soilborne or seedborne fungus which causes various symptoms of root rot, crown rot, and overall wilting.

Purple spot is a fungus that causes sunken purple lesions on stalks and tan or brown lesions on foliage.

Rust is a fungus that produces orange spore masses on plant stalks.

Harvesting

Your first opportunity to harvest asparagus planted as crowns will happen the second spring after planting. For seed-grown asparagus, it will take an additional year for spears to be ready. As you make your first harvest, go easy. Cut no more than two or three spears per plant. In subsequent years, harvest pencil-thick spears when they are about 6 to 8 inches (15 to 20 cm) tall. You can continue to harvest as long as spears are more than $\frac{3}{8}$ inch (1 cm) in diameter. You'll know it's time to stop harvesting when most new spears remain small and bud tips start to expand and open. Those remaining ferns will continue to grow, providing energy for the plants below ground.

When harvesting asparagus, you can cut or snap the spears off near the soil level. But here's my advice. Take each spear between your thumb and forefinger, and snap it near the base. What ends up in your hand is the best part, which is exactly that part of the spear you want to eat. If instead you cut the spear near the base, you don't know if you're also getting some of that tough and woody part.

Try to have asparagus on your menu for the same day that you harvest (or at least as soon as possible). Asparagus is best when enjoyed extra fresh from the garden.

BEETS

Beta vulgaris
(Conditiva Group),
Amaranth family

The Down and Dirty

Preferred climate	Warm days, cool nights
Sun	Full
Soil	Well-drained and cool
pH range	6.5–6.8
Sow seeds	Outdoors, 10–12 weeks before first frost for fall crop or 3 weeks before last frost for spring harvest. Indoors, one seed cluster per cell.
Sowing depth	½ inch (1.3 cm)
Days to germination	About 5
Germination temperature	60°F–85°F (16°C–29°C)
Note	Soaking beet seeds in warm (but not hot) water for an hour (or overnight) before sowing can speed up germination.
Transplant seedlings	Carefully so as not to disturb the roots
Spacing	3–4 inches (8–10 cm) for beets to be eaten or stored, can use tighter spacing if more greens are desired
Days to maturity	45–65

Notes from the garden

I love beets so much that I grow two crops every year—one in spring, and another in fall. I know a lot of people find their flavor too earthy, but not me. I enjoy them roasted, boiled, grilled, baked, or pickled, in salads or tossed with goat cheese. I've even been known to chop them up and use them as a pizza topping! And I especially love that even the tender green tops of the plants are edible, a delicious addition to soup or stir-fry, or simply sautéed and served as a side.

And if you really don't like the taste, know that new varieties, 'Badger Flame' is one, are being bred that are nutritious and delicious, but without the earthy taste. Beets that don't taste like beets!

But even if I didn't like to eat beets, I would still grow them in my vegetable garden, if only for the aesthetics. I'd rank beets in a top three list of the most beautiful edible you can include in your garden (along with Swiss chard and red

Exercise extreme care when transplanting tender beet seedlings, as their root systems are very delicate at this stage.

You can't tell from this photo, but the 'Badger Flame' variety of beet doesn't even taste like traditional beets.

mustard). Plus, beets are very low-maintenance and leaf out fairly quickly—giving a big boost of near-instant gratification and confidence.

Conventional wisdom says to direct-sow beet seeds outdoors since they're a root crop and the seedlings are quite fragile to transplant. But I have great success starting one wave of beets in midwinter for early spring planting, and then another in mid-summer for planting in early fall—being careful when handling so as not to disturb the roots.

My favorite varieties

- 'Avalanche' This striking All-America Selections winner is a white beet with green stems. It's an open-pollinated variety that's mature in 55 days, with a root diameter of 2 to 3 inches (5 to 8 cm).
- 'Boldor' This golden beet has 2-inch (5 cm) roots that are brilliant yellow inside. The tops are green. This variety is known for good germination and sweet flavor. It matures in 55 days.

- 'Chioggia' An Italian heirloom variety, this beet has pretty red and white circles inside. Tops are green with purple streaks on the stems. Two-inch (5 cm) roots are round and semi-flat, and ready to harvest in 65 days.
- 'Early Wonder Tall Top' A fast grower in cool soil, this open-pollinated variety is typically mature in just 45 days. You'll note deep red globes that are 3 to 4 inches (8 to 10 cm) in diameter, with green leaves that feature purple stems and veins.
- 'Red Ace' A hybrid with high disease resistance, the uniformly round roots are best when picked at 3 to 4 inches (8 to 10 cm) wide. Ready for harvest in 55 days, the green tops and bright red stems are also especially tasty.

Choosing what to grow

If you're growing beets with an eye toward color, be aware that seeds are often sold as "rainbow mixes." Mixing up the varieties you grow will add color to the garden, but will also result in different harvest times, even if all the beets were planted at the same time.

Beets are another great crop to add around the perimeter of other planting beds to make the most of every bit of space.

Don't wait too long to harvest your beets. If left in the ground too long, they become woody and tough.

Planting

I like to plant beets around the perimeter of my leafy greens beds for efficient use of space. Stagger plantings over several weeks to extend the harvest.

Beet seeds are large clusters that actually contain between three and five seeds each. It's not necessary to break the clusters apart for planting, but thinning will be necessary.

Once seedlings reach 3 or 4 inches (8 to 10 cm) tall, thin them to one plant every 3 to 4 inches (8 to 10 cm).

Mid-season care

Add a 2- to 3-inch (5 to 8 cm) layer of light mulch once seedlings reach 5 inches (13 cm) tall. This suppresses weeds, aids moisture retention, and keeps the sun off the tops of the beetroots as they grow, improving their flavor.

Fertilize beets about every three weeks with an organic fertilizer low in nitrogen but higher in phosphorus and potassium and follow the manufacturer's application rates.

Pests & disease

Aphids can feed on beet leaves and excrete honeydew, which attracts ants and other insects. Knock them off with a sharp stream of water or use insecticidal soap.

Cutworms feed on roots and stems. Since the insect overwinters as eggs or larvae underground, row cover won't prevent an infestation. If you have

a problem, turn over the first few inches of soil two weeks prior to planting to expose the worms to hungry birds.

To reduce occurrences of beet diseases like leaf spot, root rot, powdery mildew, rust, and scab, use seed only from a trusted source and practice good garden sanitation. Crop rotation is also effective.

Harvesting

When your beets have reached their maturity date by variety, pull back the mulch and inspect the "shoulders" of the beetroots to check the size. Follow the size guidelines listed for the variety grown, as beets left in the ground too long will become woody and tough. Picking too early generally isn't a problem. The leaves taste even better when picked early, and the beetroots are sweeter.

Pull beets out of the ground by hand. Deeply watering the soil a day prior makes the job easier.

Beets are best enjoyed fresh. If you plan to consume the tops, place them in a bowl of water and agitate gently before cooking or eating.

Storage

Bruised or damaged beets don't save well. To store beets, don't rinse them off. Lightly brush off the soil and then cut off both the green top and the thin bottom part of the root. Place the beets in a sealed bag or airtight container for up to two weeks. Beets may be canned for longer-term storage.

BLUEBERRIES

Vaccinium corymbosum,
Heath family

The Down and Dirty

Preferred climate	**Cool to mild**
Sun	**Full**
Soil	**Well-draining, moist, and acidic**
pH range	**4.0–5.5**
Transplant plants	**In spring or fall**
Spacing	**5–8 feet (1.5–2.4 m) apart, according to variety, 8–10 feet (2.4–3 m) between rows**

Notes from the garden

They're not vegetables, but blueberries are a staple at my GardenFarm™. You can't beat the fruit they produce for snacking while you work, and you'll love the plants themselves for the aesthetic value and color they add throughout most of the year. They're especially popular as ornamental elements in the foodscaping (or "edible landscaping") movement (See Chapter 1).

Blueberries are also, pound for pound, one of the most nutritious foods you can eat. Packed with antioxidants, Vitamin C, and fiber, they're ideal all alone as healthy snacks or handy for making into preserves or pies, topping many of your favorite foods, tossing into a smoothie or yogurt or oatmeal, and canning or freezing for use all winter. Best of all, growing blueberries is easy. They need lots of sun, plenty of water, acidic soil, and very

little else. They're largely pest-free and can be grown in nearly every kind of climate.

I have a ring of blueberry plants around the perimeter of my vegetable garden, as they love the same full-sun exposure as my veggies. But since they're off on their own, I can easily tweak the soil pH to meet their unique needs. And passing my blueberry bushes every time I enter and exit the garden ensures that I can eat my bodyweight in blueberries over the course of a hard-working day!

Choosing what to grow

There are three primary types of blueberries. Which type you plant could be determined by where you live. Within each type, you'll have a number of varieties to choose from that produce early-season, mid-season, or late-season berries.

Lowbush varieties are the hardiest of the blueberries and will do well even under snow cover or in cold regions where it gets as cold as -30°F (-34°C). In the spectrum of blueberries, lowbush varieties are the smallest. These "wild blueberry" plants reach 12 to 36 inches (30 to 91 cm) tall and spread out 5 to 8 feet (1.5 to 1.8 m) wide.

Highbush varieties, as you might have guessed, get taller—up to 7 feet (2.1 m). Best in mild climates, they can be further divided into northern highbush and the less cold-tolerant southern highbush types. Your local garden center will have the type best suited for your area.

Rabbiteye blueberry plants are the most heat- and drought-tolerant. They also are most forgiving of poor soil conditions. They can get 12 feet (3.7 m) tall (or more) and spread 5 to 6 feet (1.5 to 1.8 m) wide.

Flowers on your blueberry plants are good! They're self-pollinating plants, but you can help them along by planting different varieties near each other.

Blueberry hybrids are also available. For example, **half-high** berry bushes combine the hardiness and short profile of the lowbush varieties with the heavier fruiting tendencies of highbush varieties.

Be aware that, although blueberries are self-pollinating, you'll want to plant at least two varieties that flower at the same time in close proximity to each other. This will increase the pollination rate and crop yield of both varieties. You'll also get bigger berries and, if you mix and match early-, mid-, and late-season varieties, a much longer harvest!

Planting

Blueberry plants are picky about soil pH. They prefer soil that's much more acidic than most other plants, absolutely no higher than 5.5 (which is well under neutral). You'll want to perform a soil test in your planned location and adjust as needed, likely with a sulfur-based soil acidifier. (Learn more about the all-important soil test in Chapter 2.)

Finely-ground shredded pine bark mulch, pine bark nuggets, or peat moss will also lower your soil pH and should be mixed into the entire growing area.

Clayey soil will need lots of acidifier (sandy soil requires significantly less). Remember that soil will naturally return to its native pH over time, so repeat your soil test every two years and adjust as needed.

Plant blueberry plants in a hole two to three times wider than the rootball, but no deeper. With the base of the stem just above ground level, backfill with plenty of acidic organic matter and water in. Add 2 to 3 inches (5 to 8 cm) of acidic organic mulch—like rotted pine needles or finely ground pine bark. This layer will help acidify the soil as it breaks down, while retaining moisture and suppressing weeds as it does.

Careful with That Compost!

Blueberries don't thrive in rich soil the way most plants do. So when I tell you to add "organic matter" as you backfill around blueberries, don't use that beautiful compost you've been making! Not only is it not helpful for blueberries, it can also even be detrimental. Use finely ground pinebark instead. It's slow to break down, low in nutrients, and will last a long time. My friend (and blueberry master) Dr. Lee Reich mixes a bucketful of peat moss with the native soil he's pulled out of a fresh planting hole. Once a new plant is in place, he backfills with that mix. I'm a huge fan of compost, but save it for the plants that truly benefit from it—every plant in the garden besides your blueberries!

Blueberry plants like it moist. A drip irrigation system puts water right where it needs to go with no extra effort required from me.

Mid-season care

Your blueberry plants require plenty of moisture. The old saying says the soil should stay as wet as a wrung-out sponge. I use a drip irrigation system on mine, aiming for 1 inch (2.5 cm) of water per week right at the roots.

Try applying soybean meal, alfalfa meal, or cottonseed meal once a year to provide an organic nitrogen source. One pound (0.4 kg) per 50 square feet (4.6 m²) of bushes is about right. Blueberry bushes should be pruned while they are dormant, in the period of time before leaf buds have formed on the stems. Prune out branches that are rubbing against each other or arching downward toward the ground.

Keep track of the age of your blueberry bushes. Their production will start to decline in about their sixth year. Help them along by pruning out older stems and cut down to the ground any that are 1 inch (2.5 cm) or more in diameter. Keep four to six of the healthiest new shoots that remain and remove the rest.

Pests & disease

Blueberry maggot is usually first noticed in its adult, fly stage. Traps hung among the plants are an easy scouting solution.

Spotted wing drosophila (SWD) is a type of fruit fly that's drawn to underripe fruit. Plant early-ripening varieties, as the SWD doesn't strike until early August.

Salvaging Your Blueberry Crop

Both types of maggots listed here develop inside the fruit of blueberry plants. Refrigerating your berries for 48 hours before eating them will kill any that are inside. Or test berries by mixing 1 teaspoon (5 ml) of salt to 1 cup (237 ml) of water and submerging berries in the solution for 10 to 15 minutes. If maggots are present, they'll start crawling out.

Yellow-necked caterpillars are covered in long white hairs and have large yellow bands around their heads. They hit at least a few of my blueberry plants every fall without fail, showing up en masse and going to work quickly stripping the foliage. Use Bt or hand-pick as an easy organic control, but thankfully, since they show up just before the plant's natural leaf drop, they're not a huge threat to the long-term sustainability of your blueberry plants.

Your most common blueberry pests will be birds, deer, raccoons, and other wildlife. Heavy-duty netting can be draped over the plants as berries begin to ripen to discourage feeding. But due to the risk of birds getting caught, I prefer planting enough to feed ourselves and the critters.

Mummy berry is a wind-borne fungus that causes berries to actually mummify and fall to the ground before they're ripe. If you see this on your bushes, remove mummified berries and discard them to avoid further spread. (And don't add them to your compost pile.) At season's end, spread 1 to 2 inches (2.5 to 5 cm) of mulch around the base of the plants to create a barrier and keep the fungal spores from spreading.

Harvesting

Your berries turning blue, oddly, is not an indication that they're ripe for picking. That blue coloration *does* mean it's almost time, though. Difficult as it may be, leave the berries on the bush a few days longer for optimum taste.

Try "tickling" the berry clusters to test for ripeness. Give them just the gentlest of touches. The ones that are perfectly ripe will fall away from the stem, leaving unripe berries attached.

And check often during the warm summer days. Once they're ripe, blueberries won't wait around long before falling to the ground.

I like to add finely-ground pine bark to each planting hole for new blueberry bushes. It will help acidify the soil around the plant roots.

Berries turning blue doesn't automatically mean they're ripe, but they're close. Get ready to get hands-on to know for sure when it's time to pick.

The foliage of blueberry plants is especially picturesque in autumn, a nice fall bonus for this summer favorite.

BROCCOLI

Brassica oleracea
(Italica Group),
Cabbage family

The Down and Dirty

Preferred climate	Cool and steady
Sun	Full, but light shade can delay bolting
Soil	Moist and well-drained
pH range	6.0–7.0
Sow seeds	Indoors, 8 weeks before last frost
Sowing depth	¼–½ inch (0.6–1.3 cm)
Days to germination	10–14
Germination temperature	60°F–85°F (16°C–29°C)
Note	Thin to one seedling per cell after sprouting
Transplant seedlings	4 weeks before last frost
Spacing	12–18 inches (30–45 cm) apart, with 15 inches (38 cm) between rows
Days to maturity	50–75 for most; a few varieties can take up to 220

Notes from the garden

Broccoli is one of my favorite plants to eat. Steamed, roasted, or even fried, it's one of the most nutritious and vitamin-packed vegetables you'll find. And since the entire plant—florets, stems, leaves, stalks and all—is edible, broccoli provides more bang for your buck than almost any other crop in the garden.

But broccoli is also one of my favorite plants to grow. Related to cabbage, cauliflower, kale, collard greens, and brussels sprouts, broccoli similarly performs best in climates where it stays relatively cool all year long. Summers get downright hot where I live, so I always adjust my planting times and plant two crops a year. My early spring planting is harvestable before the real heat comes, and then I plant it again in my cool-season garden. That way, just as temperatures start to drop, this second wave of broccoli hits full maturity and is at its sweetest when there's little else happening in the garden.

‘Belstar’ is one of the broccoli varieties I enjoy growing most, since it performs well in either warm or cool climates and is resistant to many diseases.

Cabbage worms will do plenty of damage to your broccoli, too. Floating row cover will prevent them from laying eggs on your crop.

My favorite varieties

- ‘Belstar’ Suitable for both warm and cool weather, this uniform broccoli has tight 6-inch (15 cm) heads of blue-green florets. Good disease resistance, it matures in 66 to 75 days.
- ‘De Ciccio’ Old Italian heirloom variety with blue-green heads 3 to 4 inches (8 to 10 cm) wide. A vigorous grower, it reaches maturity in 60 to 70 days, but the plants will reach maturity at different times for an extended harvest period.
- ‘Express’ Deep blue-green heads can grow up to 7 inches (18 cm) across. Tender side shoots also make a tasty treat. Plant in spring or summer; it matures in 60 to 70 days.
- ‘Gemini’ Can be planted in spring or even late summer since it's a fast grower and ready to harvest in just 50 days. Florets are light green and domed on 6-inch (15 cm) heads.
- ‘Purple Sprouting’ A truly unique variety with sweet-tasting, loose, purple florets that turn green when cooked. Plants reach 24 to 36 inches (60 to 90 cm) tall and are hardy to 10°F (-12°C) and colder. An open-pollinated variety, it takes 220 days to mature, so it's typically planted in late summer and harvested in early spring.

Planting

Seed-started plants should be hardened off before planting outdoors. (See Chapter 6 for details.)

Broccoli can typically be planted outdoors four weeks prior to the last frost date in your area, but if you use a cold frame, row cover, or cloches to shelter your plants, you can plant outdoors even earlier, by as much as three weeks. (More on these season-extending practices in Chapter 10.)

Amend planting soil with compost and well-aged manure; this improves drainage and provides key nutrients for broccoli.

Mid-season care

Broccoli likes soil that is consistently moist; aim for 1 to 2 inches (2.5 to 5 cm) of water per week. Use a drip irrigation system for supplemental watering if needed. A good layer of mulch around the plants will retain moisture and keep soil temperatures cooler.

Broccoli is a moderately heavy feeder, so I apply a balanced organic fertilizer throughout the growing season to help my broccoli plants thrive.

Pests & disease

Cabbage loopers and cabbage worms affect all brassica plants. Be on the lookout for small white butterflies fluttering over your plants in mid-spring and early fall. They're looking for a place to lay their eggs. Row cover (installed at planting) prevents them from doing so on your broccoli plants. Handpick caterpillars as you find them or use Bt as a biological control.

Flea beetles are very small black or bronze jumpers that will chew through your broccoli crop if they can get to it. Use row cover or plant a more preferable trap crop, like radishes nearby.

Cabbage root maggots are fly larvae. If you have them, your plants will show wilt and stunted growth. A physical barrier is your best defense.

Most diseases that affect broccoli are from wet foliage. If you eliminate overhead watering, you'll go a long way in discouraging problems like Alternaria black spot, ring spot, Botrytis stem blight, clubroot, and downy mildew. If you have diseased broccoli plants, remove them. Practice crop rotation by not planting any brassicas (cabbage family) in the same spot for at least three years to let the pathogens cycle out of the soil.

Harvesting

Harvest broccoli when unopened flower buds are just starting to swell. Target morning hours, when moisture content is highest, and cut the stalks several inches below the head at a 45-degree angle. Once you harvest the main crown, smaller crowns typically develop from the plant's side shoots. Consistently harvest these to encourage even more production.

Harvest broccoli in the morning, when the moisture content is highest. New, smaller crowns can continue to develop even after the first harvest.

BRUSSELS SPROUTS

Brassica oleracea
(Gemmifera Group),
Cabbage family

The Down and Dirty

Preferred climate	Cool, with soil temperatures below 70°F (22°C)
Sun	Full
Soil	Well-draining
pH range	6.6–7.8
Sow seeds	Indoors or in a cold frame 4-6 weeks before last frost date
Sowing depth	¼ inch (6 mm)
Days to germination	5–8
Germination temperature	60°F–85°F (16°C–29°C)
Transplant seedlings	After last hard frost
Spacing	18 inches (45 cm)
Days to maturity	85–145, depending on variety

Notes from the garden

Nothing complements a main dinner course in the fall quite like fresh brussels sprouts straight from the garden. I love their crunch and their nutty flavor, whether they've been roasted, steamed, sautéed, or even served raw.

Brussels sprouts with their miniature cabbagelike heads that grow on thick stalks are always one of the coolest-looking plants in my vegetable garden!

Fittingly, then, brussels sprouts fare better in cooler climates and even improve with a little frost and snow! They're worth trying for any gardener looking to take their growing season well into winter. They require a bit of planning and patience, but I think the rewards are well worth it!

My favorite varieties

- 'Diablo' A good producer with uniform sprouts of medium size, this hybrid grows to more than 2 feet (61 cm) tall and matures in 110 days. Harvest in late fall or early winter.
- 'Gladius' Intended for early- to mid-fall harvest, this hybrid grows to more than 30 inches (76 cm) tall, but matures in just 98 days. Blue-green sprouts have a long shelf life.
- 'Long Island Improved' This variety dates to the turn of the 20th century. It grows 2 feet (61 cm) tall with 1-inch (2.5 cm) sprouts and matures in 90 days. The seeds, however, take longer to germinate at 10 to 21 days.

- 'Nautic' This hybrid variety is resistant to black rot and Fusarium. Tightly wrapped 1-inch (2.5 cm) sprouts are spaced far apart, helping them dry quickly and avoid disease. Plants mature in 120 days.
- 'Redarling Hybrid' Large red-purple sprouts are sweeter than green varieties, and grow on plants that reach 30 to 40 inches (76 to 101 cm) tall and take 140 to 145 days to mature.

Mid-season care

Brussels sprouts require 1 to 2 inches (2.5 to 5 cm) of water per week. Water at the base of the plants to prevent pathogen transmission via wet foliage.

Organic fertilizer that's high in nitrogen, such as blood meal, cottonseed meal, or manure, will help the plants' overall development and production. For a fall harvest, fertilize by side-dressing every 3 to 4 weeks through the end of summer. Too much fertilizer will result in plants with lots of leaves but paltry sprouts. Stop fertilizing once the plants are reaching maturity and starting to produce. Staking will likely be needed to help keep plants upright—especially for taller varieties.

As the plants mature and sprouts start to form on the stalk, consider removing the leaves from the bottom up as the sprouts start to enlarge. This can help accelerate sprout maturity.

Remove brussels sprout leaves from the ground up (giving the plant a more tree-like appearance). This helps accelerate sprout maturity.

Pests & disease

Since they are the same species as cabbage, many of the same pests can pose problems for brussels sprouts: cabbage loopers, cabbage root maggots, cabbage worms, slugs, cabbage aphids, and flea beetles.

You can discourage many of the most common pests by covering brussels sprouts plants with a floating row cover upon transplanting until the plants are well-developed. You can even leave the cover on until harvest if you wish, as brussels sprouts do not depend on pollinators to mature.

Insecticidal soap and Bt can help control cabbage worms and cabbage loopers.

Harvesting

Brussels sprouts reach peak flavor after a few frosts, though sprouts can be picked as soon as they're firm. Harvest from the bottom of the stalk up. Break off the leaf below each sprout, then cut the sprout where the bud meets the stalk. Smaller, more compact sprouts tend to be sweeter.

Many gardeners choose their varieties based on days to maturity and overall plant size. But be on the lookout for the uniquely colored brussels sprouts that can add striking color to the garden as well as your dinner plate.

Some varieties may be topped about four weeks prior to the first frost to encourage more budding in a shorter time.

Check for firm sprouts, smaller sprouts are sweeter.

CABBAGE

Brassica oleracea
(Capitata Group),
Cabbage family

The Down and Dirty

Preferred climate	Cool to cold
Sun	Full
Soil	Fertile, well-drained
pH range	6.5–7.5
Sow seeds	Indoors, 6–8 weeks before last frost date for spring cabbage. Direct-sow, 4 weeks before last expected frost. For fall cabbage, start seeds indoors 6 weeks before transplanting or direct-sow 10–12 weeks before first frost.
Sowing depth	½ inch (1.3 cm)
Days to germination	4–7
Germination temperature	75°F (24°C)
Transplant seedlings	In spring, after last hard frost. In fall, 8–10 weeks before first frost.
Spacing	Closely follow recommendations by variety to avoid overcrowding.
Days to maturity	50–100 days, depending on variety

Cabbage loves it cold and can tolerate temperatures as low as 20°F (-6°C).

Notes from the garden

From cole slaw to sauerkraut to kimchi, cabbage is a wonderful crop for the gardener looking to bring classic Old-World flavors to their cooking, and is perfect for those interested in getting into home pickling and fermenting.

Like all brassica crops (broccoli, cauliflower, kale, brussels sprouts), cabbage thrives in cold weather, tolerating temperatures as cold as 20°F (-6°C). Hot weather will force cabbage plants to bolt—they'll send up flower stalks well before the plant is ready to harvest—and turn the cabbage bitter. That makes it ideal for either starting your gardening season in very early spring or extending it late into the fall. Fall-grown cabbage, since it matures in cool weather, is far less likely to bolt and will have a sweeter taste.

From a visual standpoint, there aren't many more impressive sights in the garden than an entire bed of beautiful softball-sized cabbage heads tucked inside their surrounding nests of massive, showy green leaves. But allow plenty of space. Cabbage plants can get large, and overcrowded plants are more prone to disease due to poor air circulation and may even fail to form heads.

My favorite varieties

- 'Fast Vantage' A quick-maturing variety that can be added to salads well before other cabbage varieties are ready.
- 'Pacifica' Great for slaws and soups, this is a bolt-tolerant cabbage variety that hot-weather gardeners may favor.
- 'Ruby Ball' This red cabbage matures a little later than most, but is a reliable and consistent favorite that's also resistant to splitting.

Remember that if you plant only one variety of cabbage all at the same time, all the plants will mature at the same time. Stagger your planting times and consider using several varieties to prevent an overabundance come harvest time.

Don't pull cabbage plants out of the ground. Use a knife instead to cut off the head at the base of the plant.

Mid-season care

Cabbage is a heavy feeder, so supplement with a balanced organic fertilizer before planting and lightly work in a generous addition of compost to the top layer of soil.

Although cabbage is cold-hardy, a frost blanket, row cover, or mini hoop tunnel may provide extra protection for young seedlings as they get established.

Cabbage needs even moisture levels during its steady and uninterrupted growth cycle.

No Trespassing—Cabbage Roots at Work

A layer of mulch is especially important for cabbage as a weed suppressant. The very shallow roots of cabbage plants don't like to be disturbed by nearby weeds. Mulch will help smother weeds before they sprout and cause problems.

Pests & disease

Several garden pests actually have cabbage right in their name, giving you an idea of how inviting this crop can be to many of nature's foragers. Cabbage loopers and cabbage worms are common, but slugs, aphids, and flea beetles like cabbage, too.

Thankfully, none of these pests are devastating, and all can be easily controlled with a lightweight and translucent floating row cover. Put it on at planting and leave it in place until the plants are well-established and growing strong. Cabbage does not need to be pollinated, so blocking access to insects won't affect growth.

Be on the lookout for small white butterflies around cabbage plants in mid-spring and early fall. They're cabbage butterflies, looking for a place to lay eggs. A floating row cover will encourage them to go elsewhere.

Bacillus thuringiensis (Bt) is a biological control that will selectively eliminate caterpillar larvae, including cabbage worms and cabbage loopers without harming beneficial insects.

Cabbage diseases include Alternaria black spot, black leg, ring spot, Botrytis stem blight, clubroot, and downy mildew. To lessen the occurrence of all of them in the first place, refrain from overhead watering. Wet foliage invites pathogens, so keep your watering directed at the base of the plants. If you do find diseased cabbage, remove the affected plants to limit the spread. Rotate crops in subsequent seasons. Brassica-specific diseases will not affect other crops.

Harvesting

Cabbage heads are ready to harvest when they have grown to full size, according to variety, and firmed up. Do not pull out the plant entirely, but cut off the head at the base of the plant instead.

For fall cabbage, don't feel the need to harvest your heads just because frosty nights are in the forecast. Late-season cabbage can easily handle such conditions.

Allow plenty of room for your cabbage plants to grow. Even when mature, they'll need good air circulation.

CARROTS

Daucus carota,
Carrot family

The Down and Dirty

Preferred climate	Cool for sweetest taste, down to cold with season-extending help. Avoid harvesting in summer heat.
Sun	Full sun to light shade
Soil	Deep, loose, loamy fertile soil that's well-draining but with good moisture retention
pH range	6.0–6.8
Sow seeds	Indoors, not recommended. Outside, 3–5 weeks before the last frost of spring and/or mid- to late summer. Sow so that once thinned, spacing is 2–4 inches (5–10 cm) between seedlings. Sow every 3 weeks for a continuous harvest.
Sowing depth	¼ inch (6 mm)
Days to germination	5–21
Germination temperature	45°F–85°F (7°C–29°C)
Note	Prevent soil from crusting, which can inhibit seedlings pushing through the surface.
Transplant seedlings	Direct-sow only. Carrots do not like to have their roots disturbed.
Spacing	2–4 inches (5–10 cm) apart, 12–18 inches (30–45 cm) between rows.
Days to maturity	60–100 days, depending on variety

Notes from the garden

You can never replicate the taste of garden-fresh vegetables with what you buy at the grocery store. But that's especially true for carrots, more so than maybe any other vegetable in this book.

While nothing compares to a homegrown carrot, they can be a challenge to grow. You may get lucky your first time around, or you may become very frustrated in repeated efforts that only yield so-so results. Fortunately, the obstacles that usually thwart a successful carrot crop are avoidable.

For me, the biggest challenge every season is making sure the seeds stay moist enough to germinate, which because of the time they take (5 to 21 days), can be a challenge to monitor. I've learned some tricks along the way to help with that, such as covering the seeds with burlap fabric. I use coffee bean sacks. The fabric is

I cover my carrot seeds with old burlap sacks from my local coffee roaster. The fabric keeps the soil nice and moist for the long seed germination period.

As much as I enjoy eating homegrown carrots, I think I love the bright green foliage that the plants provide to my garden almost as much.

permeable, allowing you to water from above and they keep the baking sun from evaporating moisture at the soil surface. I can easily pull the fabric back to check on my seeds' germination status, and then remove it once that begins to happen. And one last thing. I love seeing the bright-green ferny foliage of the carrot tops every time I walk into the garden. No matter what the weather is like, or what else is growing in the garden (and later in winter, there's sometimes not much else), those frilly, fresh carrot tops always seem to lift my spirits.

My favorite varieties

- 'Atlas' A small, rounded variety that matures more quickly and is better-suited for subpar soil.
- 'Bolero' A sweet variety that is more resistant to common diseases and leaf pests. Slightly tapered roots are 7 to 8 inches (18 to 20 cm) long.
- 'Danvers' An orange heirloom variety, it tolerates heavier soil. Roots grow 6 to 8 inches (15 to 20 cm) long.
- 'Dragon' A purple-skinned carrot with orange-flesh. Seven-inch (18 cm) roots produce a sweet but spicy flavor. Good for heavy soil. Fun fact: this variety's lycopene content equals that of tomatoes.
- 'Yaya' A faster maturing variety that produces 6 inch (15 cm) blunt barrel-shaped roots. Great for warmer regions where you're looking to grow that classic carrot before heat becomes an obstacle.

Planting

Carrots grow and taste better when they mature before or after the hotter months of summer, so pay attention to timing. Cool soil that is under 70°F (21°C) is the key to growing sweet carrots.

Keeping Your Carrots on the Straight and Narrow

Spend any amount of time on social media sites devoted to gardening, and you're sure to see cute pictures of carrots that bear a striking resemblance to a human torso from the waist down, often with far more anatomical detail than can be mentioned here. They make for clever posts, but they're not the desired outcome if you're serious about growing good carrots for the kitchen. Deformed, stunted, disfigured, or split roots with multiple appendages are avoidable if you simply maintain deep, loose, rich, fertile, evenly moist soil.

Proper preparation is the key. Work the soil well in advance of planting to achieve the ideal growing environment. I start weeks ahead of time with well-rotted shredded leaves and plenty of compost. Remove any stones or pebbles, or any obstructions that can obstruct a clear path to straight roots. It's the most important step in

Oddly shaped carrots are often the result of the roots trying to grow through soil that's not loose, or sometimes packed with obstructions.

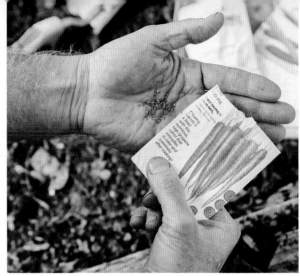

Carrot seeds can be tricky to work with, given their tiny size. Pelleted seeds allow the gardener to sow them more easily and consistently.

setting up carrots for success. Raised beds and deep grow bags are superb options for growing them, as the soil can be more easily managed.

Carrot seeds are the size and color of the typical poppy seed, so sowing them evenly at 1 inch (2.5 cm) spacing is difficult, to put it mildly. I've tried a number of ways, but have since settled on using pelleted seeds (seeds coated in a natural, degradable source that allows for greater ease and consistency of spacing).

Mid-season care
Floating row covers can be installed from the moment of germination to prevent access to plants by the carrot rust fly and other pests. Avoid excess nitrogen fertilizer, which can cause excess top growth to the detriment of root growth. Keep up with weeding to reduce competition for moisture and nutrients.

Thinning is a tedious process. Trying to remove seedlings thickly sown, while earnestly attempting to leave only one carrot plant every 2 to 4 inches (5 to 10 cm) will try your patience. Plan on devoting some time to this important task.

Pests & disease
The adult carrot rust fly is a small dark fly, but damage is caused by white maggot larvae below ground. It bores into roots and creates tunnels that become mushy.

Foliage damage from flea beetles appears as small shotholes. Excessive damage can kill the plant, with youngest foliage being most susceptible.

In the case of root-knot nematodes, microscopic worms in the soil form galls or thickened roots, split roots, stunted roots, or clusters of hairlike roots.

Wireworm damage is caused by larvae feeding on roots and shoots.

If you have black canker, root markings will appear as black, purple, or brown lesions mainly on the shoulders and crown. On carrot foliage, symptoms will appear as small rust-colored lesions.

Harvesting
Carrots become sweeter once they're exposed to a few periods of frost, as colder temperatures cause them to store energy in the form of sugars.

Harvest carrots within 3 weeks of maturity. Pull carrots by their tops if the soil is loose. If carrots break, loosen the soil with a garden fork. Once harvested, cut top growth 1 inch (2.5 cm) from the root.

Carrots can also be kept in the ground in cold frames through winter.

CAULIFLOWER

Brassica oleracea
(Botrytis Group),
Cabbage family

The Down and Dirty

Preferred climate	Cool to warm; heat will cause bolting
Sun	Full
Soil	Fertile, well-draining
pH range	6.5–7.5
Sow seeds	Indoors, 4–5 weeks before last frost; outdoors, after last frost
Sowing depth	¼–½ inch (0.6–1.3 cm)
Days to germination	6–10
Germination temperature	As low as 50°F (10°C), but 80°F (27°C) is ideal
Note	For fall harvest in cool climates, sow seeds 12 weeks before first frost
Transplant seedlings	In early spring, after last hard frost. In fall, 8 weeks before first frost.
Spacing	18 inches (45 cm) apart, 18 inches (45 cm) between rows
Days to maturity	50–100, depending on variety

Notes from the garden

Cauliflower gets a bad rap for being fussy to grow. Yes, it has its quirks, but it's well worth your time and effort. It's in the cold-hardy group of brassicas, making it a great addition to your cool-season garden. And while it traditionally has white heads, other varieties can be found to produce yellow, green, purple, or even orange.

This nutritious vegetable may be the most versatile of that entire brassica bunch. I love dipping it raw, but it's also wonderful roasted, steamed, or sautéed. And in recent years, cauliflower has exploded in popularity as a sneaky (but tasty!) replacement for less-healthy foods. Riced cauliflower can replace white rice, buffalo cauliflower can take the place of boneless buffalo wings, and cauliflower pizza crust can be so delicious you'll never miss the real thing.

Get a soil test (as discussed in Chapter 2) before committing to growing cauliflower, though. It requires a soil pH that falls within a fairly narrow window to discourage a disease called clubroot, so get your pH right well before planting to avoid headache later.

Cabbage butterflies, white in color, usually mean cabbage worms or cabbage loopers, which can cause damage to cauliflower. Install a floating row cover.

Manually securing a cauliflower plant's leaves over the head protects it from too much sun, which can affect taste.

Choosing what to grow

As cauliflower matures, the heads need to be protected from the sun, as too much will affect the color, texture, and taste. Some varieties need intervention to manually fold the leaves over the head and use a clothespin, rubber band, or string to secure them in a process called blanching. Some varieties are self-blanching, meaning the leaves naturally wrap around the head.

My favorite varieties

- 'Amazing' An open-pollinated white variety that's tolerant of both heat and cold, it's also self-blanching. Matures in 68 days.
- 'Cheddar' A bright orange hybrid that matures in 58 days. It does not have great heat tolerance, so it's best for a fall harvest.
- 'Lavender' This bright purple hybrid can be grown in spring, but is best-suited as a fall crop. Allow 70 days for maturity.
- 'Snow Crown' Known for unusual vigor, this white hybrid variety tolerates frosty temperatures down to 25°F (-4°C). It matures in 50 days.
- 'Romanesco' Actually an old cross between cauliflower and broccoli. Reliable newer varieties include 'Puntoverde' and 'Veronica'.

Planting

Amend soil (of proper pH levels) with plenty of compost prior to planting, and shield your cauliflower crop with floating row cover as soon as it's in the ground. This physical barrier will prevent many insects from laying eggs. If daytime temperatures are 75°F (24°C) or warmer, use a shade cloth to protect tender seedlings.

Mid-season care

Cauliflower needs constant moisture. Consider using drip irrigation to maintain 1 to 2 inches (2.5 to 5 cm) of water per week, enough to keep soil moist but not drenched. Underwatered cauliflower can develop heads with purple coloration on the underside. It's safe to eat, but the flavor is less than optimal.

A heavy feeder, cauliflower benefits from a balanced ratio of organic fertilizer throughout the season. But follow the manufacturer's directions on application rates. Overfertilized cauliflower can result in hollow stems and being more vulnerable to pests.

Pests & disease

Cabbage loopers and cabbage worms may be your primary foe. Hand-pick any caterpillars you find. Bt is also an effective biological control.

Clubroot, black leg ring spot, Botrytis stem blight, and downy mildew are all diseases that can affect cauliflower. The risk of all of them can be lessened by refraining from overhead watering. Remove affected plants or foliage to reduce the disease's spread in the garden and practice crop rotation (no brassicas in that spot for the next three years).

Harvesting

Harvest cauliflower while heads are still compact. The average target size is 6 to 8 inches (15 to 20 cm), but earlier is better for best taste and quality. Cut the plant at the base of the neck.

Store cauliflower in the refrigerator, whole in an unsealed bag, for up to two weeks. Alternatively, it can be chopped up, blanched, and then frozen.

COLLARD GREENS

Brassica oleracea
(Viridis Group),
Cabbage family

The Down and Dirty

Preferred climate	Cool to cold for best taste despite heat tolerance
Sun	Full sun, will tolerate light shade
Soil	Well-draining, fertile and rich in organic material
pH range	6.5–7.5
Sow seeds	Indoors, 4 or more weeks before setting out in the spring garden when ground is workable. For a fall crop, sow indoors about 3 months before the first frost and transplant 4-6 weeks later. Outdoors, direct-sow from early spring up to 3 months before first frost.
Sowing depth	¼–½ inch (0.6–1.13 cm)
Days to germination	3–10
Germination temperature	75°F–85°F (24°C–29°C)
Note	Where temperatures are milder and seldom go below freezing, you can plant seedlings from fall through winter.
Transplant seedlings	In later winter or early spring once ground is workable so that plants mature before summer heat comes on. In fall (preferred), plant out to allow 2 months of growth before freezing temperatures.
Spacing	24 inches (60 cm) apart in all directions
Days to maturity	70

Notes from the garden

I've always been under the impression that collards are just a Southern U.S. thing, with not much appreciation for them anywhere else. That would be a real shame if that's true. Although they are heat-tolerant, they save their best work until after they've been exposed to several frosty nights. That's when their sweetness really shines through. Collards are incredibly delicious, and one of the hardiest and easiest plants you can grow in your garden. Start them from seed indoors, direct-sow seeds outdoors, or plant them as seedlings. They're not fussy at all.

I grew up eating collards when they would show up on the family dinner table, simmered in grease from several bacon slices along with a meaty ham bone tossed into the pot. Even as a kid, I found collards tasty enough (likely due more to the bacon and ham). Yet I don't recall ever going back for seconds. And I should note, those collards were neither homegrown nor farm-fresh.

But since becoming an avid vegetable gardener in my adult life, I love to grow and eat collards. And for years now, I've lived on mostly a plant-based diet, so there's no bacon or ham in the collards I make. Now I know what truly fresh, homegrown collards really taste like. I prepare just the fresh leafy greens, along with a little vegetable broth, some chopped carrots and onions, and garlic (all homegrown as well). A dash or two of hot vinegar sauce adds a subtle kick and the finishing touch for a vitamin- and nutrient-rich, delicious dish— fresh from the garden.

My favorite varieties
- 'Champion' Hardier and more compact in size at 24 to 36 inches (60 to 90 cm), this bolt-resistant variety has blue-green foliage. Plus, the waxy leaf surface makes it less inviting to cabbage worms.
- 'Georgia' A classic heirloom from pre-1880, I have great success with this reliable, carefree variety, thanks to its tolerance to heat, frost, and fluctuating temperatures. This large variety, up to 36 inches (90 cm), has tender leaves and mild flavor producing an abundant crop well past first frosts. Not picky about soil quality.
- 'Green Glaze' While not as high-yielding as more prolific varieties, rated highly for its taste, and resistance to cabbage worms, likely due to its glossy, waxy leaves.
- 'Vates' Large blue-green leaves and slow to bolt.

Planting
Direct-sow seeds or plant seedlings into well-amended soil that's high in organic content and drains well. Add a generous layer of natural mulch. Once seedlings are thinned, allow for 18 inches (45 cm) between plants.

Mid-season care
Maintain consistent soil moisture of between 1 to 2 inches (2.5 to 5 cm) including rainfall per week.

Cover with shade cloth during the hottest days to provide some relief from the heat.

Pests & disease
As a brassica, collards are targeted by cabbage worms and cabbage loopers. They're the main threat in cooler months. In summer, several common garden pests sample their thick leaves, including grasshoppers, aphids, and harlequin bugs. Fortunately, because collards are not dependent on insect pollination, row cover placed over the plants serves as an effective barrier to prevent most of the common pests from impacting the plants.

Regarding diseases, collards are susceptible to the same diseases impacting other members of the brassica family. A few of the most common include downy mildew, Alternaria leaf spot, and Cercospora leaf spot, along with clubroot and black rot.

Harvesting
Collards are considered mature once they reach the size of a dinner plate. Harvest leaves rather than remove the plant itself. The plant will keep growing for months, making collard greens an ideal cut-and-come-again crop. While leaves can be harvested at any time throughout the year, they're at their best once they've been exposed to moderate frost.

Leaves are ready for harvesting when they reach the size of a dinner plate.

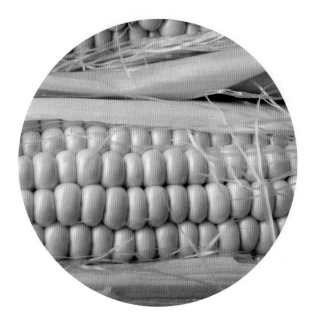

CORN

Zea mays,
Grass family

The Down and Dirty

Preferred climate	**Warm**
Sun	**Full and unfiltered**
Soil	**Loamy, well-draining**
pH range	**6.0–7.0**
Sow seeds	**Outdoors, beginning one week after last frost date. (Start dates also vary greatly depending on variety; follow seed packet directions.)**
Sowing depth	**2 inches (5 cm), one seed per cell**
Days to germination	**Up to 12**
Germination temperature	**60°F–95°F (16°C–35°C)**
Note	**Starting corn seeds indoors is not recommended.**
Spacing	**Every 4–6 inches (10–15 cm) in rows 30 inches (76 cm) apart**
Note	**Corn is wind-pollinated, so a single row is unlikely to produce ears. Plant several short rows instead. Stagger sowings by 2 weeks for a longer harvest window.**
Days to maturity	**68–120**

Notes from the garden

Maybe you've never considered growing corn because you assume it's best left to professional farmers who have acres upon acres of cornfields. While it's true that the most planted crop in the United States is grown on a grand commercial scale, there's no reason why you can't enjoy fresh-picked corn straight from your own vegetable garden.

Beware, though. Corn is one of those crops that taste so much better when you grow it yourself that you may never want to touch that bin in your grocery store's produce department ever again.

Choosing what to grow

Know the main types of corn so you can select varieties that match how you plan to enjoy the harvest. Most home growers choose sweet corn. This type allows you to have fresh corn in all its iterations: steamed, roasted, boiled, or grilled corn on the cob.

Beautifully colored flint corn is frequently used in autumn decorations and fall centerpieces, but it's perfectly edible, too.

Flint corn features kernels in all different colors. It's what you typically see used in rustic fall decorations, but flint corn is edible, too. Traditionally, it's used to make hominy, which in turn is used to make tortillas.

Flour corn is used to make corn flour. Popcorn is actually its own type, grown specifically for corn meant to be popped.

My favorite varieties

- 'Big N' Tender' A sweet corn variety with a mix of white and yellow kernels on 8-inch (20 cm) ears. Plants can reach 8 feet (2.4 m) tall and mature in 79 days. This variety is resistant to northern corn leaf blight and Stewart's wilt.
- 'Dakota Black' An interesting open-pollinated popcorn variety with pointed kernels so dark red they appear black. Also good for ornamental purposes. Plants reach 4 to 6 feet (1.2 to 1.8 m) in height, with ears that grow 5 to 7 inches (13 to 18 cm) and are mature in 95 days.
- 'Glass Gem' A wildly popular variety in recent years due to kernels in a rainbow of iridescent colors. Plants reach 6 to 7 feet (1.8 to 2.1 m) tall with three or four, 3 to 8 inch (8 to 20 cm) long ears on each. This open-pollinated variety is a flint corn, but can be used for cornmeal and popcorn, too.
- 'My Fair Lady' A sweet corn intended for organic growing. Ears are white and yellow and reach 7 or 8 inches (18 or 20 cm) long. Plants reach 5 feet (1.5 m) but are high-yielding. Mature in 78 days.
- 'Sugar Buns' Mature in 70 to 80 days, this sugar-enhanced sweet corn has creamy yellow kernels on ears 7½ inches (19 cm) long. Plants stay around 5 to 6 feet (1.5 to 1.8 m) tall and are resistant to several common diseases.

Mid-season care

Stay on top of watering, as moisture-stressed corn plants will produce ears with missing kernels. Use soaker hoses or a drip system to supplement rainfall, aiming for 1 inch (2.5 cm) of water per week. Hot and dry spells may call for 1½ inches (4 cm) per week. Avoid overhead watering, since this can disrupt tassel pollen.

Corn is a heavy feeder that needs plentiful nitrogen. Amending soil prior to planting with a green manure like clover or vetch is ideal. After planting and once stalks reach 10 inches (25 cm) in height, side-dress with organic fertilizer such as blood meal, feather meal, chicken manure, alfalfa meal, or cottonseed meal. Or use a liquid nitrogen fertilizer (such as fish emulsion) and reapply every two weeks. In all cases, apply again when corn begins to tassel.

Corn is also susceptible to blowdown. The stalks are shallow rooted and easily blown over in high winds. Consider placing stakes at either end of your rows and running twine down both sides of the plants, tying off each length at the stakes. The twine will support the stalks from both the front and the back. For even more strength, weave the twine in and out of the plants in a zigzag pattern to really hold the stalks upright.

Pests & disease
Armyworms are striped moth larvae that attack during cool, wet springs. Remove eggs and caterpillars by hand or use Bt.

Corn borers and corn earworms can be detected by the use of pheromone traps. An application of Bt will control them if found.

Corn flea beetles and corn leaf aphids can be kept off your crop by the use of a floating row cover when plants are young. Keep beds weed-free.

Corn rootworms, cutworms, and seedcorn maggots overwinter in soil. Rotate crops to prevent a population buildup in the soil. Turn soil two weeks prior to planting to expose larvae to hungry birds.

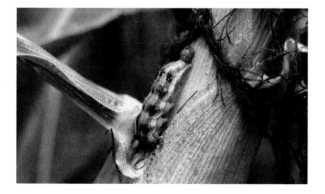

Corn earworms are just one pest that can wreak havoc on a crop. Thankfully, they're easily controlled.

Japanese beetles are identified by their telltale greenish-coppery wing covers. They do their damage by cutting corn silks and preventing pollination. Grubs can be controlled with *Bacillus thuringiensis galleriae* (Btg) or parasitic nematodes. Adults can be hand-picked.

Racoons, squirrels, birds, and deer can also be a problem with corn. A physical barrier is your best chance at protecting your crop. Balloons, ribbons, and scarecrows can be effective but require frequent relocation around the garden. Motion-activated sprinklers are another option. Depending on your personal stance, electrified fencing can also be employed.

Corn can be affected by various plant diseases, like anthracnose, crazy top, leaf blight, leaf spot, maize dwarf mosaic virus, and Stewart's wilt. Keeping pathogen-transmitting pests off your crop is a major start to preventing these conditions, but also practice crop rotation. Wait four years before planting corn in the same spot.

Harvesting
Sweet corn is ready to be harvested when silks turn from light yellow to dark brown. Harvest early in the morning when kernels are at their highest moisture and sugar levels. Keep sweet corn in its husk until ready to cook. Husks can remain during roasting or grilling. The sooner you can eat corn after harvesting, the better. That's when corn is at its sweetest. As soon as ears are picked, the sugar begins turning to starch, and that fresh-picked sweetness begins to fade.

Flint corn can wait until just before the first frost. Popcorn and flour corn should be harvested when kernels are hard and glossy. Peel back husks and store in a dry place until kernels reach desired state.

To harvest any type or corn, grasp the ear, twist and pull downward.

CUCUMBER

Cucumis sativus,
Cucumber family

The Down and Dirty

Preferred climate	Warm
Sun	Full
Soil	Fertile, well-draining
pH range	5.5–7.0
Sow seeds	Indoors, 3–6 weeks before transplanting. Outdoors, 2 weeks after last frost risk.
Sowing depth	1–1½ inches (2.5–4 cm)
Days to germination	3–10
Germination temperature	60°F–95°F (16°C–35°C)
Transplant seedlings	2 weeks after last frost risk
Spacing	Seeds: 2 inches (5 cm) between seeds and 5 feet (1.5 m) between rows. Transplants: 12 inches (30.5 cm), or in soil mounds: 3 feet (90 cm) apart in all directions.
Days to maturity	55–60 days

Notes from the garden

I have to confess, cucumbers are not on my top-ten list of favorite edibles to grow. I do love to eat them but getting them to that point (at least in the hot and humid place I call home) requires real fortitude. Beetles eat the leaves, worms bore holes into the fruit just as it ripens, and a variety of diseases will challenge your patience along the way.

That said, I do grow cucumbers every year. I marvel at the flowers, which are magnets for bees and other pollinators, and the vines, which wrap their tactical tendrils around anything.

Cool and crunchy, they're wonderful raw in salads or smoothies, roasted, sliced for sandwiches or drinking water, or used to make homemade pickles. Bumpy and short varieties tend to pickle best (and fit in canning jars nicely). Also look for "burpless" or "seedless" varieties. These lack cucurbitacin, the compound that can give heat-stressed or overripe cucumbers a bitter taste.

My favorite varieties

- 'Bush Champion' Productive bush-type variety for containers or small gardens. Fruits are 8 to 12 inches (20 to 30 cm) long despite small plants. The plants are resistant to mosaic virus and produce superior-tasting cucumbers.

- 'Itachi' Long and slender, this white cucumber is popular for stir-fry. Fruits are 10 inches (25 cm) long with thin skin, superb taste, and no bitterness. Vines reach 4 to 5 feet (1.2 to 1.5 m). Fruits will grow straight when trellised or curved when on the ground.
- 'Little Leaf' Open-pollinated, disease-resistant, stress-tolerant. Bright emerald green fruits grow to 3 to 6 inches (8 to 15 cm) and are tasty either fresh or pickled. Compact vines. Mature in 57 days.
- 'Summer Dance' Japanese burpless variety with 9-inch (23 cm) long curved fruit. Plants are high-yielding and resistant to downy mildew and powdery mildew. Plants spread 3 to 4 feet (90 to 120 cm) and grow 18 to 22 inches (45 to 56 cm) tall. Mature in 55 days.
- 'Sweet Success' English cucumber with nearly seedless dark green fruits that grow up to 12 inches (30 cm) long. This variety is resistant to viruses and leaf spot. It spreads 4 to 5 feet (1.2 to 1.5 m) and matures in 58 days.

Planting

Sow seeds indoors in moist seed-starting mix, three per 4-inch (10 cm) container.

Before planting outdoors, acclimate seedlings to sun and wind by hardening them off, as described in Chapter 6. Plant vining cucumbers away from other plants. Choose a location near a fence or install a trellis prior to planting.

Sowing seeds directly in rows or mounds is easy and they germinate quickly. In fact, unless you absolutely need to start them indoors for some reason, you can't beat the simplicity of direct-sowing. If direct-sowing outdoors in rows, allow seedlings to reach a couple inches tall, then thin the rows to one plant every 12 inches (30 cm). If using the soil-mound method, sow three to six seeds per mound.

Mid-season care

Cucumbers want even, consistent watering throughout the season. But wet cucumber foliage can easily invite diseases. soaker hoses or drip irrigation set on automatic timers are ideal for cucumbers. (See "Getting the Watering Right" in Chapter 9.) Aim for 1 inch (2.5 cm) of water per week, but more may be required in the hottest part of summer.

Don't Let Your Cukes Get Bent out of Shape

Perfectly straight cucumbers are the goal in the garden, and they're certainly easier to work with in the kitchen. But that straight shape is determined by what happens as they're growing. Misshapen fruit often comes from uneven or inconsistent watering. Pollination also plays a major role. Without adequate help from pollinators, your cucumbers could end up underdeveloped. One more reason to attract more bees, butterflies, and birds to your vegetable garden!

Misshapen cucumbers are often a result of uneven or inconsistent watering. Pollination can be a factor, too, so encourage those butterflies and bees to visit your garden!

The tendrils of your growing cucumber plants will cling to anything they can find, including nearby plants! Proper spacing and a support structure for them to climb is essential.

Cucumbers are heavy feeders. Start them in soil that's well-amended with compost and use a balanced slow-release fertilizer in the top layer of soil. Be sure to follow the manufacturer's directions for fertilizer coverage; too much will boost foliage growth but reduce fruiting.

Cucumber tendrils will latch to anything they can find as they grow. String, twine, wire mesh panels, even chicken wire installed vertically with poles, stakes, or A-frames make good trellis systems for cucumbers. Trellising also allows you to grow more cucumbers in a smaller area and helps keep fruit from contacting the ground.

Pests & disease
Most cucumber pests can be thwarted with a floating row cover, but be aware of your varieties. *Parthenocarpic* (seedless) varieties don't need pollination, so a floating row cover can be left in place full-time. For varieties that require pollination, though, any physical barrier must be removed when the vines flower or they will never set fruit.

Cucumber beetles can be striped or spotted, but both chew holes in leaves and pass on a pathogen that kills plants within days. Choose wilt-resistant varieties, hand-pick beetles as you find them, and practice crop rotation to avoid recurrence in subsequent years.

Use floating row cover to prevent squash bugs. (Obviously, this is only practical for cucumbers grown along the ground!) If they become an issue, remove old leaves and vines from the garden at season's end to keep them from overwintering in the bed.

Aphids chew leaves and vines, excreting a substance that attracts ants and other insects. Knock them off your cucumber plants with a sharp stream of water.

Alternaria is a leaf blight that causes small, yellow-brown spots that become holes in leaves. Older leaves will be affected first, curling up and dying. Avoid overhead watering and practice crop rotation.

Anthracnose is a fungus that affects ripe and over-ripe fruit. You'll see small, round, yellow depressions that enlarge over time. Remove infected fruit, as the spores will spread to other fruit and to the soil. Do not save seeds from infected fruit.

Downy mildew and powdery mildew are fungal diseases that can be prevented by proper spacing of plants and good air circulation.

Fusarium wilt and Verticillium wilt are caused by soilborne fungi. Start with clean, compost-rich soil at planting or premium potting mix in containers as a preventative.

Harvesting
Cucumbers can grow fast, so check plants frequently. It's not uncommon for me to have to check my cucumber plants twice a day once the fruit sets. If left on the vine too long, cucumbers turn yellow and bitter. Regular harvesting will result in more productive vines and better-tasting fruit.

Smaller fruit tends to be crisper and better tasting than fruit at its maximum size.

Use pruners or snips to remove cucumbers from their vines. Enjoy immediately or store dry and at room temperature for a couple of days. And don't forget cucumbers are great candidates to be preserved by pickling and don't even require special equipment.

EDAMAME

Glycine max,
Legume family

The Down and Dirty

Preferred climate	Warm to hot
Sun	Full
Soil	Well-draining
pH range	6.0–7.0
Sow seeds	indoors, 4–6 weeks before last frost. Outdoors, after last frost.
Sowing depth	1 inch (2.5 cm)
Days to germination	5–10
Germination temperature	70°F (21°C)
Note	To increase yields, use a nitrogen-fixing inoculant formulated for soybeans.
Transplant seedlings	After frost-free date, when soil temperature is at least 55°F (13°C).
Spacing	2 inches (5 cm) apart in rows 12–24 inches (30–60 cm) apart
Days to maturity	65–80 days

Notes from the garden

Not everyone recognizes soybean by its other name, edamame (used when referring to the immature soybean pod). But when the beans mature, harden, and dry in the pod, they're used for making tofu and soy milk. That's not why I grow it, though.

If you've ever enjoyed edamame in stir-fry, salads, or Asian cuisine, you know (and probably love) this vegetable. My favorite way to enjoy edamame is from a bowl of hot, salted, steamed pods. In fact, my kids even love edamame this way. I don't mention that it's the only vegetable that includes all nine essential amino acids. Now that is a powerful little packet of protein!

As a legume in the garden, it stores nitrogen in the soil to feed my plants. While frozen edamame pods are readily available (like everything else) these days, you just can't beat the deliciousness of fresh from the garden. I find edamame very easy to grow.

My favorite varieties
- 'Agate' Quicker to harvest than most, this variety maintains the classic buttery, nutty flavor.
- 'Envy' This popular variety is a good short-season option and ideal for succession planting.
- 'Manitoba Brown' This rich-tasting variety does better in cooler climates.

Planting
After the last risk of frost, transplant seedlings 6 inches (15 cm) apart in rows 1 to 2 feet (30 to 60 cm) apart. Or direct-sow seeds 2 inches (5 cm) apart and thin to 6 inches (15 cm) between plants once they've reached 4 inches (10 cm) tall. In all cases, a layer of natural mulch will maintain moisture in the bed, minimize weed growth, and suppress diseases in the soil.

Plant edamame every 10 days through mid-summer for a succession of delicious pods.

Mid-season care
Keep the soil evenly moist, and don't let it dry out during flowering and pod set. Scout for pests and diseases.

Pests & disease
Mexican bean beetles can turn leaves into lace quickly. Stay vigilant and you can keep this threat in check. Use insecticidal soap on the early stages of Mexican bean beetles if you see them.

Edamame seedlings should be thinned once they reach 4 inches (10 cm) tall. Allow 6 inches (15 cm) between plants when thinning or transplanting.

Whiteflies favor edamame, too. Floating row covers work well. Use insecticidal soap, making direct contact on whiteflies.

Critters love edamame and deer, rabbits, and woodchucks will gladly wipe out your crop. A physical barrier is the best defense.

Bean rust and powdery mildew are two diseases to look out for.

Harvesting
Edamame is ready to harvest when the beans within the pod have filled out but the soybeans are firm, not hard. At this time, the pods start to dull from their bright green color. There should be a bit of give as you lightly squeeze the pods. But that window of ideal harvest time is short—just a few days.

To harvest, you can pull the entire plant from the ground. Edamame pods are all ready at the same time and the plant won't continue to produce new pods. Use your thumb and forefinger to pop the pod from the stem.

How much edamame would a woodchuck eat? Pretty much all of it, as I was unlucky enough to find out one season.

When your pods start to dull from their bright green color, it's time to harvest. They should be firm, but not hard.

EGGPLANT

Solanum melongena,
Tomato family

The Down and Dirty

Preferred climate	Warm
Sun	Full
Soil	Well-draining, compost-rich
pH range	5.5–7.0
Sow seeds	Indoors 4–8 weeks before last possible frost date
Sowing depth	¼ inch (6 mm) in small pots rather than flats (to minimize transplant shock)
Days to germination	7 days
Germination temperature	85°F (29°C), use a germination mat to maintain temperature
Note	Use grow lights above pots to produce sturdier stems, use a gentle fan on young seedlings to help prevent damping off disease. Transplant to a larger pot at about 4 inches (10 cm) tall or when roots are growing out the bottom of their original pots.
Transplant seedlings	After last possible frost date or when overnight temperatures are above 60°F (16°C)
Spacing	24 inches (60 cm)
Note	Acclimate seedlings to outdoor conditions by hardening off. Put pots in the sun for 30 minutes on the first day, then increase the time gradually over 7 to 10 days so that by the last day, plants are exposed to a full day of sunlight.
Days to maturity	58–90

Notes from the garden

Eggplant may be an acquired taste for most children (and plenty of adults) I know, but for my money, there's nothing quite like eggplant parmesan with homegrown ingredients.

For the gardener, eggplant is a pleasure to grow. It has a reputation for being tricky, and it can run into some of the same pest and disease issues that affect its nightshade cousins. But if you've grown tomatoes or peppers, you're already off to a good start with eggplant. It's a warm-season crop, but can be successfully grown in cooler

Most people know eggplant to be deep purple in color, but some varieties can be different shades, streaked with white, all-white, or even green. Even the shapes vary widely by variety.

'Black Beauty' is among the most popular eggplant varieties.

climates with a little extra care. Also eggplant seedlings are easier to grow than eggplants from seed, even if they're more expensive and more limited in the varieties.

The classic varieties come in all shades of purple and are sometimes streaked with white. Some varieties are all-white, and some are even green at maturity. Along with the different fruit shapes— bulbous, round, long, skinny, curved—and the purple flowers. Aside from the fruit (which I love), eggplant adds visual interest to my vegetable garden with its shrublike form and striking foliage.

My favorite varieties

- 'Black Beauty' A classic heirloom variety with large, dark purple fruit, the plants grow 18 to 24 inches (45 to 60 cm) tall. Fruit is ready to harvest 74 days after planting.
- 'Galine' This productive hybrid variety is reliable in northern climates. The "black bell" fruits reach 6 to 7 inches (15 to 18 cm) and are mature 65 days after planting.
- 'Listada De Gandia' A European heirloom, the 14-inch (36 cm) plants produce purple-and-white-streaked egg-shaped fruits that reach up to 8 inches (20 cm) long. The fruit has mild flavor and tender, thin skin. Maturity is reached in 80 to 90 days.
- 'Pot Black' The compact plants are ideal for containers, with 3-ounce (85 g) fruits that have no bitter flavor. Allow 58 to 62 days to maturity.
- 'White Star Hybrid' White varieties tend to be less bitter than their purple counterparts. This one has shiny white fruit that's sweet and tender. The plants can grow 30 to 36 inches (76 to 90 cm) tall. The fruit reaches 5 to 7 inches (13 to 18 cm) in length.

Mid-season care

Warm soil, at least to 70°F (21°C), is crucial for eggplant. In cooler climates, plant through slits cut into black plastic that has covered the bed for a few weeks to capture solar energy and heat the soil. Use floating row cover if needed until summer heat sets in. Eggplant is self-pollinating, so allowing insect access to the plants isn't necessary.

Blood meal or cottonseed meal may be used at planting, but be sure to amend the soil with plenty of finished compost.

Thank You for Your Support

Employ stakes or, preferably, tomato cages or cones early. Some varieties of eggplant get quite heavy and can even break their branches, so keep them well-supported!

Eggplant needs at least 1 inch (2.5 cm) of water per week, and up to 2 inches (5 cm) weekly during the hottest parts of summer. Inadequate watering results in small and bitter fruit.

Once flowers begin to develop, any fertilizer used should be either balanced or have more phosphorus than nitrogen to promote fruiting over foliage growth. Follow package directions. More fertilizer is not better and will not yield more fruit.

Pests & disease

Flea beetles are the most common eggplant pest. Look for pin-sized holes when leaves are young and tender. By summer, the plants are big and strong enough to survive on their own. Plant a nearby trap crop of radishes, as flea beetles prefer them to eggplant. Or use a floating row cover.

Aphids can be knocked off plants with a sharp stream of water. Hand-pick the eggs of fruitworms and armyworms from under leaves and on fruit. Pick off any caterpillars you find. Bt can control moth and butterfly larvae.

Eggplant sees many of the same diseases as tomato plants (since they're in the same family). However, diseases are not nearly as common with eggplant. Verticillium wilt is a soilborne fungus that can linger for years without remedy. Starting plants with compost-rich soil and premium potting mix in containers is your best precaution. Anthracnose is a fruit-rot fungus found on ripe and overripe fruit that presents as small, round depressed areas that enlarge over time. Remove infected fruit from the garden and do not save seeds from the fruit. Phytophthora blight shows up as leaf spots, fruit rot, crown rot, and dieback of the growing tip. Overwatering allows the fungus to thrive. Dispose of affected plants and do not add them to compost.

Harvesting

Know your eggplant variety so you can track when to harvest. Most varieties can be picked when fruits are halfway to mature size. Smaller fruits often have better flavor, and frequent picking encourages additional fruit. Harvest when the fruit is still glossy. Dull fruit is past its prime. The fruit should feel firm but with a slight springiness. Carefully cut fruit off the plants—don't pull or yank—and enjoy right away.

Pin-sized holes in your eggplant are a sure sign that flea beetles have invaded your garden.

I use shorter versions of my tomato cages for my eggplants to help support maturing fruit.

Tulle, commonly used as bridal veil material, is one of my favorite row covers.

GARLIC

Allium sativum,
Amaryllis family

The Down and Dirty

Preferred climate	Variety-dependent
Sun	Full sun to light shade
Soil	Well-draining for biggest heads
pH range	6.0–7.0
Sowing	Direct-sow cloves instead of seeds, at least 2 weeks before first frost
Sowing depth	2 inches (5 cm)
Days to germination	2–8 weeks
Germination temperature	55°F–85°F (13°C-29°C)
Spacing	4 inches (10 cm)

Notes from the garden

If you're looking to grow a crop that you'll use often in your own kitchen, it's hard to beat garlic. It's seemingly in every recipe you'll make, and it's an easy-to-raise crop that provides an extra benefit for your garden while it grows. Best of all, once you get started with growing your own garlic, you may never have to buy it again!

Garlic is in the *Allium* genus, along with onions, shallots, leeks, scallions, and chives. Like several of those crops, garlic can be stored for long periods of time—when properly cared for.

Varieties

Softneck garlic varieties have pliable stalks that can be braided for storage and make an attractive display. They're best suited to southern climates. Softneck garlic usually has all-white bulbs and a mild flavor. The cloves are on the small side as compared to hardneck varieties, with more cloves per head. They generally last longer in storage, though.

Hardneck garlic is identified by woody and stiff stalks, hues of purple and pink in the bulbs, and more intense flavor. They're more cold-hardy and do better in northern climates. Hardneck cloves are easier to peel and tend to be larger than their softneck counterparts.

Hardneck garlic also grows a flower stem called a scape. This bonus crop can be used to make pesto, mixed into a stir-fry, or substituted for

Hardneck garlic varieties have woody, stiff stalks that run all the way through the head.

Scapes are a bonus crop that come with hardneck garlic varieties. They can be cut off and eaten long before the heads are ready.

green onions in most recipes. Scapes appear as curly garlic stems in spring. They can be cut off and enjoyed weeks before the garlic heads are ready. (Removing them also forces more of the plant's energy into a larger head of garlic.)

Choosing what to grow

Rather than starting garlic seeds (more accurately, bulbils) it's easier and more practical to grow garlic from cloves. In fact, when you see gardeners refer to "seed garlic," they're actually talking about garlic heads that are intended to be separated into individual cloves for planting.

Can grocery store garlic be used as seed garlic? Not usually. The garlic at your local store is almost always from China or California and, although it depends on where you live, there's a good chance it's not suited to grow in your region. Instead, look to a local farmer's market or farm stand for seed garlic that will reliably produce well where you live.

Planting

Exact dates vary according to geography, but most garlic is planted in or around October. Aim for at least two weeks before the first frost, but definitely plant before the ground freezes. Garlic will have greater yields when cloves are planted

early enough to establish full vegetative growth in fall. The more vegetative growth, the greater the bulb when day length increases and temperature warms.

Well-draining soil that's rich in organic matter will produce the biggest heads. Since garlic benefits from moderate nitrogen into early spring, amending the soil with nitrogen (such as blood meal) before planting will help with early foliage development.

Break apart a head of garlic into individual cloves just before planting. Use the biggest ones for planting, leaving the "paper" intact. Plant with the pointed end up (root end down) and cover with soil until the surface is level, then water.

Ward Off Vampires...Or Squirrels

Squirrels and other mammals hate the taste and smell of garlic, so they'll generally leave your garlic plantings alone (and maybe nearby vegetables as well). For that reason, many gardeners use garlic as a protective border plant in beds where critter foraging is a problem.

A generous layer of loose straw or shredded leaves will help insulate the soil and allow garlic to grow through.

Finally, rotate your crop to avoid planting garlic in a spot where garlic, onions, or another member of the allium family has been grown in recent years.

Mid-season care

Garlic requires ½ to 1 inch (1.3 to 2.5 cm) of water per week. In the winter, when the ground is frozen or when outdoor temperatures are below freezing, pause supplemental watering until the ground thaws and temperatures rise again.

In late-winter, side-dress with a nitrogen-based fertilizer such as blood meal, soybean meal or cottonseed meal, composted chicken manure, or another slow-release nitrogen source to help below-ground bulb development. Avoid later nitrogen applications, which can inhibit bulb development.

Harvesting

In warm climates, fall-planted garlic may be pulled up as early as May or June. In cooler regions, harvest will likely be mid-July to mid-August.

Popular advice says garlic is ready when the first four leaves (counting from the bottom) have browned and flopped over. This is about a third of the stalk's height. When at least half of your garlic plants reach this stage, cease watering for a week, then test by pulling up one bulb. Use a trowel to carefully loosen the soil around the bulb. It should come out easily. If the test bulb appears much smaller than according to variety, water the remaining garlic, giving bulbs another week to grow before repeating the test.

Garlic for storing must be cured. Curing toughens the bulb and improves the flavor. Shake off loose dirt, but don't rinse or scrub the harvested garlic. In a well-ventilated space and out of direct sunlight, place your garlic plants on wire racks or hang them roots-up. They should be spaced out or lattice-stacked to allow good airflow and if possible, run a fan.

After 14 days, the outer skin of each head of garlic should be dry and papery. At this point, the stalks can be cut off and composted. Keep garlic heads whole until cloves are needed.

Store garlic heads in a dry, dark place to discourage sprouting. A garlic keeper jar with holes for ventilation or a paper bag works well. Never put garlic in a plastic bag or an airtight container, as trapped moisture will cause mold.

If you set aside your largest bulbs each year and plant the largest cloves, you can repeat the cycle indefinitely and your garlic will continue to improve.

Garlic's not as attractive above-ground as some crops, but there's plenty of flavor developing just beneath the surface!

Curing garlic takes some time and a dedicated space with the right conditions, but the results are well worth it.

GREEN BEANS

Phaseolus vulgaris,
Pea family

The Down and Dirty

Preferred climate	**Most any**
Sun	**Full**
Soil	**Fertile, well-worked**
pH range	**6.0–7.0**
Sow seeds	**Indoors, 3 weeks before last frost date. Outdoors, after last frost date.**
Sowing depth	**1 inch (2.5 cm)**
Days to germination	**5–10**
Germination temperature	**60°F–85°F (16°C–29°C)**
Note	**Bean seeds germinate quickly and reliably in warm soil. To conserve indoor seed starting space, skip the indoor sowing and direct-sow outside. In warm climates, sow more seeds 10 to 12 weeks before first frost for fall crop.**
Transplant seedlings	**Once soil temperature reaches 70°F (21°C)**
Spacing	**Bush, 4–6 inches (10–15 cm) apart, in twin rows 12 inches (30 cm) apart.** **Pole, 3 per vertical support.**
Days to maturity	**Most varieties, 54–70**

Notes from the garden

Green beans go by many names: snap beans (for how they're broken prior to many preparations), string beans (even though most modern varieties no longer have a fibrous string down the pod seam), or even haricot verts (when they're feeling fancy and French).

Whatever you call them, they're a must-grow for every summer garden. They germinate reliably (and quickly) wherever you plant them, and they waste no time getting down to business once they do. Bean flowers are self-pollinating, and soon you'll have a bean pod factory that you may be hard-pressed to keep up with.

The magic is in picking them while they're young and extra-tender. But try to resist the temptation to eat too many as you harvest. I often fail at following my own advice on this. It's a highlight of my harvesting time, as I find green beans are best fresh from the garden.

And remember, green beans don't even have to be green! Yellow, purple, and multi-colored varieties can be found to add even more interest to both your garden and your dinner plate.

Choosing what to grow

Decide early if you want to grow bush beans or pole beans. Bush beans don't climb or twine. They grow to a certain height, produce fruit, and then stop growing. Repeat plantings every 10 days will ensure a longer harvest.

Pole beans need to climb a vertical support like a trellis, stake, or teepee. They keep climbing upward until they're killed by heat or frost, producing fruit the whole time. No need to plant a second wave as pole beans are quite prolific.

My favorite varieties

- 'Antigua' Bush bean with 5-inch (13 cm) dark green pods and good disease resistance. Plants grow to an upright 18 inches (45 cm) with mature fruit in 55 days.
- 'Blue Lake Pole' Popular pole bean that grows 7 feet (2 m) tall with long pods that are great for canning. Plants mature in 75 days. A bush-type Blue Lake is also available.
- 'Dragon Tongue' Bush bean with pods flecked with deep purple. The pods can be eaten as a snap bean when young or left to ripen and then shelled. The plants grow 24 to 30 inches (60 to 76 cm) tall and mature in 60 days.
- 'Kentucky Wonder' A very popular heirloom pole variety with straight silver-green pods that reach 6 to 8 inches (15 to 20 cm) in length. The plants can climb to 8 feet (2.4 m), reaching maturity in 70 days.
- 'Wyatt' Bush-type bean with deep emerald-green pods on productive and uniform plants. The tender pods can grow to over 6 inches (15 cm) long and are mature in 54 days.

Planting

Water green beans immediately upon planting. Once they germinate, cover the ground with a layer of mulch, about 2 to 3 inches (5 to 8 cm). Mulch will act as a barrier between the plant foliage and soilborne pathogens.

For pole beans, provide a climbing support right away. Buy a garden trellis or make one yourself with simple bamboo stakes, strips of lumber, or long tree branches tied at the top into a teepee formation.

Mid-season care

Like all legumes, green beans work with nitrogen-fixing bacteria to produce their own fertilizer. Supplemental feeding from you shouldn't be necessary, so give them good soil rich with compost and let them do their thing.

Green beans are shallow rooted, so careful and consistent watering is a must. Strive to provide 1 inch (2.5 cm) of water per week, more during the hottest part of summer. A soaker hose or drip irrigation system makes this easy, while keeping water off the plant leaves.

Pests & disease

The Mexican bean beetle is the green bean's most common foe. It's often mistaken for the beneficial lady beetle with its pale orange back and small black spots. The Mexican bean beetle eats the foliage of your bean plants and can be tough to control once established. Look for yellow egg clusters on the undersides of the leaves, or hatched larvae, which resemble chubby and spiky yellow alligators. Remove eggs or larvae by hand or try neem oil. The flowers on beans don't need help from insects for pollination, so floating row cover is convenient and helpful as a pest barrier for bush beans but obviously impractical for pole varieties.

Aphids feed on plant sap and invite disease and other insects. Check under the leaves, knock them off with a sharp stream of water, or if necessary, use insecticidal soap.

Leafhoppers are small, light-green or gray wedge-shaped insects that suck out plant juices and spread disease in warm weather. They can be controlled with organic insecticides containing pyrethrin (derived from chrysanthemum), although even this treatment can kill other garden beneficials.

You may spot the Mexican bean beetle on your plants in any one of its phases. Just be careful not confuse it for the beneficial ladybug.

Bean common mosaic virus creates a mosaic pattern on leaves, stunting or killing the plant. Remove affected plants and discard, but do not add them to your compost pile.

Bean rust is a common fungal disease (especially on pole beans) that presents on foliage as dark red spots or blotches that look like rust. Avoid overhead watering, and don't touch the foliage or harvest the pods when the leaves are wet. After the harvest, remove and destroy the infected plants.

Harvesting

Don't let green bean pods hang on the plant too long or they'll get tough and stringy. Pick bush beans when they're young and tender. Not only are they at their best then, but you may get a second or even third crop. With pole beans, harvest at least twice a week to keep the plant producing. Pay attention to the listed ideal pod length for cues on when to harvest.

I like to use both hands to pick beans off my plants. That helps keep the vines from breaking as I pull the pods away.

Use harvested beans while still fresh or store them whole and unwashed in your refrigerator's crisper drawer for up to a week. If you have more beans than you know what to do with, remember they freeze or can especially well.

Beans are best when they're young and tender, so don't wait too long to pick them. Plus, the sooner you pick, the better your chances are of getting a second crop!

HERBS

The Down and Dirty

Preferred climate	Varies by type
Sun	**Full**
Soil	**Well-draining**
Sow seeds	**Indoors, late winter to early spring**
Sowing depth	**¼ inch (6 mm)**
Days to germination	**7**
Germination temperature	**70°F–85°F (21°C–29°C)**
Note	**Use sterile seed starting mix, keep seeds under grow lights. If roots become compacted or grow through bottom holes, transplant to larger pots. Harden off before planting outdoors.**
Transplant seedlings	**After last frost date**
Spacing	**According to plants' mature size**
Note	**Herbs need soil that is well-draining for optimum growth. Amend soil as needed before transplanting. Consider growing in containers.**

Notes from the garden

I wanted to include culinary herbs in this book because I can't imagine growing a vegetable garden without including them. But it does open up something of a can of worms. There are dozens upon dozens of different herbs I could list in this section...but they would mostly read the same. The guidelines for growing parsley just aren't that different from the guidelines for growing oregano or dill or cilantro or basil. If you can grow one, you can likely grow them all. So I hope you'll indulge me by letting me provide one catch-all guide to growing pretty much any popular herb and trusting that you can take it from here.

Culinary herbs are by far the easiest way to start growing edible crops. You don't even need a garden. Pots, containers, window boxes, even glass jars on a sunny countertop provide all the space you need to keep your kitchen well-stocked in homegrown herbs. Terra cotta pots are especially suited for herbs since the porous clay material allows for air exchange and for the plants' root systems to drain well.

Terra cotta pots are perfect for growing herbs. The porous clay material "breathes" to allow for drainage as well as the exchange of air.

Fresh herbs are easy to grow, bring pollinators to your garden, and instantly improve the taste and quality of everything you cook in the kitchen.

Herbs couldn't be easier to grow, they're undemanding, they produce prolifically throughout the season, they improve the taste of everything you cook, and they can't be beat for attracting beneficial pollinators to your garden to make all of your other crops more productive, too.

My favorite herbs

Basil Sometimes called "the king of herbs," basil is used in cooking worldwide, but most closely associated with Italian cuisine. From pesto to a pizza topping, it's also used in everything from soups to sauces to salads. And like many other herbs, it can even be used to make a wonderfully flavorful infused cooking oil. Sweet (or Genovese) basil is the most common variety in North America, with a subtly minty flavor that's between sweet and savory. Lettuce leaf basil features extra-large leaves that are less sweet. Bush basil stays short and compact and has an intense flavor. Most basil is green, but purple varieties can add visual interest. It's an annual, but cuttings can be taken and grown indoors.

Cilantro This member of the carrot family produces leaves that are chopped fresh for use in many Mexican favorites, from tacos to guacamole to salsa. A cool-season annual, it can reach 2 feet (60 cm) tall in the garden. If you're one of the people (some studies estimate it's as much as 15 percent of the population) whose genetic makeup causes cilantro to taste like dish soap, you may choose to grow it simply for the pretty flowers that attract pollinators. Additionally, if you wait for the plant to bolt and go to seed, cilantro seeds are known as the spice coriander.

Dill The herb that's responsible for making dill pickles, dill is also great as a garnish on fish or in potato salad. Dill will grow 2 to 4 feet (60 to 120 cm) tall and is highlighted by delicate yellow flower clusters. Most herbs are naturally resistant to pests thanks to their strong scents, but dill is irresistible to the black swallowtail butterfly and acts as a host plant. You'll find the black-and-green-striped caterpillars with their telltale yellow dots munching away on the tops of your dill plants. Watching them go through their transformation is like having a front-row seat at a magic show for me, so I typically plant a lot more dill than I need so I can leave the caterpillars undisturbed.

Fennel doesn't get the love that many culinary staples like basil, oregano, and parsley do, but even if you don't eat it, it's worth growing for all the black swallowtail butterflies this aromatic herb will bring to the garden.

With its woodsy scent, you can't miss rosemary in the garden. And since more and more hardy cultivars are being developed, many gardeners can plant it once and enjoy it for years.

Fennel This aromatic herb likes it a little cooler than most other herbs. As with dill, it's a host plant for the black swallowtail butterfly. With a flavor reminiscent of licorice, fennel seeds can be used in sausage-making, fennel pollen can replace fennel seed in some recipes, and fennel stalks can be used instead of celery. Some varieties grow an above-ground bulb that's used in cooking.

Mint A fast-growing perennial, mint stays under 2 feet (60 cm) tall but can spread to overtake a garden space in a hurry. When I grow it, I always do so in a container. Its taste and fragrance is like nothing else in the garden. Fresh spearmint leaves are a nice touch in a glass of lemonade or iced tea. Apple mint can be used to make jelly. Chocolate mint and orange mint have hints of their namesakes in their aroma profiles.

Oregano A staple of Mediterranean cuisine, oregano is actually a member of the mint family and ranges in flavor from sweet to spicy. Greek oregano has green leaves tinged with gray that are hardy and flavorful. Italian oregano is milder

in taste, with larger leaves. Oregano can establish itself in the garden, survive winter, and come back in spring. If the flowers are not removed, oregano will self-seed and spread extensively.

Parsley Another relative of the carrot, parsley is grown as a root vegetable in some places. It's a vigorous grower that will produce a profuse amount of foliage that can be used in cooking and as a garnish. There are flat-leaf and curly-leaf varieties. Flat-leaf parsley is considered more flavorful for use in recipes, while curly-leaf parsley makes a more attractive garnish when whole leaves are used. Parsley is a biennial, meaning it will grow a rosette and tap root in its first year and flower and die after its second. It's another host plant of the swallowtail, so plant extra.

Rosemary This perennial herb may provide my all-time favorite smell in the garden. With a lemony pine flavor, its needlelike leaves are used either fresh or dried on everything from chicken to fish to roasted potatoes. While growing, it produces flowers in white, pink, or purple, depending on the variety. Rosemary is particularly drought-tolerant. Some varieties have a low, creeping habit, while others can reach 5 feet (1.5 m) tall; be sure to check the expected size before you purchase. Some varieties are meant to be ornamental only.

Sage With its pungent, earthy flavor, sage is a must-have flavor in many classic autumn dishes, complementing everything from pork to poultry to

Thanksgiving stuffing. Its woody stems and gray, fuzzy leaves make it a standout in the garden, too. It's a perennial in many climates and stays around 2 to 4 feet (60 to 120 cm) tall.

Thyme Related to oregano, thyme is spicier in flavor, making it perfectly suited to many Old-World dishes. It's a perennial evergreen that does well in winter, often putting on tiny flowers that attract pollinators in milder locations. Different varieties offer a wide spectrum of flavor profiles, from spicy and pungent to citrusy to earthy.

Mid-season care
Some herbs, like rosemary, are notably drought-tolerant, while others, like basil, will quickly wilt if the soil dries out. That said, most herbs do just fine with 1 inch (2.5 cm) of water per week, whether from rainfall, supplemental watering, or a combination of the two. Remember that herbs grown in containers may need to be watered more frequently than in-ground plants.

Herbs can grow quickly, and some types produce woody stems. To keep new growth (and what you harvest) on the more tender side, mid-season and regular periodic pruning will offer a more pleasing (and tastier) culinary experience. Make your cuts about one-third to halfway down on the stem, just above a set of leaves. This kind of regular pruning also helps to maintain a more compact, bushy plant.

Basil and tomato don't just go together in the kitchen; they're excellent companion plants in the garden, too. A row of basil plants can keep damaging hornworms away from your tomato crop.

Most herbs don't need fertilizer and actually perform better without it. This is important to remember if, like me, you interplant herbs with vegetables—especially the heavy feeders. Basil and cilantro are the exception. For them I apply a balanced fertilizer every few weeks.

To Protect and Serve: Herbs as Companion Plants
Herbs are robust plants that typically don't have a lot of pest issues. In fact, they can sometimes even help repel pests from neighboring edibles! Basil that's planted near tomatoes, it's said, can help keep tomato hornworms away from the entire crop. And cucumber beetles may steer clear of your cukes entirely if there's dill planted alongside. Now, that's not an ironclad guarantee against all pest issues, but if you're planting these crops anyway, why not take advantage of the symbiotic relationship between some of these companion plants?

Harvesting
Snip whatever herbs you need for cooking at any time once the plant is established. Remember that a little goes a long way when it comes to fresh herbs.

Storage
Extra cuttings can be hung and dried, then ground or crushed. You can even freeze herbs for use throughout winter months.

Or take cuttings from healthy plants in fall before the first frost. Dip the plant stems in rooting hormone powder and propagate new plants in potting mix or seed starting mix. Many herb cuttings will readily root when placed in a container of water. Overwinter cuttings indoors and plant outdoors in spring.

KALE

Brassica oleracea
(Acephala Group),
Cabbage family

The Down and Dirty

Preferred climate	Cool to cold
Sun	Full, but can tolerate light shade
Soil	Well-amended, cool and moist
pH range	6.0–7.0
Sow seeds	Indoors, 6–8 weeks before last frost. Outdoors, direct-sow when soil temperature reaches 65°F (18°C) in spring. For fall direct-sowing, late summer to early fall.
Sowing depth	½ inch (1.3 cm)
Days to germination	5–10
Germination temperature	70°F–90°F (21°C–32°C)
Note	While moist soil is key during active growth, discontinue watering when temperature first drops below freezing to improve hardiness and flavor.
Transplant seedlings	4–6 weeks after last hard frost
Spacing	10–18 inches (25–45 cm)
Days to maturity	50

Notes from the garden

My cool-season garden every year always includes kale. Yes, it gets bonus points for being just about the easiest above-ground edible you can grow, but it has many other virtues that should earn it a place at your table season after season.

Besides its ease of growing, kale is beautiful. If you haven't figured it out yet, I love growing edibles that do double duty in the garden. Kale is a great choice in your foodscape garden, as it rivals any ornamental plant. There are varieties that are deep dark green, light green, green with pink, purple, smooth-leaf options, and tall curly ones, too (my personal favorite). There are even dwarf varieties.

Kale is also one of the toughest, most undemanding plants you can grow. Provide it with good compost-rich soil, come back every now and then to supplement with a little organic fish emulsion, and that's it. It's rich in vitamins and minerals, and it is rarely bothered by pests (other than aphids, that love to show up on kale late in the season).

As for hardiness, I'd put it up against brussels sprouts (a champion for cold-season hardiness) all day long for its ability to take on winter without any supplemental protection. In fact, like many cool-season crops, kale tastes even sweeter when kissed by a few frosty nights.

But here's the deal closer. When my non-vegetable-loving daughter started *asking* for sautéed kale for dinner, you better believe I started growing plenty of it! For her, it was love at first bite. It should be worth noting, though, just like with other store-bought veggies, there is no comparison between what you find at the grocery store and sweet homegrown kale that you pull fresh from your own garden.

My favorite varieties
- 'Dwarf Green Curled' This frost-tolerant variety from northern Germany is a compact and showy variety that produces excellent flavor on tightly ruffled leaves. A high-yielder, plants reach 18 inches (45 cm) in height.
- 'Red Russian' Bright purple stems and slate-green, deeply lobed leaves are tender and very sweet. Taste improves with cold temperatures, making this variety very popular in salad mixes. Very cold tolerant, it reaches 24 to 36 inches (60 to 90 cm) tall.
- 'Redbor' A productive variety, it features tall and deeply curled leaves that are dark red in color. Flavor is improved by cold weather; the color intensifies as well. An ideal choice for overwintering.
- 'Vates' Highly productive in spring and fall, this variety is popular served raw in salads, made into kale chips, or even used in soup! Leaves resist yellowing in cold and heat. Sturdy and compact plants up to 24 inches (60 cm) tall.
- 'Winterbor' Ruffled blue-green foliage with excellent flavor, produces best in spring and fall. Plants are tall, 24 to 36 inches (60 to 90 cm), and provide excellent yields of densely curled greens. Vigorous with good cold hardiness, it can overwinter in southern gardens.

Planting
Direct-sow or plant seedlings in well-amended, compost-rich soil so the seedlings will get off to a fast start. Add mulch around the base to retain soil moisture and reduce weed competition.

The cold never bothered it anyway. Kale's taste actually improves after it's been hit with a little frost or snow.

Mid-season care
Kale is a low-maintenance plant. However, it will reward you with faster and more vigorous growth if you provide a steady nutrient supply. Continue to maintain even soil moisture and feed every 2 to 3 weeks with an organic liquid fertilizer (such as fish emulsion) with a balanced ratio.

Pests & disease
Aphids are common on kale plants, especially late in the season. Inspect your plants often and blast aphids off with a stiff stream of water. Kale is a tough plant and can usually handle the water. Alternatively, you can spray insecticidal soap, or (ideally) be patient and do nothing as predatory insects will always move in and take over. Even kale with aphids present on the leaves can be harvested and then washed off to enjoy.

Harvesting
Harvest from the bottom up. New growth will continue from the top. Cut leaves from the main stem or snap leaves off by hand by grabbing at the base of the leaf. Leaves are harvestable any time, but younger leaves are more tender and better-suited for eating raw in salads.

KOHLRABI

Brassica oleracea
(Gongylodes Group),
Cabbage family

The Down and Dirty

Preferred climate	**Cool**
Sun	**Full**
Soil	**Evenly moist, well-drained**
pH range	**6.0–7.0**
Sow seeds	**Indoors, 6 weeks before transplanting outside and soil can be worked.** **Outdoors, early spring after ground thaws and late summer.**
Sowing depth	**¼ inch (6 mm)**
Days to germination	**4–7**
Germination temperature	**50°F–80°F (10°C–27°C)**
Transplant seedlings	**In spring, about 2 weeks before last frost. In fall, up to 60 days before first frost.**
Spacing	**4–10 inches (10–25 cm)**
Days to maturity	**50 days**

Notes from the garden

Without a doubt, kohlrabi is the strangest-looking vegetable you will ever grow in your garden, due to its edible swollen stem. I've heard it described as a spaceship, an alien, or some mythological creature that just showed up in your garden. It is, if nothing else, a conversation starter for friends who visit your garden. But beyond its odd look, I think it's beautiful, too. Colors range from creamy white to pink and purple, with attractive foliage, too (that's edible when young).

It almost looks too strange to be delicious. But it is delicious and a very versatile crop in the kitchen, either raw or cooked. It provides a sweet crunch to salads and stir-fry and makes a great addition to soups and more.

Kohlrabi is a fast and easy-to-grow cool-season crop that I start from seed indoors in early February (and again in mid-summer) and transplant outdoors about 6 weeks later on both occasions. It doesn't take long for the unique above-ground bulb to form and then, (or any time after), it's ready to harvest.

It may not win many beauty contests, but kohlrabi can add visual interest to the garden with a nice range of colors and attractive foliage.

Kohlrabi is a fast grower in the cooler months. It won't take long for the uniquely shaped bulb to form after seedlings are transplanted.

My favorite varieties
- 'Kolibri' A hybrid variety with 3- to 4-inch (8 to 10 cm) bulbs, crisp texture, and deep purple, tender skin.
- 'Kordial' Another hybrid, this one has early, crack-resistant bulbs with crisp centers, rich flavor, and satisfying crunch.

Planting
Kohlrabi grows best in cool weather, in moist soil that is well-draining and compost-rich. A top-dressing of shredded leaf mulch (or similar) will benefit the health and vigor of this plant.

Mid-season care
Kohlrabi is happy with minimal care. It's a moderate feeder when it comes to nutrients, but along with rich soil, supplement every two weeks with a balanced soluble or liquid concentrate organic fertilizer such as fish emulsion.

Pests & disease
As a member of the cabbage family, kohlrabi can be attractive to cabbage worms, cabbage loopers, flea beetles, cutworms, cabbage aphids, and thrips. Floating row cover is effective to block access to some pests. Regular monitoring and hand removal is usually all that's necessary.

The disease that's perhaps most common to kohlrabi is clubroot, a soilborne fungus that stunts growth and disfigures roots. Leaves wilt during the day and then recover at night. Planting certified seed offers a good head start, but this fungus is difficult to control once present.

Alternaria leaf spot is a fungal disease that may present during cool, damp weather. Look for round or angular gray to brown lesions with concentric rings. Treat with fungicides approved for this disease.

Harvesting
Kohlrabi is ready to harvest when the bulb-like swollen stems are 2 to 3 inches (5 to 8 cm) in diameter. A simple pull will extract the plant from the soil. Cut off the leaves and roots and refrigerate for up to 6 weeks. Alternatively, kohlrabi will wait right in the garden for you until you're ready to enjoy it, all the way through fall and even into early winter. For extra protection when temperatures drop, cover the plants with mulch.

LEEKS

Allium ampeloprasum
(Porrum Group),
Amaryllis family

The Down and Dirty

Preferred climate	Warm to cool (check variety)
Sun	Full but can tolerate some light shade
Soil	Loamy and fertile, evenly moist, compost-enriched
pH range	6.2–6.8
Sow seeds	Indoors, in mid- to late winter, about 8 weeks before last frost risk. Outdoors, direct-sow in early spring: ¼–½ inch (0.6–1.3 cm) deep, 2 inches (5 cm) between seeds and 24 inches (60 cm) between rows.
Sowing depth	¼ inch (6 mm)
Days to germination	5–7
Germination temperature	60°F–85°F (16°C–29°C)
Note	Similar to tomatoes, leek seedlings are planted deep. The absence of light leaves the underground portion white.
Transplant seedlings	After risk of frost has passed, plant seedlings that are ideally pencil-thick, 8–12 inches (20–30 cm) tall.
Spacing	6 inches (15 cm) between plants in rows 24 inches (60 cm) apart.
Days to maturity	70–110

Notes from the garden

Leeks are a non-bulbing type of onion with a milder taste, used as a culinary crop for over 4,000 years. They're easy to grow and in moderate climates can overwinter in the garden with light protection.

The unique quality of leeks is their thick, long, white (blanched) stalks—the edible portion of the plant. The key to blanching as much of the stalk

as possible (which means more edible portion) is to prevent light exposure. This is accomplished by drawing soil around the stalk as it grows, a process referred to as *hilling*. As more of the stalk is covered, more leaves grow higher up the plant which results in a longer blanched stalk. Some leek varieties mature faster than the classic full-sized leek. Quicker-to-mature varieties (known as short-season leeks) have thinner stems and won't keep as long in storage. For the classically sized, longer-storing leeks—grow long-season leeks. They obviously take longer to mature but for me, they're well-worth the wait.

My favorite varieties
- 'Alto' Although not winter-hardy, this is a good variety to grow in spring for a summer harvest. A tall, fast-growing, full-flavored leek when harvested at maturity (85 days), it can alternatively be harvested earlier for a milder flavor.
- 'King Richard' A fast-growing, medium-sized leek with a white shaft and dark blue-green foliage. More cold-tolerant than other varieties and can overwinter in moderate climates.
- 'Lancelot' A classic, open-pollinated leek with excellent large white stalks averaging 12 to 14 inches (30 to 35 cm). A good variety for summer and early fall harvesting.
- 'Tadorna' A vigorous grower producing dark green leaves on a good-sized stalk, this variety is adapted to many regions and a good cool-weather option. Good disease resistance to leaf blight, it reaches maturity in about 110 days.

Planting
If sown indoors, you can spread seeds generously into an open flat or container. Once seedlings reach about 3 inches (8 cm) tall, separate and plant into individual cells. After the last risk of frost has passed, plant them deeply into trenches so that most of the plant is below the soil when you backfill. Only 1 or 2 inches (2.5 to 5 cm) of the seedling leaves will be above ground at this point. Don't compress soil around the stem.

Mid-season care
Leeks are easy to grow and undemanding, but they do like a steady supply of nutrients. If you start with rich soil at planting, a supplemental feeding of a balanced organic fish emulsion every 2 weeks almost until harvest time is sufficient.

Pests & disease
Onion maggot is the larva of an adult fly that lays its eggs at the base of the leek plant. When the larvae hatch, it bores into the plant. Thrips are tiny insects that feed on the foliage and can discolor or distort leaf tissue. Grow them under row cover to deter these two pests.

Leaf blight is the most common disease affecting leeks, but there are varieties that have some resistance to this.

Other foliage challenges include leek rust and downy mildew.

White rot is a fungus that lives in the soil.

Harvesting
Once plants reach the average size for that variety, loosen the soil around the stalk with a spading fork and lift from the soil.

Hilling, or drawing up more and more soil around your leek stalks as they grow, will ensure a larger blanched portion of the plant that can be eaten.

When transplanting leeks, bury them deep. Only 1 or 2 inches (2.5 to 5 cm) of the seedling leaves should be visible above ground.

LETTUCE

Lactuca sativa,
Sunflower family

The Down and Dirty

Preferred climate	Cool
Sun	Full, but can tolerate shade
Soil	Well-drained and fertile
pH range	6.5–7.0
Sow seeds	Indoors, usually 3–4 weeks before last frost date (but up to 8 weeks for some varieties). Outdoors, after last hard frost. Fall harvest, 6 weeks before first frost.
Sowing depth	Under a fine layer of soil (lettuce needs light to germinate)
Days to germination	5–14
Germination temperature	40°F–60°F (5°C–16°C) for best results
Note	Lettuce seeds will germinate in soil up to 75°F (24°C), but not as consistently.
Transplant seedlings	After soil is workable
Spacing	Roughly 8 inches (20 cm) between plants, 12 inches (30 cm) between rows. Check variety for specifics.
Note	Can be planted closer together if you intend to harvest as baby greens.
Days to maturity	30–100 days, depending on variety

Notes from the garden

At my house, we eat a lot of lettuce. So, in the garden, I'm always looking for ways to grow more of it. Luckily, lettuce is a fast grower that allows me to sow successive plantings throughout spring and fall for a continuous bounty of my favorite varieties for much of the year.

But even though lettuce is a cool-season crop (and is surprisingly cold tolerant in spite of its tender leaves), it can take a little heat. I love to incorporate lettuce in beds with other plants that I know will grow tall by the time temperatures rise so a little shade from those plants can keep lettuce from bolting. (Bolting happens when a plant sends up a flower stem as an emergency measure in extreme heat, and when it happens to lettuce, the leaves become irreversibly bitter-tasting.)

In addition to the cool and crunchy taste of fresh lettuce, lettuce adds a beautiful visual element to the vegetable garden, thanks to a vast array of leaf colors, sizes, and textures.

I love the contrast lettuce provides to most other plants in the garden and will look for any opportunity to tuck in a few heads here and there.

I enjoy growing loose-leaf lettuces because I can continue to harvest them a little at a time all season long.

Choosing what to grow

With countless varieties, you have a lot to consider with lettuce. Also, decide if you want lettuce that you'll harvest as individual leaves or the full head.

My favorite varieties

There are four main types of lettuce. Each type boasts many different varieties.

- **Butter** lettuces are also called butterhead, bibb, or Boston lettuces. They have small, roundish heads that are somewhat loose and quite sweet. 'Buttercrunch' has a buttery flavor and texture. It's also heat-tolerant. 'Grandma Hadley's' is green with purple-tinged edges. 'Yugoslavian Red' has red leaves with green centers and a mild flavor.
- **Iceberg** lettuces, or crisphead lettuces, are heat-sensitive and best-grown in cooler climates. Green, spherical heads are mild-flavored and crunchy, used in chopped or wedge salads or bagged salad mix. 'Crispino' does better in warm and humid regions than other iceberg varieties. 'Saladin' is particularly bolt-resistant with tight, flavorful heads.

- **Loose-leaf** lettuces are fast growers that can be harvested continuously. 'Amish Deer Tongue' is very productive, with pointy dark green leaves. 'Lollo Rossa' is compact and rose-shaped with curly purple-red leaves. 'Salanova Red Batavia' and 'Salanova Red Oakleaf' can be grown in-ground or hydroponically in water.
- **Romaine** lettuces grow tall heads with crisp ribbed leaves. Popular for their heat tolerance in the garden, romaine hearts are chopped for salads. Large outer romaine leaves are often used instead of bread or tortillas as wraps. 'Cimmaron' has an unusual red-bronze color and is very bolt-resistant. 'Forellenschluss' is a green heirloom variety with striking burgundy spots. 'Tantan' is a "baby romaine" that stays a short 6 to 8 inches (15 to 20 cm).

Planting

Quick growth is the key to sweet-tasting lettuce, so the more fertile your soil is, the faster your lettuce will mature. Amend the first few inches with a generous helping of compost, and add an organic source of nitrogen. (Nitrogen boosts leaf growth, and that's the part of lettuce we eat!)

For continuous harvesting, stagger lettuce plantings every two weeks. This is a classic example of succession planting. You can even extend the growing season by using a cold frame to bump growing temperatures up slightly in early spring or late fall, or install shade cloth to cool your crops by a few precious degrees and keep your lettuce growing through summer. Learn more about ways to extend the growing season in Chapter 10.

Lettuce is actually a great container vegetable, too! Consider planting in a pot filled with quality outdoor potting mix, as garden soil is too heavy to drain adequately in a container.

Mid-season care

The shallow roots of lettuce plants need consistent water, especially on hot days, to provide moist, but not wet soil. A good layer of mulch (as detailed in Chapter 8) will help maintain proper moisture level and protect your plants.

Pests & disease

Aphids, armyworms, flea beetles, slugs, snails, thrips, and whiteflies all love lettuce as much as we do. A floating row cover will keep them from laying eggs on lettuce. Iron phosphate is an organic means of controlling slugs and snails. Aphids also spread lettuce mosaic leaf virus from plant to plant, causing a green and yellow mosaic pattern on leaves. The virus itself often comes from lettuce seeds, so use seeds only from a reliable source. And weed regularly around lettuce plants, as weeds may act as virus reservoirs and compete for water and nutrients. Remove and dispose of affected plants.

Downy mildew creates yellow spots on the topside of mature leaves. To reduce chances of infection, avoid overhead watering, choose resistant varieties, or apply a fungicide labeled for use to control downy mildew on lettuce.

Harvesting

Harvest lettuce in the early part of the morning before the heat of the sun. And it's best eaten that same day. Lettuce harvested midday will contain less moisture and therefore be less crisp. Oddly enough, if you wait to harvest right at dinner time, the leaves will be wilted.

For 'Buttercrunch' and loose-leaf lettuces, harvest when the leaves are the size you desire. Cut leaves from the outside of the head first to give smaller interior leaves more time to grow. Leaf lettuce can also be cut straight across the entire plant about 1 inch (2.5 cm) above the ground once the leaves are salad size. This will allow regrowth from the base and provide one or more similar harvests. Many loose-leaf varieties taste great as baby lettuce, with especially tender and fresh-tasting leaves harvested while still quite small.

For whole heads of romaine or iceberg, use a sharp knife to cut at the soil level when the plant is full-sized. A smaller head may grow back in its place.

For all lettuces, rinse immediately after harvesting and refrigerate in an airtight bag.

Strive to harvest lettuce in the early morning hours, as it will be at its most moist and crisp. Eat it that same day for best quality.

MELONS

Cucumis melo
(most melons),
Citrullus lanatus
(watermelon),
Cucumber family

The Down and Dirty

Preferred climate	Hot
Sun	Full
Soil	Well-amended, nutrient-rich, warm
pH range	6.0–6.5
Sow seeds	Indoors, one month before last frost. Outdoors, recommended, after the last frost.
Sowing depth	½ inch (1.3 cm)
Days to germination	3–4 days
Germination temperature	85°F (29°C)
Note	Melons germinate quickly in warm soil. Direct sow outside two weeks or more after the last frost.
Transplant seedlings	On soil mounds, 2–3 plants per mound, once soil is above 70°F (21°C).
Spacing	12 inches (30 cm) between plants, 6 feet (1.8 m) between rows
Days to maturity	73–100

Notes from the garden

I don't always grow melons, but if I had the room, I surely would. Few things say summer quite like biting into a sweet, juicy cantaloupe, honeydew, or watermelon. Each is a treat when eaten by itself, but they're also great in salad, as a breakfast, or even dessert. From smoothies to sorbets to salsas, you'll continue to find new and fun ways to serve up homegrown melons. (Pro tip: If you haven't tried *grilling* a wedge of juicy, ruby-red watermelon, stop what you're doing and go change your summer cookouts from this day forward. You're welcome.)

But not everyone has the garden space to grow melons. While they are certainly a sprawling plant if allowed to grow horizontally, you can trellis them, too. Their tendrils will wrap around and up vertical supports quite easily. The large and attractive melon foliage is a wonderful contrast to many of the less-showy plants of a summer garden. Learn the simple tips to grow melons easily, and what you give up in bed space will be paid back to you in the sweetest fruit coming from your garden.

Melons usually take up a lot of room in the garden. Instead, try growing them vertically on a trellis to economize space.

My favorite varieties

- 'Athena' This cantaloupe (a.k.a. muskmelon) is known for its resistance to Fusarium wilt, powdery mildew, and cracking. It matures in 79 days and boasts a long shelf life.
- 'Honeycomb' A honeydew with smooth, cream-colored skin on globe-shaped fruit. Each fruit is 5 pounds (2.3 kg) with crisp, medium-firm pale green flesh. It can be planted outdoors once soil has reached 60°F (16°C), making it a popular choice even in cooler climates. Mature in 78 days.
- 'Moon & Stars' Inside, a typical pink-fleshed watermelon. But this one is about its exterior interest—deep green skin with a large yellow spot (the moon) and myriad paint-splattered dots (the stars). Fruit can reach 40 pounds (18 kg). It matures in 100 days.
- 'Sangria' Traditional oval watermelon with dark green skin and light green stripes. Deep pink to red flesh inside that's high in sugar. Fruit matures in 87 days and can top 20 pounds (9 kg).
- 'Sugar Cube' A very sweet cantaloupe with round 2-pound (1 kg) fruit that lack ribbing but feature consistent netting. Resistant to a variety of diseases. Can be grown in both warm and cool climates. Matures in 80 days.

Planting

Since warm soil temperatures are a must for melons, many gardeners lay down sheets of black plastic to artificially warm up their soil prior to planting. While plastic can also serve as an effective weed barrier, it's not truly necessary for that purpose with melons. Their sprawling vines and large leaves will quickly fill in the area, covering the surface.

Melons prefer soil amended with well-composted manure that contains plenty of nitrogen, which will encourage vine growth.

Mid-season care

All melons benefit from 1 to 2 inches (2.5 to 5 cm) of water per week as they grow. Be prepared to supplement if you don't get that much rainfall. Be sure you water only at the base of the plant, and avoid overhead watering.

Keep your watering consistent throughout the growing cycle until the fruit reaches full size. Once it begins to ripen, though, hold off or significantly reduce any supplemental watering.

After flowering, use an organic fertilizer with a lower nitrogen number to aid in fruiting.

If using a trellis, tie the plants' vines to the vertical supports using soft, flexible fabric strips, like old pantyhose. (These also can be used as slings to hold the melons as they grow larger and heavier, preventing them from breaking off before harvest.)

If growing on the ground, keep the fruit raised off the soil surface to avoid rot and pests. It doesn't have to be much. I use an upturned flower pot saucer.

Consider reducing the number of melons per vine. By sacrificing all but the best-looking melons, what's left will be even sweeter tasting once ripe.

Pests & disease

Melon aphids are sucking insects that colonize quickly, especially under leaves and on vines. Secretions from feeding aphids attract ants and other problem insects. Be vigilant in inspecting and knock them off with a sharp stream of water or spray with insecticidal soap.

Cucumber beetles, either spotted or striped, will chew holes in leaves and pass a pathogen that causes bacterial wilt, killing your plant in a matter of days. Scrape off eggs, hand-pick adults, and rotate crops to keep the beetle population from building.

Anthracnose is a common fungal disease afflicting melons. It hits mine every year like clockwork and thrives when conditions are warm and wet. Check your leaves for water-soaked yellow spots that rapidly turn brown or black and often enlarge to take over entire leaves. Cracking and discoloration can extend to stems and even the fruit itself. Your best bet is to plant resistant varieties to start with, or try a fungicide specifically labeled for anthracnose on melons, ideally before the first signs of trouble. There are organic and synthetic options for home use. Personally, I make sure to avoid overhead watering and usually just ride it out. I've yet to have a season where I don't still get plenty of great fruit.

Powdery mildew is a fungal disease that can be avoided by proper spacing of plants for air circulation. A solution of baking soda or diluted milk can slow the spread or be used preventatively.

Harvesting

Cantaloupes are ready to harvest when the rind changes from gray-green to dull yellow. The melon should still be firm, but gentle thumb pressure to the stem will separate a ripe fruit from the plant. If it doesn't separate, wait a few days.

Honeydew can be picked when the skin turns completely white or yellow, depending on the variety. Cut ripe honeydew off the vine with shears; don't pull like you would a cantaloupe.

Watermelon tendrils give a clue to the fruit's harvest time. When the tendril closest to the fruit turns brown, it's ready to be cut from the vine. Also check the underside where the melon was resting on the ground. It will appear yellow (instead of white) when it's ripe. Of course, there's also the "knock test." A ripe watermelon sounds hollow when you give it a good tap.

Melons can be harvested before they're ripe. Just keep them stored at room temperature to ripen. Once ripe, enjoy immediately or keep refrigerated for a few days.

Yellow means "go" when it comes to identifying ripe watermelons.

OKRA

Abelmoschus esculentus,
Hibiscus family

The Down and Dirty

Preferred climate	Warm to hot
Sun	Full
Soil	Well-draining, compost-rich
pH range	6.0–8.0
Sow seeds	Indoors, 4–6 weeks before last possible frost date. Outdoors, recommended. Sow directly after last frost. Germinates reliably in warm soil.
Sowing depth	¾ inch (2 cm)
Days to germination	3–14
Germination temperature	70°F–95°F (21°C-35°C)
Spacing	12 inches (30 cm)
Days to maturity	30–60 after transplanting

Notes from the garden

On the plate, okra is polarizing. I happen to love it, but I realize not everyone is a fan. It's a staple of Southern stews as well as classic Creole and Cajun dishes like gumbo. The seed pods are great roasted, grilled, braised, sautéed, battered and fried, blanched and then served chilled, or even pickled for long-term storage.

In the garden, okra adds tremendous ornamental value to any landscape, even if you don't care for the taste. While the pods are typically green, there are numerous red varieties as well. And the striking flowers make an attractive backdrop in any setting—not surprising, since okra is related to the hibiscus.

Okra loves the heat, but it's a resilient crop that can do well in cooler climates, too, so long as you choose an appropriate variety and give it a little extra attention to create the conditions it craves.

My favorite varieties

- 'Burgundy' An All-America Selections winner, it reaches 3 to 5 feet (90 to 150 cm) tall and produces yellow cream-colored flowers. Its red pods can grow up to 8 inches (20 cm) long—but pick them at 3 inches (8 cm). This variety matures 55 to 60 days after transplanting.
- 'Cajun Delight' A high-yielding variety that was also an All-America Selections winner, it matures early, 50 to 55 days after transplanting. This is a great variety in cooler climates. Green pods are five-sided and spineless.

- 'Candle Fire' Mature just 30 days after transplanting, the pods are smooth, round, and red. This hybrid variety is highly productive and disease-resistant.
- 'Clemson Spineless' This very tall variety is the gold standard for painless picking. An open-pollinated variety, it takes longer to mature than most (60 days from transplanting), so it's better suited for hot climates. The cream-colored flowers are also edible.
- 'Jambalaya' Meaty, five-ridged pods grow on compact plants and are mature 50 days after transplanting. This green hybrid variety thrives in short growing seasons.

Planting
Okra prefers warm to hot conditions, with soil that's at least 70°F (21°C). In cooler regions, raise the soil temperature by laying black plastic over the planting location one month prior to planting.

Okra germinates quickly when direct-sown into warm soil. Direct-sowing increases chances of growing success since there's no disturbance of the roots.

Mid-season care
Okra has low water needs and doesn't like wet feet. Water only during dry spells. Strive for no more than 1 inch (2.5 cm) of total water per week.

Compost or organic matter at planting will be enough for okra to survive, but a light monthly application of fertilizer will increase yield. Fish emulsion, seaweed-based fertilizer, or a balanced 3-4-4 is ideal.

Pests & disease
Aphids may be found on leaf or stem undersides. As they feed, they excrete honeydew, which attracts ants and other insects. Control them by knocking them off with a sharp stream of water.

Armyworms are moth larvae that attack okra seedlings and eat the leaves of mature plants. The green or black and gray caterpillars can be hand-picked, as can their eggs. Bt can be used as a control, but not around butterfly larvae host plants like milkweed and fennel.

Bigger isn't always better. Harvest okra pods when they reach 3 inches (8 cm) in length. Beyond that, the taste begins to diminish and the pods get tough.

Flea beetles also damage leaves by chewing. Hand-picking these critters is difficult, so use floating row cover while the plants are young and still relatively small. That's when flea beetles tend to do the most damage.

Root knot nematodes are tiny worms that parasitize okra, stunting a plant's growth. Galls on the roots of pulled plants are a telltale sign. Your best approach is to practice crop rotation (as described in Chapter 7) for a period of four years. Blossom blight may occur with high temperatures and excessive rainfall. Remove affected blossoms and any softened pods.

Powdery mildew is a fungal disease. A solution of baking soda or diluted milk can slow the spread or be used preventatively. Proper plant spacing is the most effective strategy, as good air circulation between plants stops it from becoming an issue. Fusarium wilt and Verticillium wilt are caused by soilborne fungi. Start with fresh, compost-rich soil (or premium potting mix in containers) as a preventative measure.

Harvesting
For best flavor, most okra varieties should be picked when the pods reach 3 inches (8 cm) long. (They can grow quite fast, doubling in size overnight, so keep an eye on them!) Larger than that, the pods get woody and the taste diminishes. Frequent picking will encourage more production. Cut the stem just above the pod's cap. Store in the refrigerator for no more than 3 days.

ONIONS

Allium cepa,
Amaryllis family

The Down and Dirty

Preferred climate	Most any
Sun	Full
Soil	Loose, well-draining (sandy loam)
pH range	6.0–7.5
Sow seeds	Indoors, under grow lights 2 months before last frost. Outdoors, in spring or fall/winter, depending on climate. Two seeds per inch (2.5 cm) in rows 12–18 inches (30–45 cm) apart.
Sowing depth	¼ inch (6 mm)
Days to germination	4–10
Germination temperature	55°F–75°F (13°C–24°C)
Note	Thin by harvesting young onions, leaving one every 4–6 inches (10–15 cm)
Transplant seedlings	Just before last frost
Spacing	6 inches (15 cm)
Days to maturity	100–175

Notes from the garden

I will admit that every once in a while, I enjoy being a lazy gardener. Don't get me wrong; working with plants is my passion and my therapy, but sometimes it's nice to have a crop that just does its thing with little to no help—or even attention—from me.

Enter the onion. Considering how often we put them to work in our everyday cooking, it's amazing that they require almost no work to grow successfully. And they practically thrive on neglect. You plant them and come back when you're ready to harvest them. Pull a few when they're young as green onions (scallions) and leave the rest to keep growing. The longer you wait, the bigger the bulb until they reach full maturity.

In cool climates, plant onions in the spring. Where it's warmer, plant in fall or winter. Top growth will occur during those initial cool months, with the plant shifting its energy to bulb formation when temperatures warm up. Soon, you'll have a bumper crop of onions that you barely had to work for. We all deserve at least one autopilot plant in the vegetable garden.

Onion sets are the easiest way to grow this crop. They're simply immature bulbs that were started the previous year. Thanks to that head start, they're also the earliest to harvest!

Choosing what to grow

First, you'll want to decide whether you're growing your onions from seeds, transplants, or sets. Onion sets (bunches of immature bulbs that were started the previous year) are the most popular choice for home growers. They're the easiest to plant, the earliest to harvest, and the least prone to disease.

Beyond that, there are different onion types to choose from. Your geographical location will determine which one will perform best for you. Onion bulb growth corresponds directly to the amount of sunlight the plant receives.

- In warm climates, choose a short-day onion, which needs just 10 hours of daylight per day to bulb. Some good varieties include 'Red Grano', 'Red Rock', 'Texas Sweet', 'White Castle', and the super-sweet 'Vidalia'.
- Long-day onions require 14 to 15 hours of daylight to form a bulb. They're best suited in cooler climates, where days of that length begin around the summer solstice. Among the recommended varieties are 'Blush', 'New York Early', 'Rossa di Milano', 'Sweet Spanish', and 'Walla Walla'.
- Day-neutral onions will bulb regardless of the day length, making them ideal for those in-between regions. Day-neutral onions tend to be quite sweet. Look for 'Cabernet', 'Candy', 'Expression', 'Sierra Blanca', and 'Scout'.

If all that seems confusing, buying onion sets from your local garden center eliminates any guesswork. They will have already taken into consideration your region and stocked their shelves with types that will grow well in your climate. If you order seeds or sets online, though, you will have to decide which type you need.

Shall I Tell You About Shallots?

I debated whether to include this mention here or with garlic. The shallot is a cousin of both, with a taste that's a blend of both culinary staples. Like onions, they're most often planted as sets and prefer loose, well-drained, soil in weed-free beds. As they grow, each bulb will become a whole cluster, much like garlic. Harvest shallots after 3 to 4 months, when the tops die back, and let them cure in the sun before using or storing.

Planting

To plant onion sets, poke a hole in the soil and place the small bulb in so that the green leafy part is above the soil and the tiny roots are well covered, but no deeper than 1-inch (2.5 cm). Otherwise, bulb development can be inhibited.

Spacing is a key consideration for onions, especially if you plan to harvest some early at the green onion or scallion phase (see the next sidebar). For full-size onions, leave 4 to 6 inches (10 to 15 cm) between plants. You want them to stand "shoulder-to-shoulder" when fully mature.

Mid-season care

Once you get them in the ground, onions are pretty hands-off. Keep the soil moist (to avoid splitting bulbs) to the tune of 1 inch (2.5 cm) of water per week.

Onions don't require much in the way of fertilizer, either. In fact, any supplement high in nitrogen will result in extra leaf growth above ground—but with smaller bulbs below the surface. Start with fertile, compost-rich soil. In spring, side-dress with a small amount of additional compost or a light application of a balanced low-dose liquid or granular fertilizer.

The tiny roots of onion sets need to be well covered when planting, but don't go deeper than 1 inch (2.5 cm).

I generally plant a lot of onions, knowing that I'll harvest many of them early to use in the kitchen as scallions.

Green Onions: Always a Classic

You know the tune, even if you don't recognize it by name. But gardeners of a certain age (cough, cough) can't say "green onions" without also humming the iconic 1962 R&B instrumental song of the same name by Booker T. & the M.G.'s for the rest of the day.

But green onions, or scallions, deserve to be in heavy rotation in your vegetable garden, too. And all onion varieties can be harvested early as scallions. Pick them when the plants reach 6 to 8 inches (15 to 20 cm) tall, while the stalks are thin and still white at the bottom. It's common for gardeners to plant their onions fairly close together and then thin them at this stage. The ones that get pulled go into the kitchen as scallions while the rest stay in the garden to fully mature.

Scallions need to be enjoyed fresh. They can't be stored like mature onions. They'll last for about a week if you keep their roots in water, or you can chop them up to freeze. And green onions are fully edible, from the crunchy green tip all the way to the mellow white bulb. Can you dig it?

You do want to be on guard against weeds, though. Onions have short, compact root systems, so they don't do well when they have to compete with weeds.

If you see exposed bulb tops peeking out above the soil, it's okay; don't try to cover them with mulch or rebury them in the soil.

Pests & disease

Onions really are a plant-it-and-forget-it crop. They don't even require much monitoring for pests or disease.

Onion maggots will sometimes find their way into your garden beds, where they'll bore up through onion bulbs to feed on the stems. Thrips can also attack foliage in summer, but you'll likely only ever know it by silvery blotches on the green growth. For both, your best defense is to keep the garden well-maintained and clear of weeds and plant debris.

Harvesting

Onions are ready to be harvested when the top foliage turns brown in color and falls over. Pull the bulbs, leaving the tops attached. Keep bulbs dry and allow them to bake in the sun for one week. Once the skin is dry, then remove the top foliage about 1 inch (2.5 cm) from the bulb.

Storage

Store onion bulbs in a cool, dry place. Mesh onion bags are a convenient way to store them. You can find them online. Onions will keep for several months in these conditions.

PARSNIPS

Pastinaca sativa,
Carrot family

The Down and Dirty

Preferred climate	Cool to cold
Sun	Full, but can tolerate light shade
Soil	Well-draining, fertile, well-composted and free of rocks down to 12 inches (30 cm)
pH range	6.0–7.0
Sow seeds	In spring, once soil is workable and 50°F (10°C). For winter harvest, sow in early summer so parsnips experience cold temperatures.
Sowing depth	½ inch (1.3 cm)
Days to germination	14–21, longer in cooler soil
Germination temperature	50°F–70°F (10°C–21°C)
Spacing	Every ½ inch (1.3 cm) in rows 18–24 inches (45–60 cm) apart
Note	Seeds older than 1 year will have a very low germination rate.
Days to maturity	95–150, depending on variety

Notes from the garden

They may look like bland white carrots, but parsnips have a distinct taste all their own. The nutty, earthy flavor of these cold-season root vegetables is made even sweeter after a few kisses of frost in winter, and they're wonderful roasted with herbs or spices or even a drizzle of maple syrup.

Parsnips are a member of the carrot family, so they follow many of the same planting rules (they don't like to be transplanted, for one) and are affected by many of the same pests (see next page).

My favorite varieties

- 'All-American' An heirloom variety, it's mature in 95 days. Taproots are 3 inches (8 cm) across at the top and can reach 12 inches (30 cm) long. This variety can be overwintered in regions where the ground doesn't freeze.
- 'Gladiator' Known for quick germination, this hybrid variety matures in 110 days. Harvest at 7 inches (18 cm) long for best taste.
- 'The Student' This heirloom originated in England and can grow to a whopping 3 feet (90 cm) long, though in most gardens, you'll want to harvest it by the time it hits 15 inches (38 cm) or so. Mature in 95 to 125 days.

- 'Tender and True' An open-pollinated RHS (British Royal Horticultural Society) winner, this variety is intended for fall or winter harvest. It's ready to be harvested in 150 days.
- 'White Spear' Another open-pollinated variety, it's known for vigorous growth and uniform taproots of about 11 inches (28 cm). Mature in 120 days.

Planting
Prepare the soil deeply, as some varieties can reach 36 inches (90 cm) or more underground. The planting area should be free of rocks, twigs, roots, and weeds to allow for easy and straight growth.

Once parsnips reach a couple inches in height, thin them to one per every 4 to 6 inches (10 to 15 cm) to allow them to grow to full-size.

Mid-season care
Parsnips sprout and grow best in soil that is moist but not wet. In quick-draining sandy soils, aim for 2 inches (5 cm) of water per week. Loamy soils will be fine with just 1 inch (2.5 cm) per week.

Once daytime air temperatures reach 70°F (21°C) consistently, apply 2 inches (5 cm) of light mulch (straw is ideal) to protect the crop from heat and retain moisture.

Top foliage that turns stunted and pale is an indicator of nutrient deficiency. Side-dress with a light application of a balanced organic fertilizer. Stay away from fertilizers high in nitrogen, as they'll cause the taproots to split.

Pests & disease
Armyworms are moth larvae that bore into parsnips. Handpick their eggs and caterpillars. *Bt* is an organic control, but installing row cover upon sprouting is a more reliable preventative measure.

Carrot rust flies are less than ¼-inch (6 mm) long as adults, with black bodies and orange heads. They lay eggs on soil near the base of plants. The larvae feed on parsnip roots after hatching. They can overwinter in soil, so practice crop rotation if affected.

Willow-carrot aphids attack parsnip foliage. Pale green or yellow in color, they spread disease.

Those aren't carrots gone bad. They're parsnips! With a distinct flavor all their own, they're one of my favorite cold-season crops to grow.

Knock them off with a sharp stream of water, and keep them at bay with row cover.

Parsnips are affected by various blight pathogens as well as mosaic viruses and root rot fungus. Crop rotation is your best defense. Wait four years before planting anything in the carrot family in the same spot.

Harvesting
Delay harvesting until after a few frosts. Cold temperatures cause the starches to convert to sugars in the taproot, resulting in sweeter taste. If the ground does not freeze in your region, parsnips can be left in the ground all winter and into spring, to be pulled when desired. (But as a biennial, parsnips set seed in their second year. When that happens, they become woody and inedible—so don't wait too long to harvest.)

Check parsnips according to varieties' mature dates. Crowns should be 1 to 2 inches (2.5 to 5 cm) in diameter; check back in a week if needed. Pull one to gauge the size of others planted at the same time.

To harvest, grab the foliage firmly in a bundle and pull up while twisting. Wild parsnips have been known to cause skin rashes, and some people experience irritation when handling. Wear gloves to be on the safe side.

Storage
Enjoy parsnips fresh or store in a refrigerator crisper drawer or root cellar for a few weeks. If storing, cut off all but ½ inch (1.3 cm) of foliage and do not wash parsnips until serving or preparing.

PEAS

Pisum sativum,
Pea family

The Down and Dirty

Preferred climate	Cool to mild
Sun	Full
Soil	Rich, well-drained
pH range	6–7.5
Sow seeds	Climbing-type, 2–3 inches (5–8 cm) apart. Bush-type, in rows 18–24 inches (45–60 cm) apart.
Sowing depth	1–2 inches (2.5–5 cm)
Days to germination	7–14
Germination temperature	45°F–75°F (7°C–24°C)
Note	While peas can be transplanted successfully, it's critical to minimize root disturbance. Direct-sowing is preferred.
Days to maturity	50–70

Notes from the garden

When I was little, the only peas I knew were the frozen kind. I have to admit, I was not a fan. But, how things changed once I started growing my own.

One of the first crops that can be sown outdoors each spring, peas are a harbinger of the growing season. With climbing-type and bush-type peas to choose from, it's easy to fit a few into almost any garden. And as nitrogen-fixing legumes, peas are a snap (get it?) to grow, with few needs and minimal pest or disease issues. In some climates, a second succession crop can be planted in late summer for a fall harvest.

As an adult, I now use fresh peas in soups and stews, or serve them blanched, sautéed, or stir-fried. But honestly, those tender young pods are so sweet that I eat more peas right off the vine than ever make it to my dinner table. They truly are like candy to me. In fact, I'd go so far as to say peas have become my favorite fresh-from-the-garden crop of all. My mom would be delighted.

There are many varieties of peas, each uniquely suited to be enjoyed a different way.

My favorite varieties

- 'Avalanche' You'll get two pods per node (instead of the usual one) with this highly productive snow pea variety. Pods are dark green and very sweet.
- 'Canoe' A shelling pea with 12 or so peas per boat-shaped pod, that takes 70 days to mature.
- 'Royal Snap II' This snap pea grows 3-inch (8 cm) purple pods on short vines. It matures in 58 days.
- 'Sugar Ann' Matures in just 51 days, this snap pea is a bush-type with short 20-inch (50 cm) white flowered vines that can be grown with or without vertical support.
- 'Wando' More heat-tolerant than most peas, this shelling pea grows on vines 2 to 3 feet (60 to 90 cm) tall. Allow 68 days to maturity.

Choosing what to grow

Mind your peas; they're not all created equal! As you decide which varieties to plant in your garden, consider how you plan to enjoy your peas.

Shelling peas are what you find in cans or bagged and frozen. Also known as English peas or garden peas, the outer pods are inedible.

Snow peas have flat, tender pods that are sweet and crunchy. Picked before the peas inside are fully mature, the pods are, in fact, the star of the show. Use them in stir-fry dishes.

Snap peas, also called sugar peas or sugar snap peas, give you the best of both worlds. Both the peas and the pods are equally delicious. Enjoy these right off the vine.

Black-eyed peas are not actually peas at all. They're beans. The same goes for **chickpeas**.

Planting

The heat of summer will not be kind to peas, so plant them as early in the spring as you can. That typically means about a month before your area's average last frost date, or as soon as your ground is thawed and the soil workable.

Stagger planting times to extend the harvest. I like to plant my first row, then follow up two weeks later with a second row, and then add a third and fourth on that same schedule if space allows.

Also, consider planting again in July or August for a second harvest in the fall, but be prepared to employ shade cloth or floating row cover to shield the tender seedlings from late summer heat in their first few weeks. Plan your timing so the plants can fully mature before frost kills the pod-producing flowers.

Give climbing types a vertical structure to cling to: a fence, lattice, chicken wire, cattle panels, or even string configured as an A-frame trellis.

Mid-season care

Peas don't need frequent water, but they do like to be watered deeply. The 1-inch (2.5 cm) per week guideline discussed in Chapter 9 should be your goal. A summer-planted crop, though, may need slightly more while temperatures are still hot.

Peas, like all legumes, produce their own nitrogen, so they don't need supplemental fertilizer. Coating the seeds with an *inoculant* (sold in powder form at your favorite garden supply center) before sowing will enhance the presence of nitrogen-fixing bacteria in the soil.

Pests & disease

If you like low-maintenance crops, just say peas, please. They're naturally resistant to pests and disease. The diseases you may encounter, like Fusarium wilt or mosaic virus, will rarely kill the plant, just stunt its growth.

Powdery mildew is the most common problem, but this fungal disease can generally be prevented by properly spacing plants.

Harvesting

For best flavor, pick peas promptly according to your variety's days to maturity. Shelling peas are ready when the pods have plumped up, but before the peas inside start to bulge. For snow peas, gauge the pod length, but pick before the peas develop fully. Snap peas can be tested when a pod is plump with full peas; if it snaps when bent in half, it's ready.

They're best fresh, of course, but if you refrigerate peas immediately after picking, you'll get up to a week out of them.

Climbing peas need a little support. Give them a vertical structure to cling to, and they'll reward you with fresh-from-the-garden taste.

Timing is everything when harvesting peas. Plump pods are your cue to get picking, but bulging peas inside the pods may mean you've waited too long.

PEPPERS

Capsicum annuum,
Tomato family

The Down and Dirty

Preferred climate	Warm to hot
Sun	Full
Soil	Well-drained, compost-rich
pH range	5.5–7.0
Sow seeds	Indoors, 8–12 weeks before last possible frost
Sowing depth	¼ inch (6 mm)
Days to germination	7–21 days, depending on variety
Germination temperature	70°F–85°F (21°C–29°C)
Note	Use heat mats to improve germination success and grow lights to encourage vigorous plants. Bump up growing seedlings to larger containers and harden off seedlings (See Chapter 6) prior to planting outdoors.
Transplant seedlings	2–3 weeks after last possible frost date, in soil above 60°F (16°C)
Spacing	12–20 inches (30–51 cm) apart, depending on variety. Plants should be close but not quite touching at maturity.
Note	Once planted, seedlings are slow to start but will begin vigorous growth once soil temperature is consistently warm.
Days to maturity	60–90 for most; up to 150 for some hotter types

Notes from the garden

Whether you like them seriously sweet, slightly spicy, or simply sweat-inducing, peppers are one of the most rewarding plants the home gardener can grow. Most are incredibly productive, churning out a bounty of gorgeous ornamental fruit in all shapes, sizes, and colors.

But for seed starters (myself included), peppers can be a little frustrating from the get-go. They take their sweet time to get growing, and it seems like an eternity before you get the tangible results you wanted. But what they lack in starting power, they make up for in going the distance once they're bathed in sunshine and warmed by the soil for a few weeks.

Peppers can present a challenge if you want to grow them from seed. They tend to take their sweet time. You can't rush Mother Nature.

Bell peppers change colors, and flavor, the longer they grow.

Peppers are relatively undemanding and will keep producing all season long, right up until, and sometimes beyond, the first frost of autumn. What you don't eat right away can be dried, pickled, or used to make big batches of everything from salsas to hot sauces.

My favorite varieties

- **Banana** This bright yellow chile pepper is curved like a banana, but just 2 to 3 inches (5 to 8 cm) long. Also called the yellow wax pepper, it's very mild and becomes sweeter as it matures.
- **Bell** The classic bell pepper has varying levels of sweetness and can be enjoyed cooked or fresh out of the garden. Some varieties start out green and bitter, gradually turning red as they mature and reach their full flavor. Others mature to orange, yellow, purple, even pink or white.

- **Habanero** Toward the hotter end of the spectrum for homegrown peppers, this chile pepper is used in hot sauces and salsas. Usually bright orange to red when ripe, mature fruit is 1 to 2 inches (2.5 to 5 cm) long and packs a wicked punch of up to 350,000 Scoville units. Milder "heat-less" varieties are available, too.
- **Jalapeno** The typical starter pepper for hot varieties, the popular jalapeno is usually picked while green, but will turn red or even black if left on the plant long enough. Older fruit will also feature "corking," white scars on the skin that indicate increased heat. Plants grow 14 to 18 inches (36 to 45 cm) tall with fruit that's 3 inches (8 cm) long.
- **Poblano** Mild at just 1,000 to 1,500 Scoville units, the large poblano pepper is popularly enjoyed stuffed in Mexican cuisine. When dried, the poblano is called the ancho chile and is often used in mole sauce.

If you like it hot, try growing your own habanero peppers to use in salsas or sauces.

Poblano peppers are a staple of Mexican cuisine and a lot of fun to grow at home.

Choosing what to grow

Most gardeners pick their peppers based on the heat of the fruit and how the peppers will be used in the kitchen. A pepper's heat is measured on the Scoville scale, which determines the concentration of capsaicinoids, the component that registers to human taste buds as "spicy." Named after Wilbur Scoville, the pharmacist who created the scale, the Scoville scale assigns a number to peppers— a higher number indicates a hotter pepper. Bell peppers are more sweet than hot. They measure 0 to 100 Scoville heat units. Jalapeno peppers range from 2,500 to 8,000 on the scale. Cayenne pepper can be between 25,000 and 50,000 Scovilles, habanero and scotch bonnet peppers can go from 100,000 to 750,000, and peppers like the 'Carolina Reaper' can top out at over 3,000,000 Scoville heat units!

Planting

Peppers like it sunny and hot, so don't jump the gun and plant them too soon. They're heavy feeders, so amend the soil well with plenty of compost and a light application of a balanced liquid or granular fertilizer. But don't go overboard. Excess nitrogen will actually decrease your fruit production.

Pepper plants can collapse under the weight of their plentiful fruit if not supported. Stake plants or install tomato cages early in the growing season.

Mid-season care

Aim for 1 inch (2.5 cm) of water per week, although peppers may want up to 2 inches (5 cm) per week during the hottest part of summer. Be sure the plants do not sit in water. Peppers don't like wet feet.

Any fertilizer used on peppers should have more phosphorus than nitrogen—for example, an organic tomato fertilizer with an N-P-K of 3-5-3. (Chapter 5 has more on N-P-K numbers.) Too much nitrogen will lead to heavy stem and leaf growth, but will cut down on the production of peppers.

Pests & disease

Peppers tend to be less susceptible to pests and disease than many other vegetable plants, but watch out for fruitworms and armyworms. These moth larvae bore into the fruits on pepper plants. Hand-pick any eggs or caterpillars (green or black and gray). Use Bt as an organic control (but not around butterfly larvae host plants like milkweed or fennel).

I treat my peppers like tomatoes as they grow. Cages help support the weight of the fruit as it gets larger and heavier.

As for disease, anthracnose is a common fungus of peppers that will often appear when conditions are warm and wet. Brown circular lesions appear on the leaves and stems. On fruit, the lesions appear sunken and water-soaked, often exhibiting a salmon-colored center.

Phytophthora blight is caused by a soilborne fungus. Your plants may suddenly wilt and die just as they reach the fruiting stage. Stem lesions may be seen at the soil line or above. Rotate crops to keep peppers, tomatoes, and eggplant out of affected beds for four years. Good drainage can be key to thwarting this disease. Plant on a raised ridge or mounded soil to lessen the chances of being affected.

Pepper mild mottle virus is transmitted by aphids and will show up as faded or yellow leaves on pepper plants. The plant's growth will be stunted, and the fruit will appear lumpy. It's a seed disease; your only recourse is to dispose of affected plants (off-site) and practice crop rotation (with seeds from a trusted source) in the next season.

Bacterial spot is a common foliar disease. Warm, wet weather is prime time for this disease to show up. All above-ground parts of the plant are susceptible. Fruit can rapidly decay. Unfortunately, bacterial spot is difficult to control in home gardens. Remove and dispose of infected plants and look for resistant varieties.

Harvesting

All peppers start out green, but most mature to a different color. Keep notes to remind you of the ideal color for each variety of pepper planted.

When harvesting, use a sharp knife or pruning shears instead of twisting or yanking fruit. Cut just above where the stem meets the fruit.

Unwashed peppers will store for a week or two when refrigerated. For long-term storage, pickle peppers or dry them in an oven or dehydrator.

If you grow peppers long enough, you're bound to run into a bout of anthracnose, a fungus that develops in warm and wet conditions.

POTATOES

Solanum tuberosum,
Tomato family

The Down and Dirty

Preferred climate	Cool
Sun	Full
Soil	Fertile, very well-draining
pH range	5.5–6.5
Sow seed potatoes	Outdoors, when soil temperature is at least 50°F (10°C) or about 3 weeks before last frost.
Sowing depth	3–4 inches (8–10 cm). For faster emergence, plant shallow at 1 inch (2.5 cm) deep in cold climates, 4 inches (10 cm) deep in warmer climates.
Days to germination	Depends on planting depth and soil temperature, as well as if tubers were greensprouted (or chitted) first (see sidebar)
Germination temperature	50°F (10°C) at 4 inches (10 cm) deep
Note	Indoor sowing not recommended
Spacing	12 inches (30 cm) in all directions
Days to maturity	Short-season varieties, 70–90; mid-season, 90–110; mid-to-late, 110–120; late varieties, 110–130

Notes from the garden

If you ask me, one of the greatest joys in life is eating fresh, homegrown potatoes. Light and creamy with a sweet earthiness, roasted in the oven with lots of garlic and olive oil—that's a taste of heaven right there! I'm referring to what most people think of as "new potatoes." They're the smaller, golf ball-sized or fingerling style, immature potatoes, as opposed to larger russet or Idaho baking potato. "New" potatoes are just a marketing term. In the farming trade, *new potatoes* refer to young potatoes in the ground, where the top growth is still green above ground. In the grocery store, "new" potatoes are really just small potatoes.

Surprisingly, potatoes are remarkably easy to grow and very undemanding. If you can provide soil that's very well-draining, nutrient-rich and consistently moist, you'll have a bounty of delicious potatoes in about 100 days.

If you're new to growing potatoes, you may experience a little distress if a cold snap comes after the top growth is up and looking spectacular. Don't worry. Frost can kill back some (or even all) of the foliage, but that doesn't mean the end of your potatoes. It takes a prolonged exposure of 28°F (-2°C) or lower for a serious setback to occur. More than likely, you'll see new growth begin to emerge within a few days.

I plant a variety of short-, mid-, and late-maturing varieties for a succession of the freshest potatoes possible.

My favorite varieties

- 'All-Blue' With its blue skin and flesh, this heirloom variety offers a stunning presentation and rewarding taste. A great addition to a red, white, and blue potato salad.
- 'Charlotte' Moderately sized, golden-fleshed tuber, it's a top performer for container growing and reliable harvest. Delicious and stores well.
- 'Reddale' An attractive red potato with moist flesh and high disease resistance to Verticillium wilt.
- 'Russian Banana' First grown by Russian settlers, this late-season, heirloom, fingerling gourmet variety offers exceptional taste from finger-sized golden tubers.

Choosing what to grow

Look for *certified* seed potatoes. Potatoes can be infected by a variety of diseases. Certified seed potatoes are produced from disease-free stock.

Greensprouting: Proper Planting Prep is No Small Potatoes

What we call "seed potatoes" are just small, young potatoes used for planting. *Greensprouting* (also known as "chitting") is necessary before planting to ensure seed potatoes have gone through the necessary dormancy period before replanting. Chitting is an optional technique to warm up the tuber to get it ready for planting.

About a month before your expected planting date, warm the seed potato up to about 75°F (24°C) and keep it dark, if possible. It takes about 7 to 10 days to break dormancy. At that point, drop the temperature to about 55°F (13°C) and turn on any kind of light. The light source will green up the tuber and stimulate the sprouts while inhibiting elongation. Don't allow the sprouts to become elongated, though, as that will reduce sprout vigor. Light makes the sprouts tough and stout so they won't be as likely to get rubbed off during planting.

Potato top growth can take a nasty-looking hit when the temperatures drop. It's okay; the potatoes underground are probably fine.

Many home gardeners have never considered growing their own potatoes. They're missing out, because a "new potato" fresh from the garden is almost as perfect as it gets.

Mound soil up around the growing plants to keep light away from the tubers which makes them turn green. Eating green potatoes can make you sick.

If you plan on planting seed potatoes within 7 to 14 days of arrival, warm them up to 75°F (24°C) to break dormancy. If it's 3 to 4 weeks before planting, keep them cool until a week before planting, then bring them out and warm them up to get them to start sprouting.

The best seed potatoes are young, juvenile potatoes. That youthful vigor produces the best tubers. You can cut a seed piece into separate pieces. If you've got a tuber the size of a large hen's egg (2.5 ounces or so), cut it in half.

Planting
In cool climates, direct-sow seed potatoes around the time that daffodils are blooming (early to mid-spring). In moderate climates, plant in late winter. In warm climates, plant in fall. Another guideline for knowing a good time to plant potatoes is to do so about two weeks after it's time to plant peas in your area.

Warm seed potatoes to 75°F (24°C) a day or two before planting. Start with whole tubers, or those weighing at least 1½ ounces (43 g). You can cut larger tubers into blocky pieces containing at least two eyes. Ideally, greensprout (chit) them first.

Mid-season care
Keep soil consistently moist throughout the growing period, especially as flowers are coming on. This is a sign that tubers are actively forming.

Also, maintain consistent fertility with a balanced fertilizer source. Potatoes benefit from all three of the primary nutrients (N, P, K). But keep nitrogen levels lower—so as not to induce excessive top growth at the expense of tuber development. Keep sunlight off developing tubers. In the presence of light, tubers will develop chlorophyll, a concentration of solanine which is somewhat toxic. Potatoes like it dark and cool. The preferred soil temperature once potatoes are growing is 60°F to 65°F (16°C to 18°C).

Hilling helps keep light off of tubers and provides a place for new tubers to form from growing points along the expanding stem with some varieties. Pull soil up against the plant as it grows or add straw mulch around the plants. Hill once plants grow 4 to 6 inches (10 to 15 cm) above the surface, then continue to do so two or three times during the season, while leaving about 6 inches

An ideal seed potato for planting is about the size of a hen's egg with two emerging buds (eyes).

(15 cm) of top growth above the soil or mulch. Crop rotation is key with potatoes. Don't plant potatoes in the same location following seasons where plants in the same family (tomatoes, peppers, eggplants) have been grown.

Pests & disease
Colorado potato beetle is the most common threat. Picking by hand is an effective and safe control.

Tomato leaf hoppers are also widespread. They are more likely to be found as temperatures warm. Potato late blight can hit a potato crop especially hard. (The Irish Potato Famine of the 1840s was a result of this blight.)

Harvesting
Harvest any time potatoes reach the size of marbles, but they're ideal once they are ping pong ball-sized or larger. If eating immediately or within a few days, harvest when the tops are still green. Be aware that flowering is not always a given. But if your potato plants do bloom, that's a sure sign your potato tubers are at a good size for harvesting. You can leave the potatoes in the ground once top growth dies back—in mild climates for 4 to 6 weeks. In cold climates, harvest sooner rather than later. Top growth dieback occurs about 6 weeks after flowering.

You can gently reach into the hill and pull potatoes out, replacing the soil. The remaining tubers will continue to grow. This results in a higher and longer yield.

When harvesting, brush soil off but don't wash. Allow potatoes to cure out of the sun for about two weeks in humid conditions around 55°F (13°C).

Storage
The ideal storage temperature is 38°F (4°C), in darkness and high humidity. Tubers will last for up to 10 months in the right environment.

Piling up straw mulch hills around potato plants will keep light away from the tubers and cool the soil, maintaining a perfect growing environment.

Brush off soil from newly harvested potatoes, but don't wash them with water. Before storing, potatoes need to cure in cool, humid conditions for about two weeks first.

PUMPKINS

Cucurbita pepo,
Cucumber family

The Down and Dirty

Preferred climate	Warm, with at least 3 months of uninterrupted frost-free growing time
Sun	Full
Soil	Fertile, well-draining soil, kept evenly moist around the base of the plant throughout the growing season, especially during flowering and fruit set.
pH range	5.8–6.8
Sow seeds	Indoors, not recommended, 3–4 weeks before transplanting into warm soil. Outdoors, direct-sow once risk of frost has passed and soil temperature has warmed to at least 70°F (21°C).
Sowing depth	½–1 inch (1.3–2.5 cm)
Days to germination	5–10
Germination temperature	70°F–90°F (21°C–32°C)
Transplant seedlings	Allow several days for hardening off tender seedlings before planting into warm soil which is at least 70°F (21°C).
Spacing	Varies greatly, depending on pumpkin size and vine length.
Note	Vining pumpkins need at least 50–100 square feet (4.6–9.3 m²) to grow unencumbered. Small pumpkins need about 24 inches (60 cm) between plants, medium pumpkins need 36 inches (90 cm), and large pumpkins need 4–6 feet (1.2–1.8 m) between plants. Row spacing depends on growth habit or vine length. Bush varieties need 4–5 feet (1.2–1.5 m) between rows, short vine types need 6 feet (1.8 m) between, and long vine varieties need about 12 feet (3.6 m) between rows.
Days to maturity	90–120 days

Notes from the garden

Pumpkins are a fun crop to grow if you have the space and time. And fortunately, there are more options than ever for space-challenged gardeners, opening up the possibilities for many more wannabe pumpkin growers.

Even so, pumpkin vines still need room to spread out, and I've never wanted to dedicate a chunk of prime growing space to something that is, for me, a novelty crop. But pumpkins don't have to grow in your prime garden space. I know lots of gardeners who have an open sunny spot with

Pumpkins are fun to grow, provided you have a lot of space to do so.

Old-fashioned wisdom says to plant pumpkins on hills of mounded soil. It won't hurt, but it's probably not necessary if the soil is already warm and drains well.

average soil outside their main garden where they grow their pumpkins each year. Kind of like the proverbial "back-40" or an out-of-the-way space behind a shed. Another option is to plant your seeds or seedlings in grow bags and let the vines run where they may.

Choosing what to grow

Pumpkins are space hogs. The variety you grow may be decided by growth habit; there are varieties that are bush-like, short-vining, and long-vining.

My favorite varieties

- 'Atlantic Giant' One of the largest pumpkins in the world, this long-vined variety typically grows 50 to 100-pound (23 to 45 kg) fruit—and much larger when vines are limited to only one fruit.
- 'Jack Straw' A good variety for front porch Halloween displays. A smooth-faced jack o' lantern classic with dark orange skin.
- 'New England Pie' The classic pumpkin for pies, its average weight is 4 to 6 pounds (1.8 to 2.7 kg) in a dark orange skin.
- 'Polar Bear' An extra-large white pumpkin, weighing in between 30 to 65 pounds (14 to 30 kg).

Planting

Gardeners are often encouraged to plant pumpkins on hills of mounded-up soil. This common advice holds that a raised berm will help the pumpkins get off to a faster start, in soil that's warmer and drains better. If you're looking for

every advantage possible when getting your pumpkins started quickly, you've got nothing to lose by planting in hills. But if you have well-draining soil to begin with and the soil is warm already, skip the mounds. Your pumpkins will still have a normal start with germination and early growth.

Another common recommendation to warm the soil is to use black plastic over your bed and have it in place several days or more before planting to capture the heat. Then just cut into the plastic when you're ready to plant your seeds or seedlings. Personally, I'm not a fan of using plastic any more than I have to. And I don't need it where I'm growing. My soil warms quickly in spring, so I have plenty of time to grow even large pumpkins before the first frost.

If you do feel the need to jumpstart your soil warmth with plastic, please consider a compromise. Warmer soil only helps where the roots are—you don't need to cover your entire bed with plastic. The aboveground vines don't care, and we can all do with less plastic in our gardening lives.

Mid-season care

As vines grow, stay vigilant monitoring for pests and diseases. Pumpkins are attractive to both pests and diseases so catching potential problems early goes a long way to healthier plants and a bountiful crop.

Try pinching or cutting the tips of pumpkin vines once they've spread a few feet out from the base of the plant. You'll force new branches...and more pumpkins.

If you're after larger pumpkins, albeit fewer in total, consider removing some of the developing fruit per vine to allow energy to be concentrated on the remaining one or two.

If you want more vines and therefore more fruiting opportunity, you can cut or pinch the tips of developing vines once they've grown a couple of feet out from the base. This will cause new branches to develop from each cut.

Pests & disease

Pests that favor pumpkins include squash bugs, squash beetles, squash vine borers, and cucumber beetles. The same pests go after all cucurbit crops. Barrier protection at the time of transplant or direct seeding is effective at preventing many pests of this family. Remember, though, cucurbit crops are pollinator dependent. If you're using row cover, remove it during flowering to allow pollinators access to the flowers. Alternatively, if you prefer to leave covers in place for the maximum time, you can hand-pollinate flowers.

Common diseases include bacterial wilt, Phytophthora, downy mildew, and powdery mildew. Providing good soil drainage, lots of air circulation, and rotating crops from season to season will lessen disease risks.

Harvesting

There are several clues to know when it's time to harvest pumpkins. First, check the maturity date on the seed pack (but this is always just a guideline). Next, check the color. When pumpkins are ripe, the color will be fully developed. The skin will be hard and difficult to puncture with your thumbnail. The stems will begin to shrivel and dry out.

Cut the stem from the vine, being careful to leave at least 1-inch (2.5 cm) or more of stem remaining on the fruit. The stem helps prolong storage of the fruit, so you need it to remain intact. And don't use the stem as a handle! It can easily break off, leaving you with a pumpkin that won't last very long as a result.

Cure the harvested fruit in full sun for 7 to 10 days. If frost is expected, cover the fruit or move it indoors. You can also cure pumpkins inside, but you'll need a warm environment of 80°F to 85°F (27°C to 29°C). There's no better option than sunlight, though, to help toughen up your fruit for long-term storage.

Leave at least 1 inch (2.5 cm) of stem intact when you harvest pumpkins from the vine. It helps prolong the storage life of the fruit!

RADISHES

Raphanus sativus,
Cabbage family

The Down and Dirty

Preferred climate	**Cool to warm**
Sun	**Full**
Soil	**Light, well-drained**
pH range	**6.0–7.0**
Sow seeds	**Direct sow 3–6 weeks before last frost for spring harvest; 4–6 weeks before first frost for fall**
Sowing depth	**½–1 inch (1.3-2.5 cm)**
Days to germination	**3–6**
Germination temperature	**65°F–85°F (18°C–29°C)**
Note	**For continuous harvest, sow new rows weekly until air temperature reaches 65°F (18°C) in spring.**
Spacing	**12 inches (30 cm) between rows, thin seedlings to 5 inches (12 cm) apart**
Note	**Radishes do not transplant well, so start from seed. Also, because they grow so quickly, there is no advantage to starting them indoors.**
Days to maturity	**21–60, depending on variety**

Notes from the garden

I feel like I should take a moment to apologize to the radish. It's been mentioned a lot in this book, but usually in conjunction with the less-than-flattering phrase "trap crop." True, radishes are often grown for the express and specific purpose of attracting certain garden pests to devour *them* instead of some nearby crop that's ostensibly much more desirable to the gardener.

But radishes rock in their own right, and they shouldn't be relegated to a merely sacrificial role in the garden. Sure, their peppery bite can be intense on the tongue, but radishes can also be sweet. Even the young, tender greens are a treat. And visually, radishes make any dish pop with gorgeous color (not always red and white, either). In the garden, radishes are easy to grow and quick to mature. I love to use them in succession planting, filling in small empty spaces among other slower growing crops in both spring and fall.

Choosing what to grow

Radishes are classically red in color, but aficionados seek out some of the more unique varieties for added visual interest and different flavor profiles in the kitchen. You can also find radishes in various shades of black, purple, and even green.

My favorite varieties

- 'Bacchus' A hybrid with deep purple coloring, this small globe-shaped variety is mature in just 24 days.
- 'French Breakfast' Red with a white tip, this open-pollinated variety reaches 3 to 4 inches (8 to 10 cm) long and close to 1 inch (2.5 cm) wide. Matures in 21 days.
- 'Miyashige' This Japanese daikon radish resembles a large white carrot, 16 to 18 inches (41 to 45 cm) long and 3 inches (8 cm) wide. Matures in 50 days and is intended for fall harvest.
- 'Nero Tondo' An open-pollinated Spanish variety, it's resistant to bolting. Black on the outside with a white interior, 2-to-4-inch (5 to 10 cm) globe-shaped radishes are mature in 50 days.
- 'Starburst' Light purple inside with pink streaks, this hybrid watermelon radish is mature in 60 days.

Planting

Amend heavy clay soil with compost to a depth of 6 inches (15 cm) to allow for deep radish taproots.

Use your finger (or a stick or pencil) to create a row of holes ½ to 1 inch (1.3 to 2.5 cm) deep. Place one seed in each hole and backfill gently. Consider using a floating row cover immediately after planting to protect radishes from pests.

Mid-season care

Once they emerge, thin radish seedlings to approximately 5 inches (13 cm) apart.

Radishes like rather consistent moisture to avoid becoming tough and unpalatable. Aim for 1 inch (2.5 cm) of water per week. If the soil is sandy and especially fast to drain, more water may be needed.

Supplemental fertilizer shouldn't be necessary if soil is well-composted. In fact, too much nitrogen from fertilizer can result in a smaller edible taproot.

Radishes make their presence known in any dish by adding a spicy crunch and a pop of striking color.

Pests & disease

Both larval and adult flea beetles can damage radish plants, but both can be knocked back with insecticidal soap. Also know that your radish crop will often be just fine even with a flea beetle population. The plants frequently outgrow beetle damage and still produce tasty radishes underground.

Radish root maggots are the larvae of tiny flies. Affected plants will show stunted growth and wilt. Floating row cover is a preventative measure.

Alternaria, white rust, root rot, and radish mosaic virus are diseases to watch out for. If you obtain seed from a reliable source, practice good garden sanitation, sanitize tools to avoid cross-contamination from other parts of the garden, discard diseased plant material, and rotate your crops, you'll minimize your risk.

Harvesting

Keep track of varieties planted and their locations, since some reach full maturity long before others. Radishes should be harvested promptly upon maturation. If left in the ground too long, radishes will bolt in excessive heat.

To harvest, grab the foliage at the base and pull straight up while twisting. Cut off green tops and the thin bottom part of the root. Unwashed radishes can be placed inside a damp paper towel in a zip-top bag, then refrigerated for up to a week.

SPINACH

Spinacia oleracea,
Amaranth family

The Down and Dirty

Preferred climate	Cool
Sun	Full sun to partial shade
Soil	Well-amended and organically-rich
pH range	6.5–7.0
Sow seeds	Indoors, 6 weeks before last expected frost date. Outdoors, as soon as soil is workable in spring. For an autumn crop, direct sow in late summer or early fall.
Sowing depth	½ inch (1.3 cm)
Days to germination	7–14 days
Germination temperature	60°F–68°F (16°C–20°C)
Transplant seedlings	4 weeks before last frost date. For a cool-season harvest, transplant in early fall.
Spacing	Follow packet directions according to variety
Note	If you plant to eat the baby spinach leaves as you thin the crop, plant denser than packet directions
Days to maturity	24–50

Notes from the garden

Gardeners of a certain age (like me) first encountered spinach while watching Saturday morning cartoons. Seeing Popeye save the day after downing a can or two of it was certainly intriguing, but actually tasting the canned stuff for myself was enough for me to nearly swear off spinach for life.

Thankfully, I tried it again once I got older. This time, though, I tasted fresh spinach straight from the garden. The sailor man had no idea what he was missing.

Spinach is a very easy-to-grow, low-maintenance, cool-season favorite that's always one of my first crops of spring. But because it's so undemanding and very cold-tolerant, I love planting it in the fall, too. Whether raw in salads, tossed in a smoothie for an added blast of vitamins and minerals, or sautéed for a fast side dish, you'll love growing your own spinach, too.

Choosing what to grow

There are two main types of spinach: savoy and smooth-leafed.

- **Savoy** spinach is characterized by its wavy or puckered leaves, dark green in color. Some savoy varieties are remarkably cold-tolerant, but they're also adapted to withstand high heat.
- **Smooth-leafed** spinach is also called flat-leaf spinach. This is the kind you typically see in salads. It can be harvested as baby greens for sweeter, more tender leaves.

My favorite varieties

- 'Auroch' Ready for harvest in just 24 days, this smooth-leafed spinach does best in fall, winter, and early spring. It's also highly resistant to downy mildew.
- 'Bloomsdale' A classic savoy spinach, it's known for sweet and garden-fresh flavor. Ready in 50 days. More heat-tolerant than others. Best when planted in early spring for late spring or early summer harvest.
- 'Gazelle' Smooth-leafed variety perfect for baby leaf harvest with bunches of uniform leaves. Can be harvested in 26 days.
- 'Matador' Dark green, smooth, oval-shaped leaves have a sweet flavor when mature. As baby greens, they're wonderful in salads or cooked dishes like risotto. Grows especially well when sown for fall harvest.
- 'Space' Slightly savoyed spinach with medium green leaves. Mature in 25 days. Versatile enough to be grown in any season.

Smooth-leafed spinach is a favorite for salads and can be harvested as baby greens for an even sweeter flavor.

Making a Case for Malabar

Despite the name, a similar taste, and a strong resemblance in the leaves, Malabar spinach isn't spinach at all. It's a member of a different plant family altogether—*Basellaceae*—and thrives in nearly tropical conditions. If you can provide it a hot and humid home in full sun and with constant moisture, Malabar spinach may be a way to add fresh greens to your mid-summer menu.

Malabar spinach is a vining plant, so the home gardener should employ a trellis to keep it under control. But be careful. Malabar spinach self-seeds easily and can even become invasive if left to its own devices.

Warm and rainy conditions are best to curtail blossoming, which turns the leaves bitter. Like true spinach, cut leaves for use when you have enough to use, but it can take much longer to mature than the spinach varieties listed here.

Cooked Malabar spinach doesn't wilt as quickly as real spinach, making it preferable in some soups, stews, and stir-fries. The taste, however, is much like traditional spinach. When eaten raw or used in salads, Malabar spinach brings notes of lemon and pepper, offering a unique taste that may be worth exploring for the gardener looking to try something different.

Planting

Soil that's rich with organic matter or compost should be enough to keep spinach happy, but an organic nitrogen-based fertilizer like alfalfa, soybean meal, or blood meal can boost results.

Plant a new crop every 10 days for a steady harvest that will last several weeks. Sow each crop directly, or stagger planting of both seeds and seedlings. You can continue these succession plantings until it's time for your summer crops and then start all over again in late summer for a fall harvest and beyond.

About starting spinach seeds, I consider myself a very experienced indoor seed starter. Over the years, though, I've had mixed success with spinach seeds. But "priming" seeds—soaking them in room-temperature water overnight to 24 hours and then air-drying them on a paper towel 1 to 2 days—has greatly improved my success rate in both germination time and consistency. Just be sure to plant within 7 days. And even then, be prepared for very hit-or-miss results. On the flip side, direct-sowing outdoors has never given me any issues. Seeds consistently sprout after direct-sowing within a few days.

Mid-season care

Spinach likes a lot of water so aim for 1½ inches (4 cm) weekly. Water under the foliage, at ground level, to avoid wetting the leaves. A drip irrigation (as laid out in Chapter 9) is especially ideal for spinach to keep watering slow and consistent.

Pests & disease

Proactively check for slugs. Pick them off by hand, use a pet-safe iron phosphate bait, or try placing a bowl of beer nearby at soil level to lure them away from your plants.

Adequate spacing of plants allows for good airflow and helps prevent mildew. If it becomes a problem, choose a more resistant variety.

Harvesting

True to its undemanding nature, spinach can be harvested pretty much whenever you want. It's a cut-and-come-again plant, so snip individual leaves as soon as they're big enough to use. New leaves will resprout to replace them. Or cut the entire plant an inch above the soil line—you'll get another crop of leaves in no time!

Bolted spinach is easily identified by the flower stalk sent up when temperatures get too hot. At this point, the spinach will be bitter tasting. Pull the plant out and add it to the compost pile.

Starting spinach from seed can be tricky, but I've always had great results direct-sowing outdoors.

Cut out just the spinach leaves you're ready to enjoy, and new leaves will resprout to replace them.

STRAWBERRIES

Fragaria × ananassa,
Rose family

The Down and Dirty

Preferred climate	Cool
Sun	Full
Soil	Well-draining and generously amended
pH range	5.5–6.5
Transplant seedlings	With roots spread out and the crown of the plant level with the soil surface
Spacing	See various methods below to account for varieties with runners
Note	Excellent as container plant

Notes from the garden
Okay, this one's not a vegetable. But strawberries are such a treat to eat and such a joy to grow that I couldn't leave them out of this book, just like I can't leave them out of my vegetable garden.

Choosing what to grow
There are two primary types of strawberries: June-bearing and ever-bearing.

June-bearing strawberry plants put out one crop per year, in—you guessed it—June. But the first crop won't come until the year *after* the crop is planted. Pick off any fruit that emerges in the first year to allow more energy to build a stronger plant. By the following late spring or early summer, you'll have a bounty of ripe strawberries in a relatively short window of time.

Ever-bearing strawberry plants are also called *day-neutral*. They put on a main crop the first season starting in early summer and will follow that up with a lighter second crop in late summer to early fall.

My favorite varieties
- 'Earliglow' Great flavor, disease-resistant, and it can be grown in most regions. It's a June-bearing variety, so you'll get one plentiful crop per year.
- 'Tristar' All the same attributes as 'Earliglow', but in an ever-bearing variety. You'll get two crops per year.

Planting
Choose your location carefully, as many varieties tend to ignore nice, neat boundaries. Depending on the strawberry type, use one of three in-bed spacing methods.

Varieties with runners do well in a *matted row system*. Leave 18 to 24 inches (45 to 60 cm) between plants and 4 feet (1.2 m) between rows. Don't worry, the runners will fill in those gaps. In a *hill system*, plants are spaced in double rows 12 inches (30 cm) apart in all directions. For more than one double row, allow 4 feet (1.2 m) to the next set of rows. Runners can be removed to prevent overcrowding, but this method is best with strawberry plants that send out few to no runners.

The *spaced plant system* is a sort of hybrid technique. Set plants 2 feet (60 cm) apart within rows, but with 3 feet (90 cm) between the rows. As the plants grow, remove all but four runners per plant. Those remaining will fill in the space.

Also remember that strawberries are quite happy in pots, which minimizes the sprawl in your garden.

However you start your strawberry plants, use a good layer of mulch throughout the space. In addition to the usual benefits provided by mulch (as detailed further in Chapter 8), a soft cushioning layer will help protect the tender berries.

Mid-season care
Strawberries should not be fertilized in spring, as an early season shot of nitrogen can result in soft fruit. Instead, fertilize after the harvest to give the next crop a boost.

Strawberry plants produce smaller yields as they age. Eventually, they'll stop fruiting altogether, no matter how much care you give them. Don't be afraid to start over with new plants (or vigorous runners) if yours are no longer producing well after a few seasons.

Pests & disease
Birds will likely be your biggest pest challenge. Bird netting is effective, but I'm not a fan. I've just seen too many sad stories of birds getting caught and tangled up in the netting, so I never use it. Instead, try rolls of tulle, the material used to make bridal veils. It works the same, but it won't trap birds. "Garden mesh netting" is also ultra-fine and a stronger material than tulle. Both will let in plenty of light, air, and water while humanely protecting your crop from too much strawberry snacking.

Snails and slugs can be a problem, too, but hand-picking them is generally perfectly effective. For overwhelming populations, look for a product that uses iron phosphate as its active ingredient. It's organic and pet safe.

Leaf spot diseases are likely the worst thing you'll have to deal with when growing strawberries. Keep them under control by cutting and removing infected foliage in mid-summer. Keep leaves and fruit dry by not watering overhead.

Harvesting
Strawberries often look ripe before they truly are. Give one a gentle tug. If it doesn't separate from the plant easily, wait another day or two. If you plan to use them in the kitchen later, don't wash them until just before. They'll stay fresh longer.

Most gardeners want to protect their strawberry crop from feathered flying raiders, but the netting you typically find in stores can be dangerous to our bird friends.

SUMMER SQUASH

Cucurbita pepo,
Cucumber family

The Down and Dirty

Preferred climate	Warm
Sun	Full
Soil	Generously amended with compost and shredded leaves
pH range	6.0–6.5
Sow seeds	Indoors, 3–4 weeks before last frost. Outdoors, recommended, once soil temperature reaches 70°F (21°C)
Sowing depth	1 inch (2.5 cm), two seeds per pot
Days to germination	5–10
Germination temperature	70°F–95°F (21°C–35°C)
Note	Thin to one seedling per pot
Transplant seedlings	Once soil temperature reaches 70°F (21°C)
Spacing	30 inches (76 cm) between plants
Note	Plants are very productive. You won't need many.
Days to maturity	50–65

Notes from the garden

The winter squash later in these grow guides requires patience to enjoy. Summer squash is all about immediate return on your investment. They're easy to grow, quick to mature, and are meant to be eaten right away. Roasted, sautéed, baked, or grilled, summer squash (of all varieties) is a staple on my table throughout the season, since the plants are so prolific.

And as anyone who's attempted to grow "just a little" zucchini can attest, you'll likely be looking for new and creative ways to use your considerable bounty by season's end.

My favorite varieties

There are four main types of summer squash to pick from, and I have several favorite varieties of each type.

- **Zucchini** (also called courgette) is the most well-known, usually green but sometimes yellow in color. 'Cavili' is highly productive with lime green fruit. It's parthenocarpic (does not require pollinators). 'Cocozelle' is an Italian

The different varieties of pattypan squash provide a visual feast of colors, sizes, and shapes unlike anything else in your vegetable garden.

UFOs (Unusual Fruiting Objects) in the Garden

One of the fun aspects of summer squash is the wide range, in both shape and size, of the fruit produced. But a few varieties practically defy classification with uniquely structured fruit that's unlike anything else in the garden. 'Eight Ball' is dark green, 'Cue Ball' is light green, 'One Ball' is bright yellow, and 'Lucky 8' is light green and mottled. Admittedly, the folks in charge of naming kind of phoned it in that day (or maybe they had just come from the local pool hall), but you may want to consider these spherical varieties nonetheless for a conversation starter in both the garden and kitchen.

heirloom featuring green ribbing and light green stripes. 'Golden Glory' has spineless stems and yellow fruit. 'Sunstripe' is yellow with cream-colored stripes, and 'Yellowfin' is golden yellow with superior disease resistance.

- **Straightneck** squash are—obviously—long and straight, thinner at the "neck" closest to the stem. The yellow fruit can be smooth or textured. 'Chiffon' has smooth white flesh, 'Goldfinch' is bright yellow with a unique central stem, and 'Zephyr' is yellow with a green blossom end. 'Superpick' can grow much larger than most varieties but still retain its flavor and tender quality.

- **Crookneck** squash is similar to straightneck but bent at the neck and more bulbous on the end. I like 'Delta', with its buttery yellow fruit that just keeps producing. 'Tempest' is a yellow variety renowned for culinary use.

- **Pattypan** (or scallop) squash is small and round with scalloped edges with green, yellow, white, or bicolored rinds that can also be striped or speckled. 'Benning's Green Tint' is light green with pronounced scalloping. 'Lemon Sun' is bright yellow with tulip-shaped fruit. Sunburst is deep yellow with a buttery flavor. 'Y-Star' is shiny yellow with a green blossom end ('G-Star' is the green version).

Planting

If you started your squash plants from seed, be sure to harden them off in advance of planting day.

Apply a layer of organic mulch, 2 to 3 inches (5 to 8 cm) deep, around squash plants to suppress weeds, retain moisture, and keep the leaves and fruit from coming into contact with bare soil.

Mid-season care

Summer squash plants like 1 inch (2.5 cm) of water per week, maybe up to 2 inches (5 cm) in the hottest stretch of summer, so be prepared to supplement if rain is scarce.

Squash is a heavy feeder, so I like to side-dress my plants once they're established with compost a few times throughout the season. If fertilizer seems necessary, look for an N-P-K ratio with a lower nitrogen number because you want fruit growth, not foliage growth. Keep the phosphorus number higher and follow the application guidelines to avoid overfeeding.

If you're seeing lots of flowers but no fruit, you may have a pollination issue. Try pollinating your squash plants by hand. Start by locating a female flower, identified by a small embryonic fruit between the flower and the stem. Then pick a male flower (one with nothing between the flower and stem) and peel back the petals to reveal the

Pollinating squash plants by hand is easy, but it all starts with identifying a female flower among your plants, one with a small fruit between the flower and the stem.

Squash vine borers do their damage from the inside out by eating internal stem tissue.

pollen-covered anther. Brush the anther around the tip of the stigma of the female flower, and then close the flowers with a clothespin to allow the pollination process to complete. (Playing music to set the mood while you do this is entirely optional. But Barry White or Marvin Gaye is always a thoughtful touch.)

Pests & disease

Cucumber beetles are a double headache. They chew holes in leaves and also pass a pathogen that causes bacterial wilt. Hand-pick these pests and rotate crops at season's end so a population doesn't build up.

Squash beetles are often confused with beneficial lady beetles, since both have orange-red coloring and block dots. Floating row cover can prevent adults from landing on leaves to lay their yellow eggs. Hand-picking eggs will effectively control them.

The squash bug damages foliage as it feeds and is also a vector for cucurbit yellow vine disease. Leaves that wilt, dry up, and die is a sign to watch out for. Also look for bronze-brown, oval-shaped eggs on the underside of leaves between the veins; nymphs will hatch within 10 days, and the bugs mature a month later. You'll recognize them with their flat, dark gray (almost black) bodies, just over ½ inch (1.3 cm) long and with six legs. Control them by hand-picking, installing row cover, or using insecticidal soap.

Squash vine borers destroy plants from the inside out. Eggs laid at the base of the plant (on the stem or under leaves) hatch, and the larvae bore into the plant to eat stem tissue, which eventually kills the plant. Floating row cover will keep the adults (red and black moths seen in the daylight) off the plants, so no eggs are laid. Remember to remove the cover once blooming begins so pollinators can access the flowers. Some gardeners have good luck with wrapping small pieces of aluminum foil around the first few inches of plant stems.

Downy mildew and powdery mildew are fungal diseases that affect summer squash. Full sun exposure and good air circulation are preventative measures.

Zucchini yellow mosaic virus discolors foliage and stunts fruit growth. It's transmitted by aphids, so use floating row cover immediately upon planting.

Harvesting

Once you see tiny fruit, check back often as fruit grows quickly. For zucchini, pick at 5 to 8 inches (13 to 20 cm) long for ideal taste. For straightneck and crookneck varieties, 4 to 5 inches (10 to 13 cm) is best. Pattypan, 3 to 5 inches (8 to 13 cm) in length.

To harvest, cut through the stem with sharp pruners or shears instead of pulling fruit. If the blossom is still intact, remove it and cook immediately (or within two days). Summer squash will last up to 10 days in a refrigerator compartment with high humidity at 41°F to 50°F (5°C to 10°C). Chilling injury can occur at colder temperatures.

SWEET POTATO

Ipomoea batatas,
Morning glory family

The Down and Dirty

Preferred climate	**Warm to hot**
Sun	**Full**
Soil	**Warm, well-draining, sandy loam**
pH range	**5.5–6.5**
Transplant slips	**When soil has warmed to 60°F–65°F (16°C–18°C)**
Spacing	**10–18 inches (25–45 cm) apart in rows 36–60 inches (90–150 cm) apart**
Days to maturity	**90–120**

Notes from the garden

The sweet potato is yet another case where names can be misleading. But it turns out that, botanically speaking, the sweet potato and the potato are only vaguely related to one another. Both are edible root crops. Both are delicious and versatile. But they come from entirely different plant families. And while we're on the subject of names, we should stop generically referring to sweet potatoes as *yams*. They're completely different species!

Here's what's easy about sweet potatoes, though—growing them. They're grown from rooted cuttings called *slips* instead of from seed. Once they take off, they're one of the most productive crops the home gardener can try, and they'll last for many months in storage if proper care is taken.

Starting Your Own Sweet Potato Slips

You can buy sweet potato slips from your favorite garden retailer but I almost never do, since creating them at home is so easy. And truth be told, I find it a lot of fun. Maybe it takes me back to those first gardening experiments we all tried as kids.

Start in early spring with medium-sized sweet potatoes from the grocery store or farmer's market. I cut each tuber into thirds, leaving me with two ends and a middle. I save the middle section for baking; the two ends will produce my new slips.

Insert three or four toothpicks into each cut sweet potato end so that you can suspend the potato, cut-side down, into a glass of water. The toothpicks simply hold the potato over the glass so that it's roughly half-submerged in the water.

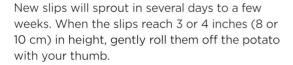

Slips are the rooted cuttings from which sweet potatoes are grown.

You should see new roots sprouting within two weeks, signaling that the slips are ready for planting.

New slips will sprout in several days to a few weeks. When the slips reach 3 or 4 inches (8 or 10 cm) in height, gently roll them off the potato with your thumb.

Put these slips, bottom end down, in a shallow container of water and place on a sunny windowsill. In about 2 weeks, new roots will have emerged. The slips are then ready for planting, weather permitting.

Planting

Be sure the soil has warmed sufficiently before planting sweet potatoes. Cover beds with mulch or black plastic for 2 to 3 weeks prior to planting can help raise the soil temperature.

Slips should be planted with the thicker, bottom-most portion 4 to 6 inches (10 to 15 cm) covered by soil. Bury any developing nodes.

Water immediately and keep planted slips in moist soil for about a week until they are established.

Mid-season care

If you keep beds clear of weeds while sweet potato plants are young, they'll take over the job and their thick mats of runners will smother most weeds. Don't trim these runners, as they also act as secondary roots for the plants.

In cool regions, consider applying row cover in the fall to keep sweet potato plants as warm as possible up until the harvest.

Pests & disease

Sweet potatoes have few pests, and most that damage the plants' leaves (most notably, beetles, snails, slugs, and deer) can be thwarted with floating row cover.

Wireworm damage can be prevented by avoiding fields where grass has been grown the year prior. In the warmest climates, sweet potato weevils can cause underground damage to the tubers. Crop rotation is the best defense.

Scurf is a fungal disease that affects sweet potatoes. Avoid it by practicing crop rotation and removing all foliage debris after the harvest.

Harvesting

When you notice above-ground foliage starting to turn yellow, production is slowing down. While you can harvest your sweet potatoes at this point, leaving them buried a while longer will increase their size.

But don't wait too long. Once the top growth has died down (usually from a frost), it's time to cut it back and harvest. At the very least, cut off all the foliage until you can dig the sweet potatoes up. This helps prevent disease that can travel downward through the foliage.

Use a digging fork (also sold as a garden fork) to gently get underneath the sweet potatoes and loosen the soil. Any damage to the soft skin during harvesting will make it hard for the sweet potato to survive storage. Once the soil has been loosened, use your hands to pull your sweet potatoes out of the ground.

Sweet potato plants send out thick mats of runners that smother weeds from growing in the bed; they also act as secondary roots!

Grow bags are a convenient way to keep sprawling crops neatly contained. I love to use them for growing sweet potatoes because they also make harvesting easy.

Would You Like a Bag for Those Sweet Potatoes?

In Chapter 4, I suggested using grow bags for the space-deprived gardener as a clever way to grow edibles on a deck or patio. Well, even though I'm fortunate enough to have more than enough bed space, I still like to use grow bags for my sweet potatoes, for several reasons. One, the bags tend to warm up the soil quite a bit, and sweet potatoes love that. Two, sweet potatoes can get especially viney and can take over a bed quickly. I find my raised beds are more productive with this crop contained and out of the way of my other vegetables. Just be sure to buy large grow bags, the 15-gallon (68 L) size or larger, since the underground tubers need plenty of space to grow in.

But here's my favorite reason for keeping sweet potatoes in grow bags. They make harvesting a snap. When it's time to pull the tubers, I simply tip the bag over and carefully dump the contents out. The sweet potatoes are just lying in the pile, plain as day and waiting to be harvested. There's no worse feeling than accidentally hitting a beauty with your digging fork and damaging it. This method helps me salvage every last sweet potato for the table.

Storage

Sweet potatoes need to cure for two to three weeks (to let the starches convert to sugars) before they can be eaten. Get them out of direct sunlight as quickly as possible after harvesting, but leave any excess dirt on the skin. After a few days, the skin will have toughened up enough to handle a light brushing. Don't wash sweet potatoes before curing or storing.

For long-term storage, create a warm and humid environment. This could be inside a plastic grocery bag with the handles tied shut and ventilation holes cut in the plastic. Place the bag in the sunniest spot in your house. One to two weeks at 80°F to 85°F (27°C to 29°C) is ideal.

Cured sweet potatoes will keep for six months or so, provided the space is slightly cool but rather humid.

SWISS CHARD

Beta vulgaris
(Flavescens Group),
Amaranth family

The Down and Dirty

Preferred climate	**Mild**
Sun	**Full**
Soil	**Well-draining and compost-rich**
pH range	**6.0–6.5**
Sow seeds	**Indoors, 3–4 weeks before last frost. Outdoors, after last frost**
Sowing depth	**½ inch (1.3 cm)**
Days to germination	**5**
Germination temperature	**50°F–85°F (10°C–29°C)**
Note	**Indoors, sow two seeds per cell and thin to one seedling per cell after 7 days. Harden off seed-started seedlings before planting outdoors.**
Transplant seedlings	**After last frost**
Spacing	**So they will not touch when fully mature, according to variety**
Days to maturity	**24–60, depending on variety**

Notes from the garden

When a first-time visitor is in my garden and they ask, "What is *that* plant?" it's almost a guarantee they're looking at my swiss chard. This leafy green is a nutritional superstar, with leaves that add vitamins and minerals to salads, smoothies, soups, dips, and baked dishes, or served simply as a hearty side dish when sautéed in a little oil and garlic.

Swiss chard (or, simply, chard) is a cut-and-come-again crop, meaning it can be harvested throughout the season and keeps producing for a long time, even into early winter.

But it's that fireworks show it puts on in the garden that convinces most people to try growing it. Large, puckered, waxy-looking leaves sit atop stalks that come in bright red, neon yellow, pristine white, electric orange, rich purple, and every shade in between. It's so pretty that I know people who don't even eat it but are sure to include it in their landscape beds just for the aesthetics.

A literal rainbow of colors lights up my garden beds (and containers!) from April until frost. But it's usually just the foliage that takes the hit. If I

From the bright colors to the large and puckered leaves, swiss chard stands out in the vegetable garden like no other crop does.

Swiss chard is one of those crops where proper spacing is important for healthy growth and makes for easier harvesting.

leave the roots in place, new leaves sprout by spring and the show goes on for another season. Ornamental, delicious, beautiful, *and* tough. That's my kind of plant.

My favorite varieties
- 'Bright Lights' I've grown this variety for years, and it's my favorite swiss chard of all. An All-America Selections winner, it's an absolute showstopper in the garden, with stem colors of red, orange, pink, yellow, and white, all in one crop.
- 'Fire Fresh' You won't have to wait long for this variety. Leaves are ready to eat 23 to 35 days after transplanting. With ruby stems and veins, this one also has a good degree of disease resistance.
- 'Lyon' Lime green leaves can reach over 12 inches (30 cm) long and nearly 10 inches (25 cm) wide on white stalks. This open-pollinated variety is renowned for its taste and is ready to harvest in 50 days.
- 'Perpetual' This open-pollinated variety pro-duces all summer and can last for several years in warmer climates. Its smooth leaves taste like spinach and are ready for harvest in 50 days. The plants can reach 20 inches (51 cm) tall.

- 'Rhubarb' Named for its thick red stalks that resemble rhubarb, this beautiful heirloom chard also has deep red veins in its leaves. It's ready to harvest in 60 days, but the striking color you'll enjoy as it grows makes it worth the wait.

Planting
Be sure the last risk of frost has passed before planting chard outdoors. Soil should be well-draining and amended with plenty of organic matter like compost. Chard will also appreciate the addition of a slow-release organic nitrogen fertilizer, which will promote leaf growth.

Spacing is key for swiss chard. Plan your bed so that the plants do not touch once they reach full maturity.

Apply 2 to 3 inches (5 to 8 cm) of organic mulch around swiss chard plants to suppress weeds and retain moisture.

Mid-season care

When watering, aim for 1 inch (2.5 cm) per week between rainfall and supplemental watering. Drip irrigation at the plant base allows for consistency. If hand-watering, avoid getting the foliage wet, as it promotes disease.

Provided your soil is organically rich and you fertilized with a slow-release nitrogen source at planting, swiss chard will do fine on its own. To promote more vigorous growth, you can apply blood meal, feather meal, or cottonseed meal according to manufacturer instructions. I prefer fish emulsion with a high first number (nitrogen) in its N-P-K ratio.

Pests & disease

Swiss chard is largely unbothered by pests. Aphids, flea beetles, and leafminers can occasionally be a minor nuisance, but the use of floating row cover over plants keeps all of them at bay.

My biggest pest problem with swiss chard is small slugs. They can really go to town on the leaves and wipe out your entire crop quickly. Row covers aren't effective against slugs, but sprinkling diatomaceous earth (called DE) helps and is my go-to control option.

Cut swiss chard plants just above the soil line or take stalks from the outside of the plant. Whatever's left will keep on growing.

Powdery mildew and downy mildew are fungal diseases that can affect swiss chard leaves. Plants affected by the former appear covered in white powder; the latter causes yellow spots. Planting in full sun, providing good air circulation around plants, and avoiding overhead watering are good preventative measures.

Harvesting

Begin harvesting chard when leaves are about 6 inches (15 cm) tall. Younger leaves are best in a salad or eaten like beet greens or spinach.

Harvest early in the morning. Leaves cut in the afternoon contain less moisture and wilt more readily. Cut plants 1 inch (2.5 cm) above ground with sharp scissors or garden shears. Or cut stalks from the outside of the plant, allowing the intact heart of the plant to continue to grow.

Swiss chard is at its best the same day it was cut, but can be stored unwashed in an unsealed plastic bag for up to seven days. It can also be frozen or canned.

Remember that in warmer areas plants may overwinter and provide a spring harvest. But if warmer temperatures send up a flower stalk, it's time to remove the entire plant. Bolted chard is no longer palatable.

Most pests tend to steer clear of swiss chard. Slugs, though, can do a number on your crop.

TOMATILLOS

Physalis philadelphica,
Tomato family

The Down and Dirty

Preferred climate	Well-adapted to most regions
Sun	Full
Soil	Loose, fertile, well-draining
pH range	6.0–7.0
Sow seeds	Indoors, 4–6 weeks before last frost.
Sowing depth	¼ inch (60 mm)
Days to germination	7–10
Germination temperature	60°F–85°F (16°C–29°C)
Transplant seedlings	After last frost, about 4-6 weeks after sowing indoors
Spacing	24–36 inches (60–90 cm) between plants and 4–6 feet (1.2–1.8 m) between rows. Tomatillos spread out so allow plenty of room between plants and rows.
Days to maturity	About 60–80 days from transplanting seedlings.

Notes from the garden

If you love making salsa verde from scratch in your kitchen, this is the must-grow plant in your garden. Tomatillos are easy to grow and very prolific. They're in the same family as tomatoes, but quite different in many ways, including being far less susceptible to diseases. And unlike tomatoes, tomatillos are not self-pollinating. They must cross-pollinate in order to set fruit, and they rely on insects for that. Plan on having at least two plants for successful pollination and fruit set.

The first time I grew tomatillos, I was surprised by how gangly and sprawling they were. They reminded me of those awkward early-teenage years we all went through. They're not the prettiest plant you'll grow in your garden and take up more room than you might be expecting, but these plants will take off on their own—with no fussing from you required—and produce their little green hearts out. I recommend providing some physical support (staking, trellising, caging) as these plants spread out far and wide in every direction.

Tomatillos are mature once they've filled their papery husks. The fruit inside is ready for use in all kinds of dishes, including fresh salsa verde.

My favorite varieties

- 'Purple' Golf ball-sized fruit with dark purple skin color and wrapped in a papery, purple-veined husk, this variety is not only very attractive, but it's much sweeter than green varieties.
- 'Super Verde' An extra-large hybrid variety with broad, round, green fruit. This is a productive variety with early yields.
- 'Toma Verde' The classic green fruit with an early tart flavor that sweetens as it ripens.

Planting

Plant tomatillo seedlings like you would tomato plants—deeply. Roots will develop all along the stem, so the more of the stem you bury underground, the more roots the plant will produce. More roots equal higher water and nutrient uptake and better drought tolerance.

Mid-season care

Make sure plants are physically supported as needed and monitor for pests and diseases.

Pests & disease

While tomatillos are not nearly as susceptible to what afflicts their tomato cousins, the usual suspects (listed in detail in the next grow guide plant) are what to also look out for with tomatillos.

Harvesting

Harvest when fruit has filled—or nearly filled—its papery husk and is firm and bright green (or purple, depending on the variety). Fruit that becomes soft prior to harvesting is overmature and more likely to split.

Tomatillo plants can spread wide. Give each one plenty of room to grow, and they'll reward you with many husk-covered fruits.

TOMATO

Solanum lycopersicum,
Tomato family

The Down and Dirty

Preferred climate	**Mild to hot**
Sun	**Full**
Soil	**Well-draining, organically rich**
pH range	**6.5–7.0**
Sow seeds	**Indoors, 6–8 weeks before planting outdoors. Outdoors, after last possible frost.**
Sowing depth	**¼ inch (60 mm)**
Days to germination	**About 7 (most varieties)**
Germination temperature	**70°F–85°F (21°C–29°C**
Note	**Use grow lights to encourage vigor, a fan to prevent damping-off disease.** **Pot up to larger containers and harden off plants before planting outdoors.**
Transplant seedlings	**After last possible frost date**
Spacing	**At least 24 inches (60 cm) apart**
Days to maturity after planting outdoors	**50–100, depending on variety**

Notes from the garden

Tomatoes are my favorite of all edibles to grow. And I'm not alone. They're easily the most popular home garden crop of all. A good friend of mine calls tomatoes "the gateway to gardening," since many people who would never consider themselves having a green thumb will make an exception for tomato plants. The reason? You'll never eat a tomato that tastes better than one you picked from your own vegetable garden. (Even though the tomato is, in fact, technically a fruit.)

There's a dizzying array of varieties and flavor profiles to choose from. My favorite spaghetti-sauce tomato is different from the one I prefer to slice up for a burger, and there's still other varieties that I grow to put in salads or pop whole as a garden snack.

As much as I love starting my tomatoes from seed each year, they pound me later in the season with a relentless pummeling of pests and soilborne diseases that show up like clockwork every summer in the hot, humid South. But the allure of the perfect BLT always brings me back. Tomatoes ask for knowledge and perseverance from the gardener.

Having a better understanding of your tomato plants will help you deal with challenges as they arise and make the whole experience more fun. So whether you're undaunted by the difficulties— or just numb to it all, like me—there is nothing more rewarding than a homegrown tomato. And if you ask me, it's worth every drop of sweat and tears that may be required to make that happen.

Choosing what to grow

Among the first decisions you'll want to make is whether you plant determinate or indeterminate tomatoes. A **determinate** tomato plant grows to a certain size, produces a lot of fruit in a short window of time, and then stops. **Indeterminate** varieties keep growing all season long, producing fruit continuously until the plant is killed by frost in autumn.

Next, consider growth habit. **Bush-type** tomatoes stay rather small and are good for containers or grow bags. They tend to be of the determinate variety (though there are indeterminates, too). **Vining-type** tomatoes obviously get leggier as they grow and are more frequently indeterminates.

Also, weigh hybrid tomatoes with open-pollinated or heirloom tomato varieties, as discussed in more detail in Chapter 3. Hybrids are reliable and consistent. Heirlooms bring spectacular flavor, color, shape, and historical interest to the party.

My favorite varieties

There are simply too many amazing tomato varieties to pick, and sifting through a comprehensive list of exotically named beauties, each with their own unique characteristics is half the fun. Some are old standbys, others are more recent favorites, some I try just for sheer novelty (and there are new varieties introduced every year). Here are a few of my favorites of each type to get you started.

- **Beefsteak** tomatoes are some of the largest tomatoes, some reaching over 1 pound (450 g) per fruit! These are the ones I slice to

'Sun Gold' tomatoes are one of my all-time favorites—both to eat and to grow. You'll be (pleasantly) shocked by how many tomatoes you get from just one plant.

top burgers or make a fresh Caprese salad. I love the heirloom beefsteaks like 'Black Krim', 'Brandywine', 'Cherokee Purple', 'Mortgage Lifter', and 'Lillian's Yellow'. 'Beefmaster VFN' and 'Celebrity' are good disease-resistant hybrids. Other hybrids that aren't quite "beefsteaks" but still are great slicers are 'Better Boy', 'Better Bush', 'Early Girl', and 'Summer Girl'.

- **Cherry** tomatoes are so named for their size and shape. Eat them like candy, either whole or sliced in half. These are my go-to salad tomatoes, but they're also great roasted or sautéed. Among my favorite hybrids are 'Sun Gold', 'Cherry Bomb', 'Sakura', 'Supersweet', and 'Tomatoberry Garden'. Open-pollinated varieties include 'Black Cherry', 'Gold Nugget', 'Indigo Cherry', 'Mexico Midget', and 'White Cherry'.
- **Grape** tomatoes are smaller than most cherry tomatoes and oblong in shape, but they eat the same way. Look for open-pollinated favorites 'Ildi', 'Principe Borghese', and 'Red Pearl'. As for hybrids, try 'Apero', 'Five Star Grape', 'Golden Sweet', 'Ruby Crush', and 'Valentine'.
- **Plum** tomatoes are also called paste tomatoes. If you're growing tomatoes to turn into sauce, this is what you want. 'Roma' is far and away the most popular; it's an open-pollinated determinate.

Extra Tomatoes Are for Suckers

Every gardener wants more tomato plants once the growing season gets rolling. Luckily, Mother Nature always provides us with a bonus crop that's free for the taking!

As a tomato plant grows, the stem sends out secondary shoots called suckers. If you plant these suckers, they'll become their own tomato plants in a very short time! Look for a place along the main vertical stalk where two smaller branches are growing out at the same point. One will be horizontal, growing perpendicular to the stem, and the other will be shooting out of the crotch at a 45-degree angle. That angled offshoot is the sucker.

Simply snap or cut off the sucker; it should separate cleanly and easily. Plant this sucker in potting mix in a container. Keep it watered and out of direct sun for at least a week. In a matter of a couple weeks, you'll likely find that most of the suckers are ready to be transplanted, and you'll know that another wave of homegrown tomatoes is on the way!

It's not necessary to remove suckers. Leaving them on certainly won't hurt the plant. It's a matter of preference. I tend to remove some of them, but not all of them as my plants grow. But for every one I remove, I get a new plant and extra tomatoes that I didn't even have to pay for? I'd have to be a sucker to *not* be a fan of that.

Whether or not to remove tomato plant suckers can be a topic of hot debate among gardeners, but they're easily removed and replanted to make new seedlings. Look for offshoots that grow at a 45-degree angle to the main stem.

Planting

Tomato plants can be planted quite deep. I remove all lower leaves from seedlings and bury up to two-thirds of the plant! For especially tall seedlings (or in shallow beds), I often plant them horizontally to get more of the stem underground in a method known as *trenching*. (Just be sure to have two or more sets of leaves above the soil.) It may look unorthodox, but the plant's stems will grow new roots quite quickly and produce an even more vigorous plant.

Install a tomato cage or stake for each plant upon transplanting—adding supports once plants have grown larger risks damage to the stems.

Mid-season care

Plenty of water is good for your tomato plants, up to 2 inches (5 cm) per week during the hottest past of summer. Be sure to water at ground level, under the foliage, so as not to invite disease.

Planting in soil rich with organic matter should keep tomato plants fed all season long, but I supplement with feedings every two to three weeks. Use a balanced fertilizer with equal N-P-K numbers, as explained in Chapter 5.

Pests & disease

Aphids bring ants and other insects as they feed on plant leaves. Knock them off with a stream of water or use insecticidal soap.

Two-spotted spider mites feed on the underside of tomato foliage and cause stippling. Severe infestations can lead to defoliation. To detect spider mites, use a jeweler's lens or something similar. You can also hold a sheet of white paper under affected leaves and vigorously tap leaves to dislodge mites. They'll appear on the paper as tiny specks. Effective controls include coating leaves with horticultural oil or insecticidal soap sprays.

Fruitworms and armyworms bore into the fruits themselves. Handpick eggs from stems, under leaves, and on fruit. Caterpillars may be green or black and gray. Use *Bt* as an organic control, but not around butterfly larvae host plants.

The stippling caused by two-spotted spider mites is easily identifiable. Thankfully, this pest is easily controlled.

Fusarium wilt comes from your soil. If you plant tomatoes in the same spot next season, you'll start the cycle all over again.

Early blight is common with tomatoes. Be sure to remove all affected leaves from the garden entirely to keep it from spreading.

Dark brown spots and black specks on leaves can indicate Septoria leaf spot.

Flea beetles are small black or bronze jumping leaf beetles who do damage by chewing. Use a floating row cover on young plants or plant a trap crop of radishes nearby. By summer, the plants are strong enough to withstand flea beetles.

Tomato hornworms are nasty. This green caterpillar with the scary-looking horn on its rear end can reach 4 inches (10 cm) long but is often hard to spot in the garden because it is so well-camouflaged as it chows down on tomato plant stems. Try using a UV flashlight at night to find them more easily. Hand-pick them and their lookalike pest, the tobacco hornworm. But if you find them with what looks like lots of grains of rice sticking up from their back, leave them alone. Those are the cocoons of parasitic wasps; a highly beneficial predator of hornworms has already done your pest control for you. Each cocoon will hatch a new beneficial wasp ready to do more hornworm pest control in your garden.

Alternaria, or early blight, is a common disease issue. You'll see dark, ½-inch (1.3 cm) leaf spots starting on the oldest leaves and possibly spreading to stems. It can be fatal to young plants. Remove leaf litter from the garden and do not save seeds from affected plants.

Anthracnose is a fruit rot fungus found on ripe and overripe fruit, presenting as small, round depressed areas that turn black. Don't leave infected fruit in the garden or it will spread. Do not save seeds from infected fruit. Look for resistant varieties.

Blossom end rot is technically not a disease, but a problem nonetheless. The sunken black spot on the blossom end is a symptom of calcium deficiency. It's usually due to inconsistent watering, as a calcium deficiency in the soil is rare. Double-check your soil with a soil test to be sure.

Canker is a bacterial disease that turns leaf margins brown and yellow. This happens as the bacteria clogs the veins of the plants, causing the leaves to curl and wilt. Small brown spots (sometimes with white borders) may form on fruit. Remove affected plants to reduce the spread. If the plant already has fruit, you may be able to get a harvest before the plant succumbs.

Fusarium wilt and Verticillium wilt are soilborne diseases that cause tomato plants to wilt and die. Dispose of affected plants outside the garden and practice crop rotation—no nightshades for 3 years or longer.

Late blight is a fast-spreading and deadly water mold that arrives with wet, cool temperatures from 60°F to 70°F (16°C to 21°C) late in the growing season, affecting leaves, stems, and fruit. Brown blotches appear on leaves and fruit becomes brown and rotted. Remove weeds and choose resistant varieties.

Tomato root knot nematodes are microscopic worms that form galls in tomato roots, stealing nutrients. Interplanting French marigolds may repel nematodes. If you know they are present, plant resistant varieties or practice three-year crop rotation. Heavy feeding and watering may allow an affected plant to still produce.

Bacterial wilt lives in the soil for years. It enters plants through wounds in the roots, which may be caused by nematodes, insects, or transplant damage. Symptoms include a rapidly wilting plant that remains green. Once in a plant, the bacteria will build up rapidly. You can't control bacterial wilt with chemicals, so infected plants should be removed and destroyed or thrown away. If you confirm that your plant is infected with bacterial wilt, replacing the soil or finding alternative locations for growing in subsequent seasons is your best option.

Septoria leaf spot is a fungal infection causing dark brown spots with black specks on leaves. Copper fungicide is one organic control method. Resistant tomato varieties can be found.

Harvesting

A tomato at full color with firm flesh that yields slightly to pressure is at its peak ripeness. Pick it and enjoy within a couple days. You may also pick tomatoes once they reach the "breaker" stage. This is when the fruit begins to blush or starts to show color (about 30 percent to 40 percent of its full color). At this point, you can bring it indoors (or just out of direct sun) and it will continue to ripen. (This safeguards against losing your almost ripe tomatoes to critters or frost.)

A ripe tomato will last on the countertop for a few days. Mine are rarely left to wait around that long.

Tomatoes at the "breaker" stage will continue to ripen indoors on a windowsill or countertop with no loss of quality.

The Ultimate Tomato Cage

Tomato plants need a lot of support as they grow, as the heavy fruit can quickly outweigh what the long, vines can safely hold up. Those cone-shaped wire contraptions at the garden center are easy enough to get, and they're certainly inexpensive. But I never found them to be tall enough or strong enough to fit the bill in my garden. They're flimsy, at best. And even though the basic cages are now sold in bright colors, they just don't look good enough for my tastes.

So one year I decided to make my own tomato cages, and I've never looked back. The ah-ha moment came when I was working with some livestock panels. The super-sturdy grid panels are readily available at farm and tractor supply stores, measure 16 feet (4.9 m) by just over 4 feet (1.2 m), and are constructed of heavy-duty galvanized metal wire. One panel equals one tomato cage plus one smaller pepper or eggplant cage. They're on the expensive side (about four times the price of one of those hardware store cheapies), but each one of these cages can last for decades.

These super-sturdy tomato cages require a minimal investment of time to make, but they beat anything you can buy at the big-box store and will last almost forever!

Lay out a new panel someplace flat and sturdy, like on the driveway, and cut it lengthwise six squares across with a pair of bolt cutters. Next, count nine squares from the end and cut across just above the horizontal piece at the bottom of the ninth square. This will leave long, pointy wires that are your supports to drive into the soil to anchor the cage. (For extra-long stakes, cut out the horizontal pieces at the eighth square to leave spikes that are two squares tall.) Repeat with the other end of the original panel. You should now have three pieces. The middle section can be used as a planting guide, or make a mini-cage for your peppers or eggplants.

Place a long piece of lumber lengthwise on top of one of the matching panels. Of the six squares comprising the width, leave three showing against the board's edge. Stand on the lumber and bend the panel up and toward you until you create a 90-degree angle. Repeat for the other panel.

When you sandwich the two L-shaped panels, they form a square cage that completely encloses the plant. Anchor the panels into the ground using the spiky ends. You can use nylon zip ties to secure the cage pieces to one another if you choose. I did that my first year but found the cages to be strong enough that it's not necessary.

At the end of the season, snip the ties and remove the cages. Clean them off if necessary and store the L-shaped panels in a compact and neatly stacked pile (another reason to love them!) until the next growing season.

There you have it, the ultimate tomato cage. I'm sure I'm not the first person to use livestock panels for this purpose, but I'd never seen it done before I tried it. And over the years, after recommending it to literally thousands of gardeners, I've never heard a single complaint about them not being tall enough or strong enough to handle a tomato bounty of any size. If you'd like to see a step-by-step video of how I make this Ultimate Tomato Cage, visit www.joegardener.com/tomatocage.

Use a pair of heavy-duty bolt cutters to cut a new livestock panel lengthwise. The long spiky ends are the stakes you'll use to anchor the cage into your garden bed.

By laying a long piece of lumber on the panel, standing on the board, and pulling the panel toward you, bend the cage to create a 90-degree angle.

Fit two L-shaped panel pieces together to form a square column around each tomato plant in your garden. Zip-tie the pieces together for added strength, if desired.

TURNIPS

Brassica rapa subsp. *rapa*,
Cabbage family

The Down and Dirty

Preferred climate	Cool for sweetest taste
Sun	Full
Soil	Fertile, loose, compost-rich
pH range	6.0–7.5
Sow seeds	Outdoors, 3 weeks before last frost for spring harvest; late summer for fall harvest
Sowing depth	¼–½ inch (0.6–1.3 cm)
Days to germination	4–7
Germination temperature	60°F (16°C) is optimal
Spacing	Every 2 inches (5 cm) in rows 18 inches (45 cm) apart
Note	Thin plants to one every 4–6 inches (10–15 cm) for full growth potential
Days to maturity	35–80

Notes from the garden

Turnips are among the most versatile vegetables you can grow. They can be planted as a spring crop or a fall crop, harvested for their leafy greens or their crunchy and sweet-to-spicy taproots—which can be white, purple, red, or multi-colored!

Fast growers, turnips are a great way to kick off spring planting. A row or two put in the ground before the last frost of winter can be enjoyed before the bulk of your other crops really get going. Drop in more seeds as your warm-season crops are wrapping up, don't disturb the soil, and you'll be rewarded with more fresh turnips as the weather gets cold again.

My favorite varieties

- 'Alamo' A variety with some bolt resistance that can also tolerate pests and disease, this one is grown primarily for its greens. Baby leaves resprout for multiple harvests starting in 33 days.
- 'Amelie' A bolt-resistant hybrid meant for either spring or fall harvest. Sweet, crisp, white roots grow to 2 to 3 inches (5 to 8 cm) in diameter. Mature in 50 to 80 days. Tops can also be harvested.
- 'Purple Top White Globe' Traditional turnip especially popular in warmer climates. Taproots grow purple above the soil line, white below. Harvest at 3 to 4 inches (8 to 10 cm) in diameter in 50 days. Leaves are good for cooking.

- 'Scarlet Queen' A red variety intended for use in salads, taproots mature in 43 days and reach 2 to 3 inches (5 to 8 cm) in diameter.
- 'White Lady' Mature in 35 just days, this hybrid variety is good as a spring or fall crop. White roots are crisp and sweet.

Choosing what to grow

Some turnip varieties are bred specifically to provide abundant greens; others are all about the edible root. Consider not only your growing conditions but how you plan to use the harvest when selecting varieties.

Planting

Pick through soil to a depth of 8 inches (20 cm), removing rocks and roots that can inhibit root growth. Thin to one plant per 4 to 6 inches (10 to 15 cm) once seedlings reach 2 to 3 inches (5 to 8 cm) tall.

Mid-season care

Consistent moisture is best. Aim for 1 inch (2.5 cm) of water per week. Sandy, fast-draining soils may need more water. A drip system ensures that the soil never dries out during root development.

Side-dress with a low-nitrogen or balanced fertilizer once seedlings have put on true leaves.

If growing for turnip greens, feel free to use a nitrogen-heavy liquid fertilizer such as fish emulsion, but use sparingly. If turnip roots are the goal, only use a fertilizer with a lower nitrogen number (first in the N-P-K ratio).

Pests & disease

Floating row cover installed at planting will protect your turnips from many pests like armyworms, cabbage aphids, cabbage root maggots, cabbage worms, and flea beetles.

Slugs and snails like turnip greens. Handpick them when found or use an iron phosphate-based bait for severe infestations.

Practice crop rotation to keep turnips and all brassicas out of the same spot for four years. You'll reduce the chances of diseases like Alternaria black spot, black rot, mosaic virus, and turnip crinkle virus.

Harvesting

To harvest greens, begin cutting leaves once they reach 6 inches (15 cm) long—the taste turns bitter past this point. Leaving 1 inch (2.5 cm) on the plant will encourage greens to regrow for multiple harvests. Bolted plants will have bitter leaves.

Check the portion of the turnip root sticking out of the soil to gauge readiness. Most varieties are mature at 2 to 4 inches (5 to 10 cm), but check the seed packet for precise sizing. Harvesting early is better than waiting too long, as turnips may lose flavor and become pithy as they increase in size.

In spring, harvest before hot temperatures arrive and force bolting. In fall, allowing a few frosts to hit your turnips will turn them sweeter, but harvest before the ground freezes. A 2-inch (5 cm) layer of mulch added in fall can buy you a little extra time. If the ground does not freeze in your area, turnips may be left in the ground and harvested all winter.

To harvest, grab the foliage firmly where it's attached at the root and twist as you pull up.

Cut off all but ½ inch (1.3 cm) of the foliage and the thinnest part of the root; store turnips in a crisper drawer for up to two weeks.

If you're growing turnips specifically for the greens, use a liquid fertilizer a little higher in nitrogen. It will give the above-ground foliage a nice boost.

WINTER SQUASH

Cucurbita sp.,
Cucumber family

The Down and Dirty

Preferred climate	Warm
Sun	Full
Soil	Very fertile and well-draining
pH range	6.0–6.5
Sow seeds	Indoors, 3–4 weeks before last frost. Direct-sow, recommended, well after frost risk
Sowing depth	1 inch (2.5 cm), two seeds per pot
Days to germination	7–10
Germination temperature	70°F–95°F (21°C–32°C)
Note	After sprouting, thin to two or three plants per hill
Transplant seedlings	After risk of last frost is gone, being careful not to disturb the roots.
Spacing	Several feet in all directions or near vertical trellis. Be sure to allow adequate room either up or out for these vigorous, sprawling vines.
Note	Use floating row cover on seedlings as protection from pests, but remove as flowering begins to allow access for pollinators.
Days to maturity	60–120

Notes from the garden

While its summer counterpart has a soft edible skin and should be enjoyed right away, the hard-skinned winter squash (the skin is not edible) can be cured and then stored for several months. Whether you're talking about butternut squash, acorn squash, or spaghetti squash, nothing says fall comfort food quite like winter squash.

If you have the room to grow it and the patience to wait for it, winter squash will reward you mightily during the cool and crisp days of fall. Roast it, stuff it, use it in soup, or bake it in a pie. It's wonderful as a side or an entree all its own, or can be added to everything from salads to casseroles. The flowers are tasty, too, picked before the fruit matures and either baked or fried.

My favorite types

• **Acorn** Shaped like acorns (obviously) and weighing up to 2 pounds (0.9 kg), these are fast growers and relatively small in size. Most are green or orange, though some modern varieties can be found in yellow and white. The orange flesh is sweet and nutty. 'Bush Table Queen' is a bush-type; 'Mashed Potatoes' has ivory-white fruit on compact vines.

- **Butternut** One of the most popular winter squashes, the hearty flesh of these is used in everything from soup to pumpkin pie filling. Dense vines resist pests, producing 3-pound (1.4 kg) bulb-shaped fruits in about 120 days. 'Butterbush' is an heirloom bush type. 'Puritan' is a vining type that doesn't set seed.
- **Hubbard** Interesting shapes, crazy colors, even bumpy textures. Hubbard varieties can range from 5 to 40 pounds (2.3 to 18 kg) and be pale blue, red, or bright orange—making them a popular choice for fall decorations. This type is particularly attractive to squash vine borers, though, so some gardeners like it mainly as a trap crop.
- **Kabocha** Originating from Japan, this unique winter squash tastes like a mix of sweet potato and pumpkin. 'Winter Sweet' has dark gray, mottled fruit that stores for a long time. 'Cha Cha' has flaky, sweet orange flesh encased in green striped ribbing.
- **Spaghetti** Scoop out the stringy yellow flesh and serve spaghetti squash with tomato sauce, just like its namesake pasta. Traditional varieties weigh in at about 5 pounds (2.3 kg), but 'Angel Hair' tops out at 2 pounds (0.9 kg), and the semi-bush variety 'Pinnacle' stays around 3 pounds (1.4 kg).

Planting

Winter squash can be grown in rows, but you'll often see it planted in small hills about 12 inches (30 cm) wide. Squash is susceptible to many diseases that are caused by wet conditions and temperature swings. Mounding your soil can help provide good drainage and proper air circulation, not to mention a little extra warmth which winter squash seeds and seedlings much prefer.

Mid-season care

Squash plants need 1 inch (2.5 cm) of water per week, up to 2 inches (5 cm) during the hottest parts of summer. Be prepared to provide supplemental water in periods of no rain, but avoid watering from overhead. Wet leaves are an invitation to all kinds of disease for winter squash.

Squash is also a heavy feeder. A generous application of compost at planting provides a good start, but side-dressing established plants with compost can give them an added boost during the season. If you choose to fertilize, look for an N-P-K number where the first number (nitrogen) is lower than the middle number (phosphorus). Too much nitrogen will result in vigorous vines but produce fewer fruits.

Birds Do It, Bees Do It...You Can Get in on Pollinating, Too

Winter squash requires the help of pollinators to set fruit. If you covered your seedlings with floating row cover to protect them from pests, you'll need to either remove it as the plants begin to flower to allow access to live pollinators...or manually pollinate the plants yourself! (See the hand pollination details outlined in the previous Grow Guide section for Summer Squash.)

If you want to try manually pollinating your winter squash, you'll be getting up close and personal with the male and female flowers. Or you can just take them in the kitchen and eat them.

Pests & disease

As the name suggests, the squash vine borer destroys squash plants from the inside. It starts when an adult, a moth, lays eggs at the base of a squash plant, on the stem or under lower leaves. When the larvae hatch, they bore into the plant and eat their way through, hollowing out stems and leaves as they go. The best way to control this pest is to prevent the laying of the eggs in the first place with a floating row cover (just remove it when the plants bloom so pollinators can reach the flowers). Or try small pieces of aluminum foil wrapped around the bottom few inches of plant stems. For an active vine borer problem, inject liquid Bt into the vines.

Squash bugs are six-legged insects with flat, dark gray-to-black bodies, about ½-inch (1.3 cm) long. They suck sap out of leaves, causing them to wilt, dry up, and die. (And they also transmit cucurbit yellow vine disease.) Adults usually lay oval bronze-colored eggs on the underside of leaves between the veins. Use of floating row cover is the best proactive defense, or hand-pick them when you see them.

Squash beetles are orange-red with black dots, and are easily mistaken for the common (and beneficial) ladybug. But these chow down on squash leaves and also feed on the fruit. Again, use floating row cover or hand-pick the adults and try scraping their yellow eggs off the underside of the leaves. A knife or a credit card works well for this.

Powdery mildew and downy mildew are fungal diseases of winter squash. Powdery mildew makes the plant appear as if it's been coated with white powder, while downy mildew shows up as yellow spots. Planting in full sun with adequate airflow between plants is a good preventative.

Harvesting

Leave winter squash on the vine for as long as possible, right up until just before the first fall frost. Only mature fruit will store well, so keep an eye on the temperatures and push it as long as you can.

Test winter squash by trying to pierce the outer rind with a fingernail. If you can't do it, it's ready. Alternatively, look for cracked and dry stems. Cut fruit from the vine with pruners, leaving 1 inch (2.5 cm) or so of stem attached to the squash. This will allow you to store the squash longer. Don't wash harvested squash—just wipe them with a damp cloth to remove dirt and then pat dry. Cure them for 2 weeks in a warm space to toughen up the skin.

Storage

Store winter squash below 60°F (16°C) and out of direct sunlight until you're ready to prepare them for serving.

The squash vine borer is a nasty little pest. The moths lay eggs, then the larvae tunnel into your plants and eat their way out.

You'll know the eggs of the squash bug by their bronze color on the underside of leaves.

ABOUT THE AUTHOR

Joe Lamp'l (aka joe gardener®) is one of the country's most recognized and trusted personalities in gardening and green living. With a background in horticulture and over 30 years of real-world growing experience, Joe was the host of *Fresh from the Garden* on the DIY Network, where he taught viewers how to grow vegetables from seed to harvest, with each of 50+ episodes dedicated to an entirely new crop. Currently, he is the creator and Emmy-winning host of public television's *Growing a Greener World*, which has aired for 12 seasons (200 episodes) and is still going strong. The program airs in 96 percent of the US and in numerous countries.

Joe has been an on-air contributor for NBC's *The Today Show*, ABC's *Good Morning America*, and The Weather Channel. His podcast, *The joe gardener® Show*, consistently ranks as the top-rated gardening podcast in the country. His conversations with professionals, book authors, plant breeders, and others in the green industry and gardening world are downloaded by millions of listeners every year.

As the founder and "Joe" behind the successful joegardener® brand and joegardener.com and the Online Gardening Academy™ he has created an ever-growing network of resources dedicated to all things gardening. His videos and blog posts are viewed by hundreds of thousands each and every month, and his comprehensive online courses encourage and inspire a growing number of students to become better, smarter, more confident gardeners in their own backyards. Joe and his family live on a small farm just north of Atlanta, Georgia.

ACKNOWLEDGMENTS

Little did I know over fifteen years ago when I vowed to never write another book . . . that I would write another book! For what it's worth, I tried not to. Yet to be sure, it is always flattering to be on the receiving end of book pitches, especially from one very persistent editorial director for gardening at Cool Springs Press.

So, it's only fitting that my fist huge note of appreciation goes to her—Jessica Walliser, a gardening friend, colleague, fellow plant nerd and bug geek, and one heck of an entomology author of several excellent books that I have in my own library. Thank you, Jessica, for throwing that one last Hail Mary to me for this book. You found the one topic you knew I couldn't refuse.

To be clear, I love to write. What I don't love—and what I've tried to avoid for all these years by not taking on another book project—is the vast immersion of time and energy, along with the inevitable void you create in the lives of those who depend on you. I am so blessed to have an incredibly supportive group of friends, coworkers, and family who not only embraced this project, but also jumped in wherever needed to lighten my load—even though it added to theirs.

With that, I want to start by saying thank you to my small but mighty team at Agrivana Media™ working virtually alongside me every day. I am filled with gratitude to have each of you supporting our mutual and sincere efforts to make this world a little greener every day! We all wear a lot of hats and work long hours, but it is so encouraging to be surrounded by such kind and talented people who love their work and the joint mission we share to serve and nurture our audience with this important and meaningful work.

Those cherished colleagues include Amy Prentice. If I could invent the ideal person to lead our company, it's Amy. Her passion for her work, limitless talent, and dedication to the future success of our company rings loud and clear always. I never take that for granted and give thanks every day that our paths crossed years ago via a single Instagram comment.

To Carl Pennington, creative director, and director of photography, who over the past twenty-five years has easily spent as much time with me as my family has. In fact, Carl is family. His favorite expression whenever I need reminding of his deep value in the company is: "Just remember who makes you look good." Carl's tireless effort and talent behind the camera and the results we see on screen is a gift to all of us who get to reap the fruits of his labor.

Todd Brock, another long-time friend, and former producer from my early days in television. A man of many talents, Todd's gift to all of us is his writing. Thank you, Todd, for continuing to wow me every time I read what you create from every project you take on. I don't know how you do it but please never stop.

Brendan O'Reilly is our other talented writer on the team. If you've read the show notes for the podcast, or enjoyed any of the grow guides on joegardener.com, we have Brendan to thank for that and more. And a special thanks to him for adding more to his plate than it should have held during the intersection of new fatherhood and this book writing project. Congratulations and thank you.

Tobi McDaniel: my GardenFarm™ manager and field producer for the Online Gardening Academy. Little did she know when she asked if I ever accepted volunteers at the farm that she'd quickly be swept into a new career with more work and fun than she ever imagined. Little did I know when I met her just how perfect a fit she was for enriching our company with her many talents and endless humor.

Kristine Lafond: our can-do-anything administrative support hero who we can't image life without. Kristine can catch any wild pitch we through her way. She keeps us sane against all odds and snuffs out any fire threatening to burn out of control.

David Pennington: little brother to Carl, oozes with camera and technical expertise for our television series, *Growing a Greener World*. He also manages the podcast editing, ensuring that every show is a joyful listening experience. Thank you, David, for the countless hours you endured listening to me so that you could produce a fabulous episode every week.

To my students in the Online Gardening Academy: Thank you for trusting in me by investing in yourself to become the gardener you aspire to be. I am so thankful that a bit of my mother's gift and love of teaching passed to me so that each of you could find a good and safe place to enrich your mind, body, and this planet through your knowledge and actions.

And to my many friends that I am so fortunate to have because of this work that I do, and the shared love of gardening and stewardship for this land that we all have in common: My conversations with you through podcasts, Zoom, email, cell phone, and the best of all, those occasional in-person visits—you too contributed to this book in one way or another through your positive influence, and I love that. Thank you.

To the many people I will likely never meet in person, but who have taken the time to write me with incredibly humbling and encouraging notes, letters, comments online, podcast reviews, email, or random voicemails: Your out-of-the-blue expressions of gratitude always came at the perfect time to provide just the boost I needed to energize and inspire me even more. Thank you all!

And certainly, to my wife and daughters, Becky, Rachel, and Amy. You ladies are the most precious part of my life. To be sure, having a husband and father who spends endless hours in and around the garden because of my work and passion is only made possible because of your unending patience and grace. Thank you for the room you've provided for me to grow our family's garden with such abundance and beauty.

Finally, to everyone reading this now, my hope is that you start a garden or nurture the one you already have no matter how big or small. Gardeners are special people who really can change the world. Beyond just sustaining it, let's all strive to make this land we all share better than we found it. We need that now more than ever.

Grow a garden and reap the bounty, for yourself and for those you may never know.

PHOTO CREDITS

INDEX